DATE DUE

P9-EAO-059

FULL COURT PRESS

FULL COURT PRESS

A Season in the Life of a
Winning Basketball Team
and the Women Who
Made It Happen

LAUREN KESSLER

A DUTTON BOOK

DUTTON
Published by the Penguin Group
Penguin Books USA Inc., 375 Hudson Street, New York, New York 10014, U.S.A.
Penguin Books Ltd, 27 Wrights Lane, London W8 5TZ, England
Penguin Books Australia Ltd, Ringwood, Victoria, Australia
Penguin Books Canada Ltd, 10 Alcorn Avenue, Toronto, Ontario, Canada M4V 3B2
Penguin Books (N.Z.) Ltd, 182–190 Wairau Road, Auckland 10, New Zealand

Penguin Books Ltd, Registered Offices:
Harmondsworth, Middlesex, England

First published by Dutton, an imprint of Dutton Signet, a division of Penguin Books
USA Inc.
Distributed in Canada by McClelland & Stewart Inc.

First Printing, March, 1997
10 9 8 7 6 5 4 3 2 1

REGISTERED TRADEMARK—MARCA REGISTRADA

LIBRARY OF CONGRESS CATALOGING-IN-PUBLICATION DATA:
Kessler, Lauren.
    Full court press : a season in the life of a winning basketball
team and the women who made it happen / Lauren Kessler.
        p.   cm.
    ISBN 0-525-94035-9
    1. University of Oregon—Basketball—History.   2. Women basketball
players—Oregon—History.   I. Title.
GV885.43.U56K47   1997
796.32'363'0979531—dc20   96-34640
                                                                  CIP

Printed in the United States of America
Set in Times New Roman
Designed by Jesse Cohen

This book is printed on acid-free paper. ∞

To my little girl, Elizabeth:
May she grow big and strong

ACKNOWLEDGMENTS

MANY VERY BUSY PEOPLE MADE TIME FOR ME IN THEIR LIVES and thus made this book possible. Foremost was Jody Runge. I started by interviewing her, many times, notepad lined with queries, tape recorder rolling. But as time went on, I stopped asking questions and started just being there. Jody let me be there, and she allowed herself to be who she was in front of me. Her generosity not just with her time but with her self was extraordinary. I owe a great debt to the players who let me into their lives: Betty Ann Boeving, Arianne Boyer, Cicely Brewster, Sally Crowe, Cindie Edamura, Sandie Edwards, Renae Fegent, Karen Healea and Jessica Schutt. I also want to acknowledge the other members of the University of Oregon women's basketball team who good-naturedly put up with my almost daily presence: Shanthi Barton, Mendy Benson, Courtney Kanegae, Kirsten McKnight, Uti Middleton and Kristin Nieman. Assistant coaches Stephanie Osburn, Joe Jackson and Kelly Kebe, trainer Kim Terrell, sports psychologist Karen Nelson and sports information assistant Dave Williford were all generous with their time, as were a number of other University of Oregon people: president Dave Frohnmayer, vice president for Administration and then-acting athletic director Dan Williams, former athletic director and now St. Louis Rams head coach Rich Brooks, associate athletic director Barbara Walker, university counsel Pete Swan and university archivist Keith Richards.

I want to especially thank Joanna and Dennis Runge for helping me understand their daughter, women's basketball devotee Martha Pitts for helping me capture the mood in Atlanta and Kellee Weinhold for cheering me on and sharing her insights into lesbian fans of women's sports. Ron Bellamy and Bob Rodman of the *Eugene Register-Guard* answered many questions for me. David Fletcher was a delightful source of information, anecdotes and just plain gossip, not to mention good haircuts. Wendy Maltz urged me to do this book early on and kept tabs on its progress. Duncan McDonald, who has seen me through the writing of all my books, was once again a trusted friend and reader. Kimberly Kessel made it possible for both me and my writer husband to work at home. Jackson Kessler Hager, my oldest son, happily accompanied me to many games, learning at age eight—and effortlessly incorporating into his worldview—that women can be strong and still be women. I also want to acknowledge my father, who taught me how to play, and Ellen Greenfield, who taught me how to win.

I owe a great debt to Sandy Dijkstra, my dream-come-true agent—tough, funny and wise—and the wonderful Julia Serebrinsky, my editor at Dutton, whose kindness, care and enthusiasm ought to be a model for every editor.

My greatest debt is, as it always is, to Tom Hager, partner in life and work and, by happy circumstance, the very best editor I know. My writing is so much better for his touch, as is my life.

C O N T E N T S

INTRODUCTION

I MIGHT HAVE BEEN AN ATHLETE. IT IS HARD TO KNOW. I attended high school just before Title IX, the federal legislation that mandated equal opportunity in athletics (among other areas) for girls and women. The boys at my school had a football team, a basketball team, a soccer team, a baseball team, a wrestling team, a lacrosse team, a cross-country team, a track team, a tennis team, a bowling team and a fencing team.

The girls had tennis.

I played tennis, not only because I loved the game and had learned to play well from my father and from a decade's worth of counselors at summer camp, but because it was the only sport to play. We had no uniforms. We supplied our own tennis balls. Our mothers took turns driving the team to the matches.

At the end of each year, the boys had a banquet to honor the athletes. It was, if I remember correctly, a father-son affair. Every boy who played on a varsity team was awarded a red felt letter to be sewn by a proud mother on the back of his black-and-red letterman's jacket, one emblem for each sport each year.

The girls' tennis team didn't have banquets or jackets, but at the end of my senior year, I was handed a small envelope in which was a quarter-inch-high black letter L, the first initial of my high school. It was a charm for a charm bracelet. I didn't own a charm bracelet.

At the time, none of this seemed odd or unfair to me. It

was just the way it was: Boys played; girls watched. Boys competed; girls cheered them on, either wearing little flared skirts and shaking pom-poms or yelling from the stands. I knew no girls who were serious about sports.

I had not thought of my high school athletic "career" in years and had long ago forgotten the little L charm when I met Red, one of the University of Oregon women's basketball players I was to come to know well while writing this book. I had invited her to lunch to break the ice and was watching her make her way through a third basket of French bread when she started talking about how she could have been the first girl in the history of her high school to earn twelve letters in varsity sports. That's when I remembered my little charm. I listened to myself tell her about my days in high school, and it sounded like some codger's remembrance of studying by candlelight or having a tooth pulled by a barber wielding a pair of bloody pliers. But my tale of ancient history was less than a generation old.

I came to this book not as a frustrated or would-be athlete and not, to tell the truth, as a big fan of women's intercollegiate sports. I came simply as a woman interested in the lives of women. In the fall of 1993, I began reading local newspaper stories about the University of Oregon's newly hired women's basketball coach, Jody Runge (hard g, long e). She was thirty-one at the time, and this was her first head coaching job. I knew a little bit about Title IX, and it occurred to me, counting back in years, that Jody was exactly the right age to have experienced the benefits of Title IX from the beginning. She would have just been going into eighth grade when public schools around the country were implementing the legislation. Now, after all those years of open doors, all those opportunities to compete and play through high school and college, Jody was about to start coaching a new generation of female athletes. I read the stories and, although I was no fan of women's basketball, I was intrigued by the historical moment. First-generation Title IX athletes like Jody Runge were now old enough and experienced enough to start coaching the second generation of Title IX athletes. Surely this meant something, although I did not know what.

So I went to a women's basketball game, the first I had ever seen, to find out. What I discovered, sitting high in the stands of McArthur Court on the University of Oregon campus, was first, that the game was surprisingly fast and tough, far more exciting than I expected, and second, paradoxically, that I could easily imagine myself down there on the court playing. I don't mean actually playing, of course—my body is years past that point—I mean *feeling* as if I could, watching those female bodies and realizing that my body, years ago, with lots of hard work, might have been able to do that. It was a visceral experience. When a player ran up the court, I felt it in my calves. When a player took a shot, I felt it through my shoulder blades. My gender connected me to what was going on on the court.

I had watched NBA games on television before and, in fact, was a reasonably committed fan of the Portland Trail Blazers. But watching men play, watching seven-foot-tall men who could palm a basketball and fly through the air and hang on the rim, was to me like watching an exotic species of animal: fascinating, even thrilling, but entirely alien. With the women's game, I immediately felt connected, and I was hooked.

I wanted to know who these women were and what it was like being not just a female athlete but a big, tall, strong, contact-sport-playing female athlete, a six-foot-five woman with size 12 sneakers. Women were not supposed to be this big or this aggressive. Femininity and athleticism have long been at odds with each other. The socially acceptable female sports are activities a girl can engage in without challenging the female stereotype, like figure skating and gymnastics, graceful, solitary sports, activities that consecrate the diminutive.

But these women I was watching, these hard-muscled, hard-charging women on the court, they were challenging what it meant to be female. I had to know more about them. It seemed to me that so many of the issues at the heart of growing up female in our culture—from self-esteem to body image to learning and unlearning gender roles—might be at the heart of women's sports. So I went to another game, and another. I was an outsider who just barely understood what was happening on the court, but I knew something was happening, not just on the court but in the lives of these student-athletes and their tough new coach.

I approached Jody Runge in the late spring of 1994 to see if she would grant the kind of access personally and to the team that I would need to write a book. The book was to be a "season in the life," following this young team through what I assumed would be the normal ups and downs of competition. I hoped, by getting to know the players and their coach, by insinuating myself into their lives on and off the court, that I could learn something about the experience of being female and an athlete, and could write about it meaningfully for outsiders like me. I had no way of knowing that the season I picked to write about would be a pivotal year in Jody's career, that it would be the year women's basketball came of age at this university and the year women's basketball broke through to a large, national audience.

When I talked with Jody that spring, I discovered she was beginning what would turn out to be a yearlong fight for gender equity in the sports program. She was trying to negotiate a better contract for herself, and she wanted better, more equitable treatment for her team and the women's basketball program in general. This battle became an important subplot in the season and a window into the politics of equality.

Jody was and is a very public person, accustomed to giving interviews, speaking on radio and television and hobnobbing at fund-raising events. She did not hesitate to give me access to her life, her family and her thoughts. She also allowed me access to virtually everything the team did. I went to practices. I ate at training table. I sat immediately behind the players' bench during all the home games. I was in the locker room with the players and coaches before, during and after games. I traveled with the team, riding the buses, staying at the same hotel, eating with them and sitting on the players' bench.

Of course, Jody could not grant me access to the players themselves. They had to individually agree. They thought it was somewhat interesting but mostly odd that someone would want to write a book about them. They did not see themselves as book material, which is probably why they were such good book material. These women were, for the most part, serious university students taking difficult courses while enduring a twenty-eight-game season that included, in the midst of fall and winter terms, four five-day trips up and down the West Coast. In between games, they ran, lifted weights, practiced three or more hours a day, helped recruit future players for the team and tried to eke out some kind of personal life. They were often gone from their apartments from six in the morning until ten at night.

At first, I think I was just another obligation to them. They had so many. They were used to juggling and being good sports about it. But I think, after a time, they actually enjoyed talking to me—in their apartments, in restaurants, on buses, in the hotels we stayed at on the road, late night on the phone. I was a sounding board for the feelings they could not express to their teammates or coaches, the feelings they had about themselves, their parents, their lives. After a while, they sensed what I was beginning to sense myself: I cared about them.

As I watched two stories simultaneously unfold—the story of a team and a season, and the story of a coach and her battle—I began to see many little stories: friendships, uneasy alliances, struggles with self-confidence, bouts of loneliness, denial, acceptance, small victories, small defeats. Life, in other words. What happened that season turned out to be a story about the struggle for self-esteem, equity and respect. These women, coach and players, were in it to win it.

A word about one word: *girls*. I use it throughout the book to refer to the players. Although I sometimes also call them women, *girls* is my noun of choice. I use the word consciously, very much aware that it has been used in the past to demean adult women. I have no such aim. I use *girls* for two reasons. First, it is the way the players refer to one another: "That big girl," a player will say about a strong opponent; "the girl with the attitude," a player will say about a trash-talking rival. Second, I use the word because it is lithe and playful, high-spirited and coltish. It is a fine word, and it suits them.

PROLOGUE

AT 5:30 ON A DECEMBER MORNING IN OREGON YOU HAVE TO
dig deep just to make it out of bed. About the best you can
hope for this time of year is a slate gray dawn that lightens
to a dove gray morning that slips into a pearl gray afternoon,
black firs pointy against leaden skies, clouds dark and swollen,
fog puddling in valleys and over all, over everything, a thin
gray drizzle. Jody is still not used to these black mornings
that hiss with rain. She's lived in Oregon for only a year and
a half, and the memory of the mild, bright winters of the
South, where she spent most of the previous dozen years, is
still fresh. Winters in northern Iowa, where she grew up, were
bone cold, but unlike in Oregon, the sun could be counted on
to appear with happy regularity.

   She promises herself a tall latte at Starbucks if she can
just lift her head off the pillow and reach for the light. It
works, but just barely. These early mornings are getting old.
For almost two months now, she's urged herself out of bed
in the dark, grabbed whatever University of Oregon sweatpants and T-shirt were clean, laced up her size 11 Nikes and

driven the four miles to the university to oversee morning practice. The women's basketball team practices at 7 A.M. six days a week. It's the worst practice time in the rotation. Everyone hates it: The girls struggle to get more than five hours of sleep a night, dragging themselves to the gym pale and dazed, fueled by fear of being late and dry muffins eaten on the run. The trainer Kim thinks early practices increase the chance of injuries. Jody makes sure everyone gets there on time, but she fumes about the early hour to anyone who will listen.

But the way it works is this: The men's basketball team has a permanent lock on the prime practice time, from 3 to 6 P.M. This means the men get to sleep until a reasonable hour and still have time for their classes. The men's basketball team has had this practice time as far back as anyone can remember. The women's basketball and volleyball teams have alternated for the two other practice times, the early morning and early afternoon slots. The early afternoon slot is terrible for the girls because it interferes with classes. The early morning slot is terrible because it interferes with life. It's not much of a choice. There isn't a morning that Jody wakes up without thinking about how the men get the prime time, and the women get the leftovers.

Dressing quickly, she avoids the mirror so she won't have to see how badly her blond hair needs washing. She is not a vain woman, but she is always conscious that others are looking at her. It's part of the job—being the head coach is a public position—and she's used to it. It's also part of her life: She is six-foot-three and stands out wherever she goes. People always look. This morning her hair hangs limp, but there's nothing to be done about it. The rain would make a mess of it anyway, even if she had time to fix it, which she doesn't.

Feeding the two cats and getting her gear together for the day, she can feel the anger rising. It seems as if she's always angry these days. It seems there's always something to be angry about. A few weeks back, in the middle of practice, someone started testing the fire alarm system in Mac Court, the old sports arena where the teams practice and play. At first, it was funny, such an unexpected noise on a basketball court at seven in the morning. The girls were startled. They laughed, stopped playing and covered their ears. Jody laughed too—the first time. But the alarm rang every minute or two, insistent, shrill, nerve-wracking. The practice was a mess. Jody stalked off the court looking for the culprits. Thinking about it still makes her mad.

A week or so later, she came to morning practice to find the Mac Court maintenance crew painting the bleachers with bright green enamel paint. The smell on the court was almost suffocating. After a few minutes of running through drills, the girls began to complain of headaches and blurred vision. Jody, on the sidelines, felt a little woozy herself. The trainer thought it might be a good idea to suspend practice.

"Don't they even know we're in here?" Jody yelled at Kim, even though they were standing next to each other. They were colleagues and good friends too, close after a season of working together, two career-minded, single women in their early thirties who often had dinner together or went running by the river or saw a movie. Kim knew Jody didn't want an answer. She just needed to blow off steam. Jody looked up at the men busy with their paintbrushes.

"This is just totally unacceptable," she said, clamping her jaw tight. Then she canceled practice and stormed back to her office, where she fired off a heated memo to her boss, the athletic director. "I expect that in the future there will be absolutely nothing going on in Mac Court during our practice time unless it is cleared by me first," she wrote.

This dark, sodden morning in December she is hoping for a good practice. The girls just started playing for real two weeks ago. It is only preseason, not conference play, but it still counts; it still matters. If the Oregon Ducks are to have a twenty-game winning season, which is what Jody wants, if the Ducks are to be invited back for a second consecutive year to the NCAA tournament, which is what Jody wants, the team has to win now, right from the start. There's a game Saturday against the University of Portland, not a great team, but reasonably strong, and a good test of how well the Oregon defense is coming along. Jody knows she'll be working the girls hard today and all this week.

She shifts into high gear and gets out of the house, down the hill and over to Starbucks in record time. By 6:30 she's parking her car in the lot behind Mac Court and pushing open the back door that leads to the long basement hallway. Down in the basement are the training room, the equipment room and locker rooms for all the teams that use the building. It feels like an underground tunnel down there, the walls thick and heavy, the air damp and cool. The big brick building, constructed in 1926, is the oldest campus sports arena still in use in the country. It has had a good, long time to settle into itself. The basement floor undulates. The linoleum is thin and colorless from generations of foot traffic. The gym smell is many layered, like a fine perfume, with bass notes of sweat and old shoes and wet towels, and spicier high notes of liniment and aftershave. The smell has permeated the layers of paint on the walls. It's in the linoleum. It is a strangely pleasant smell, rich and full, not acrid, the smell of seventy years of bodies in motion.

Jody checks the training room to see who's here already. The cold green fluorescent lights are blazing, and Kim is at work taping ankles. Her dog, a big, sweet-tempered Rottweiler with bad hips who accompanies her most everywhere, lies on the floor dozing. Three players sit side by side on a massage table, their long, bare legs dangling as they wait their turn with Kim. Jody stops to talk for a minute. She needs to know if there's anything she needs to know. Kim assures her there isn't.

A few minutes before 7 A.M., Jody walks up the stairs to the main level of the building. She needs to be early to set an example. When she took the head coaching job at Oregon last year, the first thing she did was tighten discipline, and one of her first edicts was: A player late for practice runs a mile for each tardy minute. This year, even with the early practice time and the wet, gray Oregon winter mornings, no one is late. The stairs from the basement open on a broad hallway that encircles the actual playing court. Lining the walls of the hallway are display cases with sports memorabilia, each case highlighting a different sport with pictures, trophies, historical artifacts, each case a tiny museum.

This morning, walking across the hallway to one of the court entrances, Jody catches something out of the corner of her eye. She stops midstride and turns to look at the wall behind her. On it hangs an eight-foot-high, five-foot-wide, gold-framed, full-color action photo of one of the seniors on the men's basketball team. It is a stunning photo: huge, powerful, commanding, celebratory. It wasn't there yesterday. Down the hall a few yards, Jody sees another enormous color photo of another men's basketball player. She keeps walking, her long legs taking long, purposeful strides. She walks around the perimeter of Mac Court, counting the larger-than-life photo posters. Two, three, four . . . There are seven of them. They take up every available wall space in the hallway, sandwiched between display cases, squeezed between doorways.

As she walks, her anger grows, until at the end of the circuit, she is, as she would say, hot pissed. To her, these photos of the men are yet another indication of how invisible the women's team is, how little respect the team gets from the university. It's another slight, purposeful or not, like running a test of the fire alarm system during practice, like scheduling painting during practice, like the fact that the team has already played four games but doesn't yet have a brochure to hand out to fans or a media kit to present to the press. She can't decide which makes her angriest: the photos themselves and how they seem to change Mac Court from neutral ground to the men's private arena, the amount of money that must have been spent to create the giant posters (she thinks about her own zero budget for promotion), or the fact that the men's team has someone to come up with these promotional ideas in the first place. After practice she'll find out what's going on. She'll call the athletic director and give him a piece of her mind. She'll demand that larger-than-life photos of the senior women find a place in the hallway.

Jody walks onto the court. As they do every morning, the girls sit in a circle in the middle of the floor, stretching and talking. This morning there is only one topic of conversation: the men's pictures. A few of the girls found out about the pictures the night before and have already had words with some of the male players.

"I told him it felt like it wasn't our stadium any longer," Roy—her real name is Renae, but everyone calls her Roy—is saying to Sally. Sally nods her head in agreement. "But ya know, he didn't have a clue about why I was upset. Not a clue." Jess, one of two seniors on the team, listens in. She is generally taciturn, not sullen or dour but serious and focused, very much aware of her position as a senior. She was so taken aback when she saw the pictures this morning, she laughed out loud, a rueful not a cheerful sound that echoed down the hallway. What's going on here? she thought to herself. I mean, is there a women's program here or not?

Red sits across from Jess in the circle. Red is the six-foot sophomore with short, curly hair the color of terra-cotta. At nineteen, she is the boldest, the most outspoken, the most self-assured of all the players. Sometimes they love her for it. Sometimes they don't. "It doesn't feel like our court anymore," she says. Her voice is louder than the others'. They stop talking and look over at her. She snorts and looks at Jody.

"Not what I would call gender equity, Coach."

Jess stands up and walks across the court, under the basket and over to an open door leading to the hallway. Through the door, framed perfectly by the door frame, is one of the men's pictures. It seems to look out over the court like a sentinel, a soldier guarding a domain. She takes a long look at it, then slams the door shut and walks back to the circle. The coach gives her a quick nod.

"All right, ladies, let's get to it," Jody says.

PART ONE

GET
MAD

JODY

JODY RUNGE HAS A BIG OFFICE—NOT PALATIAL LIKE THE
football coach, not sequestered within its own multiroom suite
with private reception area like the men's basketball coach—
but big nonetheless, three times as big as a professor's office
and about the same size as a New York City studio apartment.
It looks even bigger than it is because Jody keeps it spare,
even austere, with a large, plain desk free of clutter, two pairs
of simple, matching chairs and a bookcase for game tapes.
Across an unbroken fifteen-foot expanse of gray carpet, in a
far corner, sits a TV set. The office has all the warmth of a
Red Lion Inn meeting room. Jody likes it that way. This office
is a lot like her "game face," the expression, the body language, the demeanor she adopts on the court: authoritative,
hard-boiled, all business.

The decoration is minimal: basketball posters and two
framed archival photographs of turn-of-the-century University
of Oregon women's basketball teams, the girls dressed in
long-sleeved middy blouses and dark bloomers, their hair upswept, their expressions grave. Even the view from the big

window that runs the width of her office is unadorned. In this city built between two densely wooded buttes, surrounded by green hills and patched with forest, Jody's window overlooks a flat treeless meadow.

The woman who stands behind the large plain desk in the austere office, ear to the phone, spare hand leafing through an appointment book, can be intimidating both on and off the court. It is hard not to be when you stand six-foot-three and carry yourself like Dame Margot Fonteyn. Most tall women slouch, shoulders dropped, back slightly curved, head thrust forward, their bodies announcing their discomfort, even shame, with their size. Jody stands as if her spine were fused, as if she were forever balancing a large porcelain vase on her head.

She got her bearing from her mother, Joanna, a five-foot-eleven redhead who always wore heels and stood out in her small Iowa farm community like a palm tree in a cornfield. When Jody shot up from a not-any-taller-than-the-tallest-boy-in-the-class five-foot-nine in sixth grade to an undeniable six-foot-one in eighth grade, Joanna mounted a daily campaign to keep her daughter's back straight. For years, the first thing Jody heard when she came down for breakfast was not "Good morning" or "Did you sleep well?" but "Stand up straight" and "Tuck in your tummy." After hundreds of such morning admonishments, all her mother had to do was look at her in a certain way, and Jody's spine would straighten. Joanna's plan succeeded beyond all expectations: Jody grew up not just comfortable with her height but proud of it, a tall woman who now fashions herself even taller, sometimes wearing three-inch heels on the court. It creates a presence no player and few refs are likely to dismiss.

Jody looked even taller when she first came to Oregon in the spring of 1993. Back then she wore her hair in a bushy, two-and-a-half-inch-high perm, a hairdo halfway between poodle and Jeri-curl, the kind of hairdo you'd see on the swing shift waitress at the Denny's in Cedar Rapids. David, a hair-dresser who runs a classy one-man shop in downtown Eugene, couldn't stand it. David didn't know Jody, but he knew the hair. He saw the hair on the TV news. He saw the hair on the sports pages. And he hated it. David is a nineties version of the Warren Beatty character in *Shampoo*—a woman appreciator if not, in this era of STDs, a womanizer—and David knew he had to do something about the hair.

After Jody's first basketball season was over, David picked up the phone and called Jody over at her office. "You don't know me," he told her, "but you've got to come down to my salon right now and let me cut your hair. I've got an empty chair waiting for you." Even for a person accustomed to being in the public eye and used to phone calls from strangers—a few days earlier a guy had called Jody to say that his daughters wanted her to be their mother—she was taken aback: flattered and insulted all at once. She thought David possibly might have a few buttons missing, and at any rate figured the whole idea was silly—someone caring more about the way her hair looked than she did. But she was also intrigued and fashion-conscious enough to wonder if this guy might be right about her. She rearranged her appointments and saw David that afternoon. Now her dirty blond hair is a warm honey blond, and it lies soft, smooth and full around her face. She and David have been buddies ever since.

Jody's office sits at the end of what isn't but could be referred to as "Nonrevenue Row," a long hallway lined on one side with the tiny, windowless offices of the golf and tennis coaches and on the other, the slightly larger, windowed offices of the wrestling, softball and volleyball coaches. These are the sports that don't make money for the university. Nothing makes money for the university except men's basketball and football, whose expansive office suites are a long corridor and a world away from Jody's part of the building.

The building that houses these moneymakers and their poor relations, with their attendant publicists and trainers, ticket sellers, event handlers and administrators—the more than 110 employees of the athletic department—cost $12 million and is commonly known as "the house that football built." Financed in the early 1990s by a combination of bonds, big-money donors and the rental of football stadium skyboxes to corporate sponsors, it was named the Len Casanova Center in honor of one of Oregon's most popular football coaches. The Cas Center, as it's called, is a two-story, 102,000-square-foot concrete-and-glass building that would be at home in any office park in any upscale suburb in the country. It's a broad-shouldered building, simultaneously sleek and beefy like a well-groomed 250-pound linebacker, a building that takes itself seriously, with its curved, brick entrance plaza flanked by the ten flags of the Pacific Conference schools.

The self-consciousness of the flag-bedecked, UN-style entry would be overpowering were it not for a whimsical sculpture set on an elevated curved beam just below the flying Pac-10 flags. The sculpture, a parade of brightly painted, eighteen-inch-high figurines depicting athletes in motion, caused more of a public furor when it was installed than if Oregon had been found guilty of NCAA violations. The athletic director at the time, now long gone, hated the thing, complaining loudly and publicly that it was "not in character," by which he meant it was too playful, too light-hearted for the corporate sobriety of the building. He hated it so much that one day he called the university's maintenance department and requested that a welder with a blowtorch make an unscheduled visit to the Cas Center. Meanwhile, the sculptor, a Massachusetts man who happened to be camping in the Northwest about the time the welder was set to dismantle the fifty-four-thousand-dollar work, hurried to Eugene, dubbed the athletic director a "Neanderthal" and "a white-collar vandal" and threatened to chain himself to his work. Enter the local media; exit the welder with the blowtorch.

But that was not the end of the story. The athletic director renewed his efforts to force the university to remove the sculpture. The university answered by pleading poverty, an evasion that backfired when supporters of the athletic director's artistic taste quickly contributed thirty-one thousand dollars to have the sculpture relocated. They had in mind a back entrance occasionally used by delivery trucks in the dead of night. The battle waged in the press for weeks, until, shamed by unrelenting publicity that painted the AD and university decision makers as troglodytes, philistines—and worse yet, in tightfisted Oregon, squanderers of money—everyone backed down, and the sculpture stayed put. Today it remains an oasis of whimsy, a human touch offsetting the concrete and glass, a reminder that sports—underneath the full-ride scholarships, the big-money donors and the corporate skyboxes, underneath the bowls and the championships and the tournaments and the meets—can be fun.

This was all well before Jody's time. When she arrived in Oregon in the late spring of 1993, the sculpture was old news. Walking into the Cas Center for the first time, looking up at the arc of figurines parading across the curved beam that decorated the entrance, she had no thoughts about the artistic merit of the sculpture. But she did notice one thing immediately: Among the thirteen miniature athletes, there was not a single female basketball player.

Jody came to the University of Oregon at one of the lowest ebbs in the history of a women's basketball program that even in its good years was not much of a contender. The Oregon team had just completed its worst season in almost two decades, winning only nine of twenty-seven games overall and only three of eighteen in the Pac-10 Conference. The Ducks, as the university's team is called in humorous acknowledgment of the area's persistent rainfall, lost eleven straight games and finished dead last in the conference. Crowds were limited to a few hundred stalwart fans. The old coach, a seventeen-year veteran, was a nice guy, but women's basketball had changed during his tenure, and he hadn't kept pace. The players he had in his final, disastrous year of coaching were big, tough girls who had played competitively since middle school. Title IX of the Education Amendments Act of 1972, which mandated equal opportunity for women in public school and collegiate sports, had opened the door for them and tens of thousands like them across the country by forcing the creation of high school teams for girls. By the time these players got to college, they were more ready, physically and emotionally, for rigorous training, sophisticated strategy and serious coaching than any previous group of female athletes. They and their Title IX sisters at big universities everywhere were poised to bring the game to a new level. Some were already doing it: Powerhouses like the University of Tennessee, Louisiana Tech, Vanderbilt, Stanford and the University of North Carolina were showing the rest of the collegiate athletic world just how fast, how tough and how skilled this new generation of female basketball player could be. The Oregon Ducks were waddling far behind.

When the university made the decision to oust the old coach and look for a new one, Jody was a thirty-one-year-old assistant coach who had been paying her professional dues for ten years, moving from her alma mater, the University of Kentucky, to Florida, Alabama, Colorado State and finally Missouri. Basketball was her birthright. She had been shooting baskets since she was old enough to hold a ball. Her father, a six-foot-nine University of Iowa star of the late 1950s, couldn't wait to put up the basket in the driveway. By seventh grade, she was playing competitively. By tenth grade, she was on the high school varsity squad, where, playing the traditional Iowa six-on-six game, she averaged forty-five points an outing and once scored eighty-one points in a single game. As a junior, she led her team to the state championships.

Jody had these early competitive opportunities because she had the good fortune to live in Iowa, a state that revered girls' basketball. But all across the country, in the wake of Title IX, thousands of girls Jody's age suddenly had opportunities to play sports that their mothers—and even their older sisters—never had. The girls like Jody who went through high school in the mid-1970s were the first beneficiaries of the federal legislation. They became the first generation of Title IX athletes.

Jody's hometown of Waukon, Iowa, shut down the weekend of the Iowa State Girls' Basketball Championships, as did countless little farming communities across the state. In Iowa, for generations, high school girls' basketball has been the entertainment of choice. More than that, girls' basketball has been one of the most important shared experiences in the life of many communities, a tradition passed down from one generation of women to another. Jody's mother played high school basketball; Jody's grandmother, for her day a towering five-foot-seven, was a center.

Most people in the small towns of Iowa come out for the boys' games too, but there's something special, even mysterious about this Iowa girls' tradition. It sprang from the strong, early support of a handful of progressive male teachers and took hold partially out of small-town boredom and frigid Midwestern winters, partially out of available gym space and partially because of a ready supply of strong-backed immigrant farm girls. Their parents came from countries with rigorous national gymnastics programs where female strength and agility were seen as both natural and desirable. While physical educators around the country, male and female, were warning that strenuous sports were both physically and mentally dangerous for girls, Iowans, who worked beside their daughters and sisters in the field and in the barn, paid little heed. Iowa girls started playing basketball in 1893 and haven't stopped. Every year, the girls' state tournament in Des Moines sells out. There are always plenty of seats left for the boys' event.

In the early 1970s, after fifty uninterrupted years of state championship tournaments for girls, a *Sports Illustrated* writer visited Iowa to examine the enormous success of girls' basketball in the state. He found himself sitting at a roadside café in Story City, Iowa, talking with four high school players, two girls, two boys. The reporter probed the girls about gender equity. They seemed mystified by questions that they or their program might be treated differently than the boys. The boys, however, saw a big difference. "It's not equal," one of the boys told the reporter. "Karen and Kathy get a lot more pub-licity than we do." The kid grinned at the reporter. "But they deserve it. Right now they're playing better than we are."

Even in a state so long obsessed with girls' basketball, Jody's family was extreme. Joanna wouldn't take a full-time job because she didn't want to miss any of her children's after-school games. Dennis, Jody's father, coached or offici-ated basketball games every evening and every weekend during the season. In the summer, the Runges loaded everyone in the station wagon and traveled across the Midwest from basketball camp to basketball camp. Jody's six-foot-one younger sister was not-so-gently steered away from her nat-ural inclination to go out for the cheerleading squad. She had to be a basketball player. Jody's six-foot-nine younger brother needed no prodding. Her siblings had height and skill, but only Jody had fire. Dennis recognized it immediately and helped groom his daughter into a fierce competitor.

She didn't disappoint him. In high school, she was a three-time all-state standout. Fifteen years later, Dennis can recount these games, play by play. Like a chess master who carries a mental picture of the board, the pieces and the moves, Dennis can close his eyes and see how much time is left on the clock, how many fouls his daughter is playing with, who makes the pass, whether the ball banks off the backboard or swishes through the net. In her last two years of high school, Jody was recruited heavily. She chose women's bas-ketball powerhouse the University of Kentucky where, as the center, she led the team to the NCAA tournament three out of four years, once making it as far as the "Elite Eight," and ended her career averaging nine points and 3.7 rebounds. In college she had majored in biology, thinking that she might become an optometrist. But when her four years of collegiate play were finished, she couldn't say good-bye to the game. Instead, she started at the bottom, learning how to become a coach. There were years of learning the ropes: hopping tiny planes to remote towns to scout talent, traveling all summer to check out the up-and-coming high schoolers at basketball camps and clinics, learning how to recruit, sitting on the bench keeping stats while the head coach controlled the game.

By the spring of 1993, after being an assistant coach for eight years, she was ready to make the jump. But head coaching jobs were scarce. Although the University of Oregon was in a strong conference, the Pac-10, and as an NCAA Division I school, competed at the highest collegiate level, the Oregon job that became available with the firing of the old coach was no plum. The team was a wreck, demoralized after a humiliating season. The university was not known to be a promoter of women's basketball. At least one other coach had already turned down the job.

It was five in the afternoon on the Wednesday before Easter that Jody got the call. Oregon was offering the position. Jody had never been a head coach, but the athletic director at Oregon felt she had it in her. She had been associated with winning teams eight out of the twelve years she played or coached. She had served as Missouri's chief recruiter for the past four years, helping the team win a conference championship. At Alabama, she helped create the two teams that made back-to-back National Women's Invitational Tournament appearances. She was known to be very tough and a very hard worker.

Did she want the job? the AD asked her. Jody was hungry for the opportunity, but even after ten years of moving as far south as Florida and as far west as Colorado, she was still tethered to the Midwest. The Runges are a very close family, the kind of multigenerational rural folk who hold big family reunions by the lake every year. They stick together, and they stick close. Moving more than two thousand miles away would be painful for everyone, but Dennis and Joanna knew this was an opportunity their daughter could not let pass. That night they told her, in no uncertain terms, to go for it.

The other complication, the other tie, was Rich, Jody's boyfriend of two years. The two had had the kind of turbulent relationship that strong-minded people often have, especially if one of those strong-minded people is a woman with a job that, between the rigors of the playing season and the rigors of the recruiting season, leaves little opportunity to put the relationship first. They both wrestled with the situation: Rich was sincerely proud of Jody and supported her career, but at the same time he wanted to be number one. Jody sincerely wanted a personal life in addition to her career, but couldn't figure out how to make it work.

It was a situation that most men, in comparable positions, do not face. In NCAA Division I schools, which offer the top opportunities, 93 percent of male coaches are married, and 80 percent of them have children. But only a third of female coaches are married, and of those, only 16 percent are mothers. For women, full-time coaching careers and full-blown domestic life do not mix. Jody didn't look at it that way, as a societal issue, a gender concern. That would have smacked too much of feminism, and Jody was not, or told herself she was not, a feminist. For her, for her Reagan-era, post–women's liberation generation of women, feminism was a dirty word. It meant hating men and not shaving your legs. It was, the thinking went, a code word for lesbianism. Jody didn't see any politics in her situation; she saw only personal problems. Still, she and Rich had managed over time to carve out a relationship. It was rocky, but they loved each other. It was rocky, but they got engaged.

That night, after she got the phone call from Oregon, Jody called Rich. He was happy for her. He congratulated her. But he would not, he told her, follow her west. He would not hang on a woman's coattails. He would not put himself in a situation where Jody would have even less time for him than she did now. If she went to Oregon, she went alone. If she took the job, the marriage was off.

At 6 A.M. the next morning, she was on a flight to Eugene. At three that afternoon, she was introduced to the local press as Oregon's first female basketball coach. In the media interviews that followed, when Jody was asked about her personal life—as women always are—she mentioned the man she had decided to leave behind. "It was the hardest decision I ever had to make," she told the press.

But it wasn't really. She would have chosen the job, a head coach in one of the strongest conferences in the country, over just about anything. She didn't know the rhetoric of feminism. She didn't talk the talk. But she walked the walk. Her career was what was important, her independence, her self-worth, making a mark. If a man fit in with it, great. If he didn't, if he was too threatened by her job, her high profile, the attention she had to pay to her work, then she would do without. It wasn't that she didn't love Rich. She did. It wasn't that she didn't think about getting married, even having a child. But her real and recurrent dreams were hoop dreams.

"No one," she told the assembled sportswriters during that first interview, "will outwork us on the basketball court, in the classroom or on the recruiting trails."

The mostly male audience looked at Jody—tall, fierce, self-assured—and they believed her. But that didn't mean they were convinced she could coach a winning team. She was so excited about the job that she never asked what the salary was. It was at the press conference, after she had accepted the position, that she learned she'd be making forty-two thousand dollars a year.

"Why are you taking the job for that kind of money?" one local sportswriter asked her.

Jody didn't understand the question. Her Oregon salary would be almost double her assistant coach's salary at Missouri. It looked good to her.

When Jody arrived in Eugene in mid-April 1993, it was raining that soft, gray, unrelenting rain for which western Oregon is famous, a rain that is more insistent than drizzle but less serious than downpour, the kind of rain that drenches without seeming to, that causes hair to frizz and sneakers to sprout mildew, the kind of rain that falls for days without changing pitch: hypnotic rain; crazy-making rain.

Living out of boxes in a small, dark rental apartment down the road from the Cas Center, Jody kept count: three days, four days, a week of rain, two weeks, a month. By the end of May, she had lost faith that it would ever stop. When she came out to be interviewed earlier that spring, she hardly noticed the weather. It was raining then, but she was focused on the job, on the opportunity to coach in the Pac-10. Squired around campus and around town, she felt an intuitive affection for the place, a pleasantly sleepy small city that seemed more urbane, more arty and more liberal than the Midwestern and Southern college towns she was used to. She felt an immediate connection to the friendly, open-faced people she met. Now she wondered if she had made the right decision. She wondered if she could stand the rain.

Then, suddenly one day in early June, it stopped. The last sodden Pacific Coast front blew through; the sky blazed a deep, clear blue. The hawthorns bloomed pink. And just as suddenly, Jody changed her mind. She was going to like it here after all—at least during the dry months. In fact, she grew to appreciate Oregon so much that first summer that, for the first time in her peripatetic coaching life, when she went out on recruiting trips, she was homesick. She couldn't wait to get back. She couldn't wait to get started.

The fall, her first season, Jody was faced with four re-turning starters who had forgotten what it was like to win, and a team that was once again picked to finish last in the conference. No one expected much from the 1993–94 team—except the new head coach.

She began immediately. What the team needed, she thought, was discipline, structure and confidence. She started with discipline: Four mornings a week at 6:30, the team lifted weights. Four afternoons a week, the women jogged, rode stationary bikes or ran up and down stadium stairs. If a player was late to training—or classes, or tutoring sessions or ap-pointments or any other responsibility the coach decided to check on—she ran a mile for every tardy minute. She gath-ered them together and told them if they weren't willing to

make the commitment, they should find another way to sub-
sidize their college education. She told them to get in the boat
or get out of the boat.

When practice began that fall, she taught them a new
system of play, very structured, very precise, that made clear
where they had to be on the court and what they had to do.
In general, women's play is like this—strategic, patterned,
fundamental. Women, even the big ones, don't have the
height, strength or speed of the men who play college basketball. The men can freelance, depend on their height to
make seemingly impossible moves. The women must play as
a team, each member part of a plan, chess pieces on a board.

The team practiced two and a half hours a day, six days
a week. Still, they looked ragged, and even with the structure,
even with the new attitude Jody was trying so hard to instill,
the veterans didn't believe they could win. In fact, they lost
their first game, at an invitational tournament in Hawaii. On
the road a week later, playing a regular-season game in Texas,
the team faded in the last minute and lost by five points.

In the locker room after that game, the scene was grim.
Jody knew her team lost not because they lacked the skill but
because they lacked the attitude.

"This was a close game, and we should have won it,"
she told her players that afternoon. Her voice was stern, just
short of scolding. She didn't want to hear excuses. She told
them to go back to their hotel rooms and write out what they
thought it was going to take for the team to win. "How bad
do you want it? What kind of competitor are you? You need
to tell me what you need."

In their rooms at the Marriott Hotel in Arlington, Texas,
the women vented their frustrations and fears, some hand-
writing as many as four legal-sized pages. Those who played
were angry with themselves for making mistakes. Those who
didn't play were frustrated about sitting on the sidelines. Some
were worried about the lack of team spirit and morale, the
absence of a unified, unselfish purpose.

"Maybe I don't compete hard enough because I'm afraid

to fail," wrote one of the most talented seniors. "But I want to be able to look in the mirror after a game and say to myself that I gave 100 percent, that I not only competed but competed and won."

"There are no shortcuts," wrote another player. "Nothing but hard work is going to get us there."

"You know what it's like to give everything you have, to push yourself with power you never thought you had," wrote one of the starters. "But you can only teach us so much structure. The rest has to come from within."

The exercise forced the players to ask themselves hard questions and deal with feelings they couldn't express out loud. It was an exercise that recognized the place of emotions in the playing of the game, an exercise that came from the experience of a woman who had played the same game, faced the same fears and won. It was an exercise devised by a first-generation Title IX athlete for her second-generation players. It worked.

That night, reading the papers the players slipped under her door, Jody began to understand both the dynamics of the team she had inherited from her predecessor and what the individual players needed. And as she read, she knew she could help them, not just with tough training schedules and intense practices, but by example, by being who she was: a woman, a player, a fierce competitor with an abiding antipathy toward losing, a coach who would listen to anything but excuses. They stopped making excuses. They started expecting more of themselves.

They started winning. They came back from the defeat in Texas to take the next four games. As the season progressed, they racked up a nine-game home-court winning streak, beat top competitor the University of Washington in an intense, emotional game, drew the two largest crowds in Oregon women's basketball history—including the fourth-largest crowd ever to see a women's basketball game on the West Coast—and ended the season losing only five of eighteen Pac-10 contests. By March, the team no one but Jody had expected to go anywhere—the team that had ended the previous season in last place with the worst Oregon record in seventeen years—stood third in the conference, was ranked twenty-sixth in the nation and had secured a berth in the NCAA tournament. It was the first time in six years that the Oregon women's team had gone to the tournament. They won the first-round game convincingly in front of the largest home crowd ever to watch women's basketball in the state of Oregon. When they lost to the University of Colorado in the second round in Boulder, no one thought the less of them. They had done more and gone further than anyone other than their coach had thought possible.

TREAT US AS EQUALS

JODY IS BACK AT WORK IN HER OFFICE A FEW DAYS AFTER returning from the second-round NCAA games in Colorado when Rich Brooks pokes his head in to offer congratulations. Rich has been Oregon's football coach since 1976, a straightforward, plainspoken man who values hard work and loyalty in equal measures, a decent guy, a man respected by his athletes, admired by his assistant coaches and alternately beloved and reviled by legions of athletic boosters, depending on his erratic win-loss record. Lately he has been winning. Since the fall of the year before, Rich has taken on the additional responsibility of serving as the University of Oregon's athletic director. This is a full-time job in itself, quarterbacking a one-hundred-person-plus department, overseeing fourteen NCAA Division I sports and managing an annual budget in excess of $13 million. Rich is handling it, but just barely. He wonders what will happen when football season comes around and his other full-time job, his coaching job, must take precedence.

Rich is well schooled in the Old School, the football-and-men's-basketball-are-the-only-sports-worth-thinking-about school, but he is genuinely pleased about Jody's success. When he comes to see Jody, he is offering his congratulations both as a fellow coach, who knows what it takes to put together a winning team, and as her boss, who is proud that one of his own has made good. He is kindly and supportive, fatherly. He compliments her on a great job and discusses the bonuses she and her coaching staff have earned for bringing the team to the NCAA tournament. He also hints, now that contract time is rolling around again, that Jody can expect a raise for herself and her assistants.

Jody knows that at $42,000 she is the lowest-paid women's basketball coach in the Pac-10 Conference, but she has no clear idea what the other coaches make. Money has never been an issue for her. It's not something she discusses with her peers or asks about at meetings. Men's coaches can expect to make impressive salaries both at the collegiate and professional levels. Six figures is an expectation usually realized, often several times over. Jody's male counterpart at the University of Oregon, a second-year coach who shepherded his team through two losing seasons, makes $200,000 in salary and endorsement money. Most women in the coaching profession do not have that kind of future, and know it.

Still, Jody is pleased to hear talk of a raise. In her years as an assistant coach, she hasn't seen head coaches get many rewards. The raise would mean money in her pocket, which she can't deny would be great, but she sees it as something more, as recognition from the university not just for her but for her program. And now, after a year on the job, after the hard work that led to an unexpectedly successful season, she is ready for the university to ante up in the higher-stakes game she wants to play.

The game is called "treat us as equals," and it involves much more than salaries. To Jody, and to the players on the team, the inequities between the treatment of women's and men's basketball are so visible, so obvious and so well entrenched that it is easy to just take them for granted. Jody thinks about the locker rooms. She's happy her team has a newly refurbished space. It beats the hole-in-the-wall lined with yellow metal lockers that the girls changed in earlier in the year. But, after a $150,000 renovation of the basement of Mac Court, it is the men who have a spacious new locker room with leather couches, juice dispensers, a satellite television hookup and private offices and phone lines for the coaching staff. The women have taken over the men's old locker room, the one they moved out of because it was small, airless and a liability in recruiting.

Practice time is something else everyone seems to take for granted. Of course the men's team gets the prime time in the late afternoon. Of course the women's team alternates between two equally unattractive times that conflict with either sleep or classes. At games, only players and coaches seem to care—or even notice—that men have three officials making calls, while the women have only two. But what bothers Jody is not just that there are fewer refs to cover the court, it's also that the officials working the women's games are less experienced and often less skilled than those who call the men's games. That's hardly surprising since they earn less than 60 percent of what the men's officials take home. Jody has seen women's games turn into brutal, physical free-for-alls because of poor officiating.

Jody has spent a year quietly tallying the inequities: On game trips, the men have a chartered bus waiting for them. The women depend on their coaches to rent vans and drive them around. For scouting and recruiting, Jody must plan judiciously, buying plane tickets two weeks in advance to qualify for cheap seats and staying at hotels that offer complimentary rooms. The men's staff has the funds to fly out on a day's notice to scout a particularly crucial game. Jody's overall budget is one-third of what the men's team is allocated.

It's not an Oregon problem; it's a national problem. NCAA Division I schools spend half of their multimillion-dollar budgets on just two sports—football and men's basketball. Women's sports, all of them combined, account for only 18 percent of the budget. While she knew most of this going in, she is not interested in acting as a caretaker—however successful—of a program treated like a poor relation.

Jody wants the chance to make women's basketball important at Oregon. The recognition from Rich, the raise, might be a first step. But more than the money right now, she's interested in talking to Rich about the possibility of a multiyear contract. The football and men's basketball coaches sign multiyear contracts to protect them from being fired during "building" (i.e., losing) seasons and to bring stability to their programs. The women's basketball coach at Oregon has never had such a contract, nor have any of the coaches of the other nonrevenue sports.

Hitting the recruiting trail last summer, she realized the disadvantages of a one-year contract. As she made home visits, sitting in the living rooms of parents whose daughters were being courted by a number of schools, parents who had to decide who would be the moral force in their daughters' lives for the next four years, she was invariably asked: "Will you be around to coach my daughter through her college career? Can you guarantee that the kind of program you are talking about here in my living room is the kind of program my daughter will experience during her time at Oregon?" Jody reassured them as best she could, but she knew she was on shaky ground. She had only a one-year contract, which meant there was in fact no guarantee she'd be coaching at Oregon when their daughters arrived the following fall, let alone during their four years on the team. She could not offer much tangible proof of her stability: a first-year coach, a single woman living in a rented apartment. Her first Oregon recruiting class had not been a strong one.

A week after Rich's congratulatory visit, Associate Athletic Director Barb Walker comes into Jody's office with a salary offer from Rich: a four-thousand-dollar raise and a one-year contract. Barb is a trim, pretty blonde, a meticulously dressed woman who looks more like a buyer for Nordstrom than a sports administrator. But the job is in her blood. Her father was AD at a small college in the Midwest, and she grew up around sports, teaching, coaching, working in sports information and finally edging her way into upper administration. Six years older than Jody, Barb is above her in the hierarchy—the person Jody and the other nonrevenue coaches report to—and one of two highly placed women in the not surprisingly male-dominated department. Barb and Jody know each other from the University of Alabama in Birmingham, where they both worked in the late 1980s. When Jody arrived last year, alone with few contacts, Barb made a special effort to introduce her around. Although she makes it a rule not to get involved in the personal lives of her staff, she considered Jody an exception. Barb knew firsthand how lonely that first year could be. The two didn't become best buddies, but after Jody and one of Barb's closest friends hit it off, the three women often went out together for dinner or to see a movie.

Barb delivers news of the offer. She thinks it's pretty good news, and so does her boss, Rich Brooks. It represents an almost 10 percent raise at a time when hardly anyone at the university is getting anything. "We just don't have the money to do anything more," Barb tells her.

Since the voters of the state passed Ballot Measure 5 in 1990, the university, along with the entire state system of higher education and a number of social service agencies, has been on a short leash. Measure 5 was a property tax revolt initiative similar to California's infamous Proposition 13 of the 1970s. What the resulting drop in tax income meant to the university was an initial $10 million dollar cut in state funding, the canceling of 126 degree programs and the loss of more than 140 faculty and staff. Those who remained tightened their belts. Faculty and staff had not had a cost-of-living salary increase in two years. On top of this, the athletic department, due to lackluster football and men's basketball seasons, had run up a string of $1 million to $2 million yearly deficits. So the offer to raise Jody's salary by four thousand dollars looked decent to Barb and Rich. Given the larger financial context, it looked more than fair. About the multiyear contract, Barb had little to say other than no women's basketball coach at Oregon had ever had one, and Rich didn't see any reason to break the tradition.

But Jody did, and not just to help with her own recruiting. Jody had a vision of women's basketball fundamentally different from Rich's, a vision shared by a handful of female coaches around the country. Women's basketball, more than two decades after Title IX opened the door to athletic competition for tens of thousands of girls, was about to break through to the big time. It was, Jody and others thought, poised just short of attracting enough fans and snagging enough TV time to transform into a revenue sport—just a hop, skip and jump shot away from parity with men's collegiate basketball.

What women's collegiate basketball needed now was visible and forceful backing from athletic departments, spearheaded by athletic directors who not only believed in but publicly advocated for women's sports. They needed facilities equal to the men. They needed the money to promote themselves. They needed staff to devise marketing and media plans. Jody could see the results of that kind of support at perennial West Coast favorite Stanford, where the team was invariably ranked in the top ten, where yearly participation in the NCAA tournament was a given, where recruiting classes were among the best in the nation and where average attendance for home games was almost five thousand. That's what she wanted for Oregon.

It was all possible, she thought, because the women's game had changed so much during the past decade as bigger and bigger girls weaned on tougher and tougher competition in middle school, high school and summer camps met a new breed of women's coach—women who themselves had played serious basketball in college. It was a particular moment in the history of women's sports—first-generation Title IX athletes coaching second-generation Title IX athletes—and the difference to the game was astounding.

The women's game was faster, more physical, more exciting than anyone could have believed just ten years ago. Women were now playing with the ferocity, commitment and sheer athleticism once associated only with men. They were running the fast break; they were dribbling and passing behind their backs; they were battling for rebounds under the basket; they were scrambling for the ball. Jody—and a sizable national television audience—had watched a North Carolina player slam-dunk the ball during the NCAA women's finals earlier that month. By that single, fluid act, a barrier had been removed, a bridge had been crossed. The slam dunk was the final, dramatic proof that women could play a game recognizable to male fans of the sport.

The game had come a long way in a short time. Only a generation ago women's team sports had been seen as merely fun and good exercise played for recreation and camaraderie. The hot teams of the 1970s attracted a few hundred fans and were glad of it. Fifty was a big crowd for a University of Connecticut game. For most of its life, women's basketball had been constrained by half-court rules, where guards had to keep to their half-court and forwards to theirs, the rationale being that females didn't have the strength or stamina to play the full court. There had been other rules in the past—no dribbling, only two dribbles, no movement outside an invisible circle around each player—rules created to protect the frail female body from the rigors of athletic competition.

A hundred years ago, eminent physical educators warned against strenuous sports for women, calling competitive activities "injurious to both feminine body and mind" and "promoting of qualities that are on the whole unnecessary and undesirable." Back in 1896, dressed in bloomers and black stockings, high-necked blouses and ties, the women of Berkeley met the women of Stanford for history's first women's intercollegiate basketball game, played before an all-female audience—men having been barred from the public and in-delicate exhibition of female sweat. Stanford won, 2–1.

Jody appreciates sports history. She proudly displays photographs of turn-of-the-century Oregon teams in her office. It helps her remember how far things have come. But this is a new era; she is a new coach at the beginning of a career, and she wants to be one of the movers and shakers, one of the women who usher a new game into the new century.

She doesn't have to think long about the offer of a one-year contract with a four-thousand-dollar raise to know she doesn't want it. In fact, it offends her. The way she sees it, she came to Oregon, and in one season, she turned a team with the worst record in the Pac-10 into the winningest Oregon women's basketball team in five years. It was the biggest single-year turnaround in conference history, and her own colleagues, the other conference coaches, voted her Pac-10 coach of the year. She expects to be rewarded for this, and she doesn't see another one-year contract as either an accolade or a vote of confidence from Rich and the athletic department. If she's serious about building a tradition of winning, if she's serious about making Oregon into the kind of team that al-ways goes to the tournament, she needs to know that the uni-versity is behind her. This contract doesn't show that.

Jody likes her boss. They get along well in a daughter-father kind of way. But Rich is a fifty-year-old man who has lived and worked in the male world of football since his teens. The success he has achieved at Oregon—taking his football team to two bowl games in recent years—has come about not by attracting star players but by building teams made of play-ers taught to be selfless, expected to subjugate their own egos to the needs of the group. That's the way he runs the depart-ment too, like a team, and he expects the same kind of self-lessness. For years, the coaches at Oregon have been playing by the same rules: The revenue coaches, the football and men's basketball folks, make the big salaries because their programs bring in the bucks that pay for the other sports. The nonrevenue coaches coach for the love of it and are grateful for the opportunity. That is how the system works. And good members of the team work within the system.

Jody understands the system. She understands the game as it has been played. She just doesn't want to play it. She thinks Rich is stuck in the dark ages, that he doesn't understand the potential of women's athletics. Or maybe he's afraid of change. After all, the rise of women's sports directly threatens the hegemony of football in collegiate athletic programs.

It is football, with its one-hundred-plus-man rosters and its ninety full-ride scholarships that throws everything out of whack, including compliance with Title IX legislation. No one's exactly sure how to measure compliance, but if it means, at least in part, the same number of athletic scholarships for men and women, if it means the same percentage of male athletes and female athletes relative to the composition of the student body, then football tips the scales so precipitously that it is almost impossible to even them. It would take six basketball teams to balance the number of scholarships awarded one football team.

The men who run the NCAA and the men who run collegiate athletic programs have much to gain if women's athletics takes off: new fans, new boosters, new endorsement arrangements, new TV contracts. But they have more to lose: their traditional dominance of the field, their lock on the very notion of athleticism. To Jody, this is all Jurassic Age thinking, and Rich and his ilk are dinosaurs. She tells Barb Walker that she doesn't want to sign the one-year contract. She wants a multiyear contract. Barb goes back and tells Rich. Barb hates this middleman position. She feels like a Ping-Pong ball, bouncing between her boss and a woman she considers her friend. But it's part of the job. She does it.

Rich drops by Jody's office a few days later. He's genuinely puzzled by her unhappiness over his offer. When she was hired last March, he told her about the budget constraints, about the property tax revolt and the cutbacks. He explained to her that the athletic department was going to have to act

like the rest of the university, and that there were not going
to be raises the next year. Given this, he thinks she should be
grateful for what he considers a generous offer.

"Hey," he tells her, working to keep his voice low and
even, "you knew what you were getting into when you signed
on here. You knew the situation." Rich has deep loyalty to
those in his department who have been here for years, who
made due with cramped offices in old buildings before the
Cas Center was built, who went years without raises, who
kept quiet and worked hard. He thinks of the women's track
coach, a nineteen-year veteran whose teams won eleven conference championships, placed in the top five in the country
seven times and won a national title. That coach isn't in his
face asking for a big raise. Jody is not playing by the rules
he values.

But he does understand that a multiyear contract can help
recruiting. He is, after all, a coach himself. He promises to
talk to his boss, the vice president for administration, Dan
Williams, to see what he can do.

Most of April goes by without Jody hearing anything.

In late spring, Jody flies to San Francisco for the bian-
nual Pac-10 coaches meeting. Aki Hill is there, her opposite
number at rival school Oregon State. A small, sweet-faced
woman who stands armpit high to Jody, Aki was the first
woman in her native Japan to serve as a head coach in the
seventy-five-team amateur league. She's been coaching at
Oregon State since 1979. Like Jody, Aki is also in the midst
of negotiating a new contract. She thinks that maybe she and
Jody ought to form an informal alliance, an Oregon alliance,
to try to get their salaries more in line with the other coaches
in the conference. But neither of them knows just what everyone else in the conference makes. Aki says she'll find out.

Back in Eugene, Jody gets a fax from Aki listing the
coaches' salaries, and it's an eye-opener. Jody knew she was
the lowest-paid coach; that's no surprise. But she had no idea
how wide the gap was between her salary and the others in

the conference. From the fax, she learns that she and Aki, who makes $10,000 more than Jody, are together at the bottom of the heap. The next lowest salary is $20,000 higher than Aki's. Several coaches make in the $70,000 to $80,000 range. The coach at Berkeley makes $95,000. The University of Washington is paying its coach $108,000. At Stanford, Tara VanDerveer earns $150,000. Of course Jody doesn't expect to be compensated like Tara, who during her nine-year tenure has made Stanford a national powerhouse and this year took her team to the NCAA Final Four. But three of the other coaches in the conference are in their first year like Jody, and two of them make $80,000.

Jody sits at her desk and writes her boss a long personal letter, explaining very plainly what she wants and why she wants it. I need to buy a house, she writes to Rich. I need a place to entertain parents and kids, and I need the house to represent the commitment the university has to women's basketball. Otherwise, we're not going to be able to recruit good kids. Look, she tells Rich, I can't recruit against Tara if I'm living in a two-bedroom rented apartment—not if the University of Oregon wants a winning team. I can't recruit as an equal in the conference if I'm being paid half of what other first-year coaches are making. I got hammered in recruiting this year, she tells Rich, and I'll continue to get hammered unless I can show that this university cares about women's basketball. I understand the problems at the university, she writes, but you must understand what it takes to create a top program.

At the end of the letter, Jody spells out her request: She wants a four-year contract with graduated salary increases: $55,000 the first year, then $65,000, then $70,000, and in the final year of the contract, $75,000. This would put her no higher than the middle of the conference and, given other coaches' raises over the course of the years, would probably keep her in the bottom third. She thinks this is fair, given what she's done for the program already and given how she now sees other universities supporting their women's basketball programs. She is asking for the money not so much for what it can buy, although being able to afford a house would be a plus, but for what she thinks it symbolizes: the beginning of the university's commitment to take women's basketball seriously.

Rich reads the letter unhappily. He thought what Jody wanted was a multiyear contract, and that the money didn't matter that much. That's what he's sure she told him only last month. Now she's changing the game, and Rich really doesn't like that. He's already gone to bat for her with his boss, the vice president for administration.

Vice President Dan Williams is a sports enthusiast, a serious fan although never an athlete himself. In his mid-fifties, he is a genial, gray-haired, consensus-style manager. He doesn't see a multiyear contract as much of an advantage from the university's standpoint—coaches can and do break contracts all the time—but he understands that it could help with recruiting. After considering the idea for a while, he gives Rich the go-ahead. Now Rich has to go back to him with Jody's new salary demands.

Jody walks down the hallway to Rich's office a few days later, thinking that the two of them will negotiate based on her new graduated-increase proposal. But Rich cuts her off immediately. He tells her that it would be impossible for the university to lock into graduated raises. Legally, it just can't be done. Rich's boss has told him point-blank that state regulations do not allow for contracts that promise specific future raises. The state funds the university every two years. The university is precluded from entering into contracts that promise money it doesn't know it will have. There is truth to this, but there may also be subterfuge. In fact, the athletic department is not funded by state money. Whether the department has to play by the same rules is debatable.

But state regulations aside, the university administration is not willing to bet so much on a first-year coach. Suppose, Dan and Rich and others are thinking, this successful season was just a fluke? Suppose Jody did well only or mostly because the players recruited by her predecessor finally came into their own? Perhaps any coach would have done as well. It is too early to tell how good Jody is, how valuable she is to the program.

With Rich, it's more of a question of loyalty.

"We're all paid poorly here compared to the rest of the conference," he tells her. "We work here because we love it here." He wishes Jody would get with the program. He wishes she would play the game like everyone else, like his other stalwart coaches. "I had to wait seventeen years to get a decent facility," he tells her. "Things take time here. This is only your first year." He tells her that there is no question that there will be raises. "Trust us—you'll get raises," he says. "But we can't write it in a contract."

He gives Jody a paternal pat on the back. The top of his head comes to the tip of her nose. "You're gonna have a great career here, Jody. Just relax."

Rich isn't big physically, but he has a big persona. He's tough, direct and competitive. Jody's sense of self is no less strong. The two don't exactly clash, but they square off. In a way, the discussion about salary becomes a contest, a competition between the two of them, a game played for personal stakes.

Jody is not interested in hearing about loyalty or state regulations. She is not interested in hearing that all things come to those who wait. Although she is not asking for a salary equal to the men's basketball coach, she wants Rich to accept the idea of parity between the two programs. The basis for any future negotiation, for equality of facilities, for equal access to prime practice time, for a women's promotion and marketing budget, hinges on Rich's acknowledgment of this new era in women's sports.

"Listen," Jody tells Rich, "your men's basketball coach makes a base salary twice mine and total compensation five times my salary. He's on a multiyear contract, and"—she pauses meaningfully—"he's losing. His teams lose. My team wins, and look at what you're offering me."

"The two jobs just aren't equal," Rich tells her. You can't compare them.

"Not equal?" Jody says. There is probably no other phrase in the English language that can make her as angry. She points out that both she and her male counterpart care for and coach the same number of student-athletes, control the same number of scholarships, oversee assistant coaches, run practices, recruit and have the same season schedule in the same conference. Off season, both the men's and women's head coaches do their civic and departmental duty, from speaking to booster clubs to playing in benefit golf tournaments. "We have the same responsibilities," Jody tells him. "Where's the difference?"

Rich is quiet for a moment. It's not that what Jody just told him is new information. It's not that he's thinking it through and weighing her concerns. It's that he's momentarily taken aback that she doesn't seem to see what he thinks of as the glaring, incontrovertible difference between the two jobs. He can't believe she doesn't see it. It's not that men's basketball makes money and women's doesn't. It's not that men's basketball has a TV contract and women's doesn't. It's more basic than that.

"The difference," Rich says slowly and deliberately, "is the pressure: Jerry Green has to win or he's out of a job." He pauses. "You don't." He reminds her that her predecessor kept his job for seventeen years, despite a number of disappointing seasons. You too can have this job for a long time, he tells her.

This is precisely what Jody does not want to hear. She wants the pressure to produce a winning team. She hates the idea that she could still have a job if she were not successful with the team. It shouldn't be that way. She feels that her neck should be on the block just as the men's coach's neck is. Winning is what the game is about. Teams that win attract

fans. Fans bring revenue. Revenue makes for stronger programs. Of course Jody feels pressure to win. She expects to
feel the pressure. She *wants* to feel the pressure. Anything
less would be second-class citizenship in the world of intercollegiate sports.

The two talk for a long time. The conversation is polite,
even amiable. But neither person gives ground. And beneath
the quiet civility, there is a booming subtext. What Jody hears
is this: If you don't care if I win, then you don't care if
women's basketball is successful here, then you don't care
about women's basketball. But Rich hears this: If you don't
trust me to do right by you, then you don't trust me. If you
push for this, you care more about yourself than you do about
the department or the school. Still, Rich promises to keep
talking to Dan Williams about a new contract.

ENTER THE LAWYER

IN MID-JUNE, JODY IS HANDED HER CONTRACT. IT IS A FORTY-six-thousand-dollar, four-year deal. The multiyear contract breaks tradition in the department and will forever separate Jody from the other nonrevenue sports. It will, Rich thinks, cause morale problems among the other coaches, the veterans who have produced years of winning teams and work under one-year contracts. But he does it. He agrees with Jody that it's necessary for competitive recruiting.

Rich figures the negotiations are now over. Jody has both a raise and a multiyear commitment. Rich knows she wanted more money, but he still thinks this new contract does right by her. He figures she understands that the university can't write the graduated-raise contract she has been asking for. And, after all, Rich thinks, demands aside, she knows she's a first-year coach. She can't really be expecting more than a modest raise, can she? Besides, Rich has given Jody his word. He has told her that there will be raises in years to come, and his word has always been good enough before.

Anyway, it's the multiyear feature Jody cares most

about, he figures. If he were in her shoes, he sure would. It's one thing to come in and coach three seniors and get a winning season out of it, as Jody just did. But it's quite another to produce a winning record with the inexperienced players she now has and the weak recruiting class she has managed to bring in. No one thinks Jody will have a good season next year. But, with this multiyear contract, she's protected. She'll go for it, Rich tells himself.

But Jody sees the contract offer quite differently. She sees that the newest offer doesn't respond at all to her salary concerns. There is nothing that obligates the university to give her any raises in the future. The fact that it's a multiyear contract is good for recruiting—that's what she wanted—but it locks her into four years at a salary she can't live with, a salary she considers an embarrassment given the money her Pac-10 colleagues are making. At that salary, she will not be a player in her own department.

"We're going to do something for you," Rich tells Jody again. "Just sign the contract. Trust me." Rich feels he's not only done the best that he can for her, he's done the best he wants to do. Given his other coaches and their records, their longevity, their loyalty, anything more would be a slap in the face. He wants Jody to appreciate what he's already done for women's basketball: He's increased her budget. He's gotten her a better locker room. He's lowered ticket prices to attract more fans. Now he's offering her a multiyear contract.

Jody doesn't know what to do. It's not that she thinks Rich is untrustworthy, but she knows the basic rule of negotiating: Get it in writing. Suppose Rich isn't around next year when it's time to find the money to give her a raise? Suppose the state legislature mandates another cutback? Suppose the athletic department posts an even higher deficit than usual? Suppose she has a bad year—she knows that's the expectation—will she get a raise anyway? She decides, at least for the moment, not to sign the contract. She needs to think. She needs to talk to someone.

One of her friends in town is married to a lawyer who

knows all the personalities at the university. She talks to him about the contract and the promised raises. He assures her that the university is dealing from a place of integrity, that she shouldn't worry, that she should trust Rich. Jody listens but she continues to have doubts.

On the phone a few days later, she talks to Aki, the Oregon State coach, about the new contract Rich is offering. Aki tells her about a case down in Georgia that she's just recently read about: Apparently some lawyer almost sued the University of Georgia over inequities in salary for two coaches of women's sports, basketball and gymnastics. At the last minute, Aki tells her, the university settled and the two coaches signed lucrative new contracts.

Although she hadn't heard of the case before, Jody knows the basketball coach in question, an old friend, Andy Landers, who was coaching at Georgia when she was an assistant coach at Alabama and even before that, when she was a player for Kentucky. Jody calls him right away.

Andy tells her about Alan Manheim, a tough Atlanta trial lawyer who has developed a specialty negotiating for professional football players and draft choices. He's half agent, half lawyer, meaning he goes both for the gold and the jugular. Andy tells her that before he hired Alan, his salary was $59,000. Now he is making $97,000. Alan also negotiated a salary increase for the University of Georgia's women's gymnastics coach, from $47,000 to $80,000.

Jody sits at her desk, phone tight to her ear. "How did he do it?" she asks her friend.

"Title IX," Andy says.

In late June, Alan and Jody talk on the phone. She's impressed with the lawyer's knowledge of the world of athletics. She's impressed with his trial credentials. She's impressed with his voice, a rolling, William Jennings Bryan trial lawyer voice with just the right hint of drawl. Too much drawl and a Southerner sounds like a bumpkin. Too little and a Southerner doesn't sound like a Southerner. Alan Manheim's voice is just right. It is the voice of the New South: educated, articulate but with a preacher's lilt, the kind of voice made for telling stories or convincing juries. But what impresses Jody the most is that her friend Andy Landers trusted Alan with his career, with his livelihood. Andy is a smart man who has been in the coaching business for years. If Andy put himself in Alan's hands, that is endorsement enough for Jody.

Alan listens carefully as Jody explains her situation. She tells him about her terrific first year: putting together a twenty-game-winning season, taking the team to the second round of the NCAA tournament, being named Pac-10 coach of the year. She tells him that, after a month and a half of negotiations, she is being offered a four-year, forty-six-thousand-dollar contract.

"Tell me about the men's program," Alan says.

Jody tells him—about the two losing seasons, the coach's salary, the practice times, the locker rooms, all the issues she has been thinking about during the past year and a half. The litany of inequities is so familiar to her now that she recites by rote. Alan listens, hearing the anger in Jody's voice but also hearing the facts of what he is already coming to think of as "the case." It's familiar turf. When he worked on the negotiations for the Georgia coaches, he heard the same story: the salary gap, the unequal treatment. That wasn't supposed to happen under Title IX.

The first comprehensive federal legislation to protect students from sex discrimination, Title IX was designed to prevent gender-based inequities in admission, treatment, employment, use of facilities and access to all extracurricular activities. The law stated that no person, on the basis of sex, could be excluded from participation in any educational program or activity that received federal funding. Athletic programs quickly became the focus of the legislation, although ironically sports was neither the original impetus for Title IX nor even much of a concern during the early discussions.

When Title IX was being debated in congressional hear-ings in 1970, the issue was the discrimination against female applicants to universities and the inequitable hiring and promotion of female faculty. A Carnegie Corporation study that year had found a smaller percentage of women enrolled as undergraduates than forty years before, a smaller percentage of women receiving Ph.D.s than forty years before and, at many institutions, a smaller percentage of women on the faculty than forty years before. The concern in 1970 was that women were losing ground in educational opportunities. Sports, one of many possible activities offered within educational institutions, was mentioned only twice in the debates on Title IX, and not at all in any House, Senate or Conference reports. But, as it turned out, athletics was one of the most visibly unequal programs in high schools and colleges across the country.

When Title IX passed Congress in 1972, less than 4 percent of high school girls were playing on school teams, while almost one-half of boys were participating. In the early 1970s, 85 percent of all intercollegiate athletes were men. Colleges offered their male students an average of seven full-season (twenty games or more) sports to compete in; women were offered an average of two short-season sports (four to six games). Nationally, 1 percent of intercollegiate athletic budgets were going to support women's sports. From high school through adulthood—where thousands of men, and very few women, had opportunities to live lucrative and public lives as professional athletes—sport was the "sexual signature of masculinity," as one sociologist put it. More simply: Boys played. Girls watched.

Title IX changed that. It forced 16,000 public school systems and more than 2,700 colleges and universities to rethink their athletic programs and in the process create opportunities that had never before existed for girls and women. What exactly the law required—what "equal opportunity" actually meant in terms of access and funding and resources—and what would be the standards for evaluating compliance with the law were murky then and remain so today. But this ambiguity did not stand in the way of real and significant change. During the two decades after its passage, high school girls' participation in sports increased an astonishing 723 percent. In college, female athletes now make up one-third of all sports competitors, instead of a mere 15 percent.

From the beginning, because it challenged not just programs and administrators but ideas and stereotypes, Title IX was not a popular piece of legislation. Just a year after the provisions of the law could be enforced, the male-dominated NCAA filed a lawsuit against the Department of Health, Education, and Welfare challenging the validity of the regulations. The NCAA wanted to exempt revenue sports (that is, football and men's basketball) from the Title IX equation. That suit was unsuccessful, but a few years later, a small Pennsylvania college, faced with the threat of losing federal funds for allegedly violating Title IX, challenged the law again. In 1984, the backlash tenor of the times was right for such a challenge, and the Supreme Court's favorable ruling so narrowed the scope of the law that Title IX virtually ceased to exist. Three years later, an angry Congress overrode a veto by then-President Ronald Reagan to pass the Civil Rights Restoration Act, resuscitating Title IX and making it once again a force in the lives of high school and college students. In the early 1990s, the legislation received a boost when the Supreme Court ruled that Title IX plaintiffs could seek both compensatory and punitive damages for Title IX violations.

Even so, when the *Chronicle of Higher Education* surveyed NCAA Division I colleges in the mid-1990s, it found widespread inequalities. While women comprised more than half of the undergraduate population, they made up only one-third of the varsity athletes at the average school. Female athletes, the survey found, received a little more than a third of the money spent on all athletic scholarships.

Alan knows Title IX and its roller-coaster legal history, and, as a lawyer, he understands its litigation potential. Title IX was his close companion in the University of Georgia case, where he had to go so far as to file a lawsuit before the university got serious about creating parity between the salaries for coaches of men's and women's teams. He figures he can use the same approach with Jody's case, claiming that the salary gap in effect constitutes noncompliance with the federal law. Title IX doesn't say anything about salary, but in mandating equal opportunity, it leaves the door open to some interesting issues. At least that's the way Alan sees it.

He explains it to Jody in plain English: Your players are entitled to the same quality coaching the men have, he tells her. If they don't get that quality—if they get, in effect, bargain-basement coaching because that's all the university is paying for—then they can't be said to have the equal opportunity to become the best athletes they can be. No equal opportunity, no Title IX compliance. It's as simple as that. The argument is potent. It has the benefit of combining the law of the land with the law of the marketplace. And it is further bolstered by the Equal Pay Act of 1963, which Alan also thinks is relevant here. Filing suit under that act twenty years ago, a girls' high school softball coach won her case against a New Jersey school district that paid the boy's baseball coach substantially more. The judge ruled that the two coaches did the same job and deserved the same pay. Alan feels on firm footing here.

As he talks, Jody feels increasingly confident that she made the right choice, both in following through on her concerns and in contacting this particular lawyer. Everything Alan is telling her about Title IX and the University of Georgia situation corroborates what she's been thinking these past months. The man knows what he's talking about, Jody thinks. He's spent a lot of time in court. He wins. If I'm going to have to fight this battle, this is the guy I want to have with me.

Alan is feeling good too. If Jody is right about all she's been telling him, she's got a good case. And the beauty of it, from Alan's point of view, is that he's already ahead of the game. Thanks to his work with the Georgia coaches, he's got the case already prepared. He's even got the lawsuit written, if it comes to that. He figures he won't even have to fly out to Oregon. He just needs to make his presence known, to make some noise. He needs to show the university that Jody Runge has a lawyer behind her.

At the end of the two-hour phone call, Alan agrees to represent Jody in her contract negotiations. They don't discuss a specific salary figure, but Alan knows Jody wants a multi-year deal, and Jody has told him what the other Pac-10 women's basketball coaches make and what the Oregon men's coach brings home. He's thinking seventy thousand dollars, near the middle of the women's salaries in the conference. Alan tells Jody she can hire him for a five-hundred-dollar retainer. If he has to come west to file a lawsuit, he'll charge her for expenses. Any money he makes will come out of the settlement he feels sure she will get if the case goes that far.

"Don't sign anything, and don't talk to anyone," Alan tells her after she's agreed to the terms. "Let me do the talking. Let me be the bad guy. That's why you hired me."

Jody hangs up the phone feeling simultaneously anxious and relieved. She knows she's started something serious in motion, and it scares her. She knows she's right. She knows she's doing what's right. But that doesn't muffle the anxiety. This is dangerous business for a first-year coach. Starting a career by threatening your employer with a lawsuit is not a way to win friends—or advance a career.

But she also feels comforted. Alan has not only validated her concerns in a way no one else has been able to and given a stamp of approval to her anger, he has also shifted the responsibility onto himself. She has hated negotiating with Rich Brooks. Not that their conversations have been anything less than civil, but standing up to a powerful man old enough to be her father is disagreeable and disconcerting work. She is happy to let Alan handle it. She is, in fact, grateful.

Alan has instructed her not to talk to the media either. He wants to control what information the public gets in the hopes of molding public opinion if and when it is needed. He learned that lesson with the University of Georgia case. It is a lesson most trial lawyers know well. If he can dispense bits of information to local reporters at critical times, the media can help him exert pressure on the university. He doesn't want Jody mucking that up.

He doesn't tell Jody that. He just tells her not to talk to the press about the contract negotiations. That's going to be hard for her. Bob Rodman at the *Register-Guard*, the Eugene newspaper, has been very good to Jody and to women's basketball. She talks to him regularly. It will be difficult to chat with him about recruiting and the new season but not tell him what's really on her mind these days—that she's now working without a contract, that she's hired a high-powered lawyer, that she might sue the university if she doesn't get what she wants.

In fact, there are very few people Jody can talk to about her situation, and the loneliness she has felt since she came to Oregon, the emotional isolation, intensifies. She has been too busy to cultivate many friendships and too concerned about her public image to date casually. At work, in the Cas Center, as the word filters down about her salary dispute, colleagues and acquaintances distance themselves. They avert their eyes when they pass her in the hall. They avoid running into her in the building. Because of the lines being drawn in the department, it is now no longer possible for Jody and Barb Walker, the associate athletic director, to be friends.

Jody runs up her long-distance phone bill talking to her parents, who pump her up with their usual unconditional and enthusiastic support. Jody, her father is fond of saying, comes from a long line of hard-nosed, strong-willed people who take risks and speak their minds. He's not at all surprised that she's challenging the university to do better by her and by women's basketball. He and Joanna are concerned, of course, that Jody may be jeopardizing her coaching career. But they trust her instincts and her judgment in a way few parents trust their children, even their adult children. "Besides," Joanna tells her daughter, "whatever happens, you know you will always land on your feet. And you know you can always come home."

Jody spends a lot of time alone thinking about what she's doing. She must keep in mind the big picture, she tells herself. This is not just about my salary; it is about visibility and respect for my program. She keeps reminding herself that she is a role model to her players, that she has to fight this equity battle for them, for their future, to show them that women can and should stand up for themselves. When she thinks of it this way, it becomes a worthy crusade, not an exercise in self-aggrandizement. It becomes a bearable burden.

Even with all the parental support and the confidence-building self-talk, even with her trust in Alan, Jody feels as if she is alone and poised at the edge of a cliff. She needs to talk with someone who's been there. In late June, she tries to contact Marianne Stanley, who used to be the head women's basketball coach at the University of Southern California. When USC offered her what she felt was an unacceptable contract, she refused to sign and instead mounted a salary discrimination suit against her employer. Jody tracks Marianne down in Washington, D.C., where she and her lawyer are working on presenting her case to the Supreme Court. She has already lost in the lower courts. The two women hardly know each other, but the bond, even across the long-distance phone line, is immediate. They talk about how they both feel compelled to do what they're doing, how they both feel they have no choice but to mount the challenges. Marianne understands that this is much more than a salary dispute for Jody because that's how Marianne sees her own battle. It comforts Jody to find a kindred spirit, but it frightens her to learn how difficult, personally and professionally, life has been for Marianne since the lawsuit. The former coach has only one piece of advice, which she offers repeatedly and forcefully throughout the conversation: Don't do anything without your lawyer.

When Rich learns that Jody has retained the services of a lawyer, he understands. It's smart to confer with a lawyer during salary negotiations. But when he finds out that the lawyer is actually handling the negotiations and has instructed Jody not to talk to him, he is deeply disturbed. He feels, in a sense, betrayed. As far as he can tell, he's done his part by supporting Jody and the program. Now she is not doing hers. She isn't being a team player.

And then there's the matter of his word. The presence of this lawyer means Rich's word wasn't good enough for Jody. That's a frontal attack on his integrity. The entrance of Alan Manheim signals the breakdown of the relationship between Rich and Jody. Before Alan, it was just the two of them sparring over terms, a competition between two fiercely competitive players. Rich likes competition. He understands it.

Now, all of a sudden, things are different. Jody doesn't return his phone calls. They work in the same building just down the hall from each other, and they don't talk. Chance encounters in the hallway are awkward. Barb becomes his communications link to Jody. Jody can talk to Barb because Barb is not in a position to negotiate or make decisions. But Barb almost wishes she wouldn't. Being in the middle like this, between the growing hostility of two iron-willed people, is the single most unpleasant thing that has happened in Barb's professional life.

Jody is off traveling almost all of July, rarely stopping back in Eugene. She is scouting and recruiting in Cleveland, Terre Haute, Colorado Springs and Los Angeles. She spends long afternoons sitting on hard bleachers in high school gyms looking for big girls, girls who can shoot, girls who can play tough defense, girls who know the game and love it. Recruiting is serious business. It is the future of the team, and the future of the coach. Meanwhile, she and Alan are in constant phone contact. For several weeks, he is like an avid suitor: attentive, responsive, sympathetic, encouraging.

But as he is courting Jody, he is also striking up an uneasy relationship with the vice president for administration, Dan Williams, and Pete Swan, the university's attorney. Williams is affable but tough, a personable, genial man who is also a strong-willed career administrator. Swan is a trim, balding attorney-turned-law-professor who rides his bicycle to work every day. When he was in private practice, he specialized in product liability, antitrust and federal regulation cases, bringing perhaps one or two such cases to trial each year. Now he teaches at the University of Oregon Law School and has been representing the university in its legal dealings for fifteen years.

From the beginning of his dealings with the university, Alan demands that the president, former Oregon Attorney General Dave Frohnmayer, be involved in the discussions. This doesn't sit well with Dan and Pete. Dan, after all, is the administrator responsible for Jody's department, and Pete is empowered to write contracts. Salary negotiations are normally not within the purview of the president. But it is quite clear to everyone that this is not business as usual. No university employee in Pete Swan's memory has ever engaged an outside lawyer to conduct salary negotiations. And no one at the university is too happy about it now.

The trouble between Alan and the university contingent begins almost immediately. Partly it's logistics: a three-hour time difference and the hectic schedules of busy men. Alan and Pete, the university lawyer, spend days trying to catch one another on the phone without much success.

In truth, Jody's concerns are not on the top of anyone's list. The president not only has an upcoming legislative session to prepare for, a $150 million fund-raising campaign under way and a major university to run, but his eldest daughter has just been diagnosed with leukemia. Dan, the vice president for administration, oversees seven units in the university in addition to the athletic department, including personnel, public safety and the physical plant, the people who keep the entire infrastructure functioning. Pete is teaching classes and handling dozens of legal issues for the university, from copyright questions to protests over the demolition of World War II–vintage student housing. Weeks go by with no communication. Jody is tense and irritable.

Although some of the communication problems are caused by conflicting commitments, the basic trouble is not a matter of scheduling. It is a matter of style, a clash of cultures: the genteel academy versus the aggressive lawyer-cum-agent, the soft-spoken, consensus-building Northwesterners versus the pugnacious guy from Atlanta. The two sides have hardly begun to talk, and already they don't care for each other. Alan thinks the university administration is a bunch of dinosaurs, stuck in a past where women's athletics doesn't matter. The university folks see Alan as an interloper who knows little and cares less about Oregon, its programs and its needs.

Meanwhile, despite the presence of Alan, Rich Brooks is still trying to negotiate privately with Jody. He has managed to find another $4,000 for her, not base salary but private endorsement money from Nike. The Oregon-based shoe giant has close ties to the university and its athletic department. The man who invented the waffle-soled shoe that made Nike is the renowned University of Oregon track coach Bill Bowerman. The man who heads the company is Phil Knight, Bowerman's star athlete in the late 1950s. Nike regularly donates shoes to the players and endorsement money to the coaches. With this additional private money, Rich is now offering Jody a total raise of $8,000. He calls her with the offer and tells her that only one other coach is getting a raise this year, a mere $2,500 increase. The offer, he tells her, is more than fair. "Take it. It's a good one," he says.

Rich wants to win at this. He wants to successfully negotiate without the involvement of a lawyer. He wants to take care of his own business. He doesn't yet realize that it's out of his hands.

Rich tracks her down during one of her many recruiting trips in July. At six in the morning, he phones her hotel in Los Angeles.

"I'm not supposed to be talking to you about this," Jody says when Rich starts in.

"I do not want to talk to your attorney. I want to talk to

you," he says. "Why can't we talk. You can confer with your
lawyer, but why can't the two of us just talk?"

"I'm not supposed to be talking to you," Jody says
again. But she stays on the line.

Rich presses the new offer and brings up, once again,
the promises of future raises. "I don't understand why you
won't trust me on this," he says. Then he starts talking about
the negotiations between Pete Swan, the university lawyer,
and Alan.

"I'm confused," Rich says. "Why do you want a two-
year contract?"

"A two-year contract? I don't want a two-year
contract," Jody says. "Who told you that?"

"This is what Pete told me that Alan says you want."

Jody can't believe what she's hearing. Not only are these
guys not talking to each other with regularity, when they do
talk, they are apparently not talking about the right things.
She has never wanted, or even mentioned, the notion of a
two-year contract. She has no idea where that one comes
from. She's always wanted a four-year contract. As soon as
she hangs up on Rich, Jody calls Alan, who insists he's never
heard of nor negotiated for a two-year contract. Jody doesn't
know what to think now.

With Jody on the road, Pete in Oregon and Alan in Georgia, the at-best tenuous communication is severely strained.
Back in Eugene, the word on Jody is that she doesn't know
what she wants, that she keeps changing her mind about contract terms. First it was a raise. Then it was a multiyear contract. Then it was graduated raises. Now it's something else.

But as far as Jody is concerned, her position has been
clear: She wants a show of respect for the program and what
she's done with it. She hasn't changed her mind; she's tried
to negotiate, and over time, the terms of the contract have
changed. That's how she looks at it. Anyway, since Alan has
entered the picture, the only thing she's been seriously considering is a four-year contract with a hefty raise. Somewhere
between Alan and Pete, between East Coast and West, be-

tween high-powered hired gun and mild-mannered academic attorney, communication has broken down. Each side blames the other. Jody doesn't know whom to believe—and she doesn't much care. She just wants to see this thing resolved.

Rich, meanwhile, has come to the end of his rope on these negotiations. Barb Walker warned Jody it might come to this. There will come a time, Barb told Jody earlier in the summer, when Rich will draw a line in the sand and say, "No more. This is it. Take it or leave it." What are you going to do then? she asked Jody. When Jody returns from a recruiting trip in late July, Rich tells her, in plain language: Sign the contract or we'll go looking for a new coach.

This is Rich's last stand, however. While Jody has been traveling, Rich has been rethinking his career. The football season will be starting soon. He doesn't think he can—nor does he want to—try to handle all the decisions that go along with the athletic director's job as well as try to put together a winning football team. The budget process alone looks like a full-time job. And this problem with Jody doesn't make the job look any more inviting. By the end of July, Rich is talking seriously to Dan and the president of the university about resigning from the AD position to concentrate on football.

Rich's threat scares Jody. She wants a big raise, but she also wants to keep this job. She calls Alan. He can tell something is going on from the pitch of her voice, high and thin, on the edge.

"I've been told either I sign or they'll go looking," Jody tells him.

Alan is silent for a moment. "Does the president know about this?" he asks her. "We need to call Dave and make sure he knows what's going on here."

Alan spends the rest of the conversation calming her down, explaining options to her. If this threat about looking elsewhere for a coach is real, he tells her, we can mount a retaliation suit. She isn't sure what that means exactly but it calms her somewhat to know she isn't powerless. And don't worry about them looking for a new coach, he tells her. If it comes down to the wire, we can sign a contract that we don't like just to put us in position to sue.

Jody understands this reasoning. Refusing to sign a contract was the big mistake Marianne Stanley made at USC when she sued. It's the reason Marianne's case lost in the lower courts. Jody won't make that mistake. Alan won't let her.

After she hangs up the phone, Jody calls Dave Frohnmayer's office. The president is in Seattle, his secretary says, and won't be back for a few days. Jody explains that she needs to reach him now, today. It is late afternoon. Jody goes for a run by the river to work off some of the anxiety.

A few hours later, at home, her phone rings. It's the president. He has excused himself from a dinner meeting to return her call. Jody tells him that she's been told she has to sign the contract or start looking for another job.

"Are you aware of this?" she asks Dave. "Are you aware that my attorney will mount a retaliation suit?"

Jody is out of her league here, a thirty-one-year-old coach talking to the man who served as the state's attorney general and later as dean of the law school, a man widely considered a top candidate for a future U.S. Senate seat. But Alan has pumped her up with confidence, so she goes for it. Still, she sounds more edgy than self-assured.

Dave reacts coolly and presidentially. He tells Jody he appreciates what she has done for women's basketball at the University of Oregon. He asks her please to hold off on any action until he can review the situation personally. His plan, he says, is to discuss all this in a conference call with all parties involved. That sounds good to Jody.

It takes some arranging, and at least one false start, to get the conference call together. But finally, at the end of July, with Jody sitting at home, Alan in his office in Atlanta and Dave, Pete, Dan and Rich—in one of his last official acts as athletic director—gathered in the president's office, the conversation begins. Dave starts with his usual civility. Much of his success at the university and in public life is rooted in his ability to be unassuming and authoritative at the same time, straightforward without being aggressive, genuinely friendly without being unctuous. He is an enormously popular president. On campus, they joke that any day now the university's motto will be changed from *Mens agitat molem* (mind moves matter) to Everyone loves Dave.

Dave sets the tone, thanking everyone for arranging their schedules and making themselves available. Then he launches into a matter-of-fact summary of the university's unhappy financial situation, which has been caused by the citizen-initiated property tax limitation law. These are lean years for the University of Oregon, and Dave wants Alan to know that big raises are not in the picture. He specifically wants Alan to know that Jody's idea of four years of graduated raises is impossible. The state figures its budget every two years. The university cannot promise raises based on unknown future budgets. It's as simple as that.

Alan listens quietly on the other end of the line three thousand miles away. None of the men in the president's office know just how impatient he is until he breaks in, five minutes into Dave's discourse.

"That's not the point," Alan says. Somehow he manages to drawl and sound querulous at the same time. "The point is: What are you paying your men's basketball coach? Take a look at what you're paying him; then take a look at Jody's salary. You've got a real problem with gender equity here, gentlemen. You are in violation of Title IX here."

Dan Williams sits at the large round table that dominates the president's spacious office, listening to the speakerphone and thinking how much this guy Alan Manheim doesn't know about Oregon. He doesn't know our situation. He doesn't know our budgetary constraints. He doesn't understand the scaled-back atmosphere, the austerity, the cuts; no faculty and staff raises for two years, entire departments wiped out. Dan, like most administrators around the country, believes that men's and women's basketball certainly are not equal in at least one vital respect: One makes money, the other doesn't. In his wildest dreams he cannot imagine paying Jody what the men's basketball coach makes—or anywhere near it. Even if there were enough money in the budget, Dan would not spend it bolstering Jody's salary. To Dan, Title IX–mandated equity does not mean the equality of men's and women's sports.

Alan continues talking, now postulating his position that Title IX's guarantee of equal opportunity includes the equal opportunity for players to be coached by first-rate coaches— which translates into equal salaries. Then he begins lecturing the men in the president's office on the intricacies of Title IX.

Dave—Harvard-, Oxford- and Boalt Hall–educated, Phi Beta Kappa, Rhodes scholar, the state's preeminent lawyer for a decade, a former assistant to the secretary of health, education, and welfare, a former consultant to the Civil Rights Division of the U.S. Department of Justice—isn't accustomed to being lectured on matters of the law and doesn't much like it. He knows Title IX well. "I've been to this rodeo before," he tells Alan with mounting impatience. In fact, Dave wrote one of the first articles on Title IX, an early 1970s article in a law journal calling the university community's attention to the new legislation. At the same time, he was cochairing a national Equal Opportunities Task Force that helped publicize Title IX.

Dave does not anger easily. In fact, no one in the room, not Dan Williams, who as a vice president works closely with Dave, nor Pete Swan, who has known Dave for years and interacts with him almost daily, has ever seen Dave angry. But he's angry now. He's being condescended to. He's being lectured at. As lawyers, both he and Pete bristle at Alan's aggressive—and what they perceive as his unnecessarily combative—tone. But as lawyers, they know the chest bumping and posturing that come with the territory.

They wait for Alan to wind down. But Alan doesn't wind down; he winds tighter. He resumes his lecture on Title IX and then ends with Jody's salary demand. If the graduated raises are not possible, Jody wants a four-year, $70,000 contract. She will not sign a multiyear contract for less than that.

Jody is silent throughout the conversation, sitting on the couch in her living room, listening to the men conduct business as one would listen to the conversation of a race of alien beings. She presses her lips together. She hopes to hell Alan knows what he's doing.

Now Alan is telling Dave that if Jody can't have the $70,000, she will sign only a one-year contract. This is part of Jody and Alan's agreed-upon strategy to keep her under contract while Alan mounts a lawsuit. Even in the absence of a lawsuit, the one-year contract makes sense, as it won't lock her into the lower salary. Alan asks for a base salary of $48,000—not the offered $46,000—plus the promised $4,000 Nike money. He wants the Nike money in the contract, not as a handshake deal, the way Rich has originally proposed it.

"That's the deal, gentlemen," Alan drawls. "We're looking for a seventy-thousand-dollar four-year contract. If we can't have that, we'll take the forty-eight-thousand-dollar one-year deal. But I'm telling you, we'll be signing that one under protest. We'll be reserving our rights to sue if we sign that one." That ends the conversation.

For a half hour, Dave, Pete, Dan and Rich confer in the president's office. They are not going to go for $70,000 a year. Neither Rich nor Dan can imagine paying a second-year coach of a nonrevenue sport that kind of money. There's the question of whether the university could actually afford such a deal, and if it could, whether that's how it would choose to spend its money. And Rich makes it clear how a $70,000 contract would throw off the balance in the athletic department, what the reaction would be of other coaches with many more years and many more trophies than Jody. A half hour later, Dave calls Alan back. The university will offer Jody the one-year contract for $48,000 bolstered by the Nike money. Her new salary with compensation will be $52,000, a $10,000 raise over her first-year contract.

The negotiations are over, but the contract is a long way

from being signed. Pete has to draft it. Alan has to review it. Then Pete has to review Alan's modifications. Then Alan has to review Pete's redraft. Weeks drag on with no contract and no news of a contract. Jody feels completely out of control. As far as she's concerned, the one-year contract means there's going to be a lawsuit, and if that's what is going to happen, she wants it filed now. She wants this resolved before the girls come back next month and practice begins. She knows the case itself will take a long time, but just to have the contract in hand and know the wheels are set in motion—that's what she wants.

Jody's nerves are raw. Half the time Alan doesn't return her phone calls. At first attentive, now the lawyer seems pre-occupied with other business. Jody is used to running the show and issuing the orders. That's what a coach does. Now she's given that control to a voice on the other end of a tele-phone line. She has invested Alan with great power over her career, which is to say, over her life, and she needs almost daily assurance that she has done the right thing. More im-portantly, she needs assurance that Alan is doing the right thing. But now, all of a sudden, it seems he's always in court. Or he's ill. Or his secretary is out and the answering machine is her only connection to his office. She leaves a message, and he doesn't call back. She leaves another message and another. A week goes by. She is angry all the time.

Jody doesn't know what to think. She imagines that the university agreed to the one-year contract knowing that her chances of having a good season this coming year are slim. Okay, let her have a rotten year, she imagines her bosses thinking. She'll have a bad year, community support will dwindle, game attendance will fall off, and she'll be history. Jody doesn't want to believe that anyone wishes her or the program ill. She doesn't want to think that the university that hired her actually wants her to fail.

But in her current state of high anxiety, she will believe anything. She feels almost completely isolated. Her negotia-tions have created distances between her and the other coaches. Her relationship with Rich Brooks is over. Her relationship with Barb Walker is over. Alan has told her not to talk to Dave or Dan or anyone in the administration. Jody's one lifeline is Alan, and Alan is not communicating. Jody calls him almost daily, alternately yelling at his secretary and cursing into his answering machine but seldom speaking to him in person.

In mid-August they finally connect. Alan tells her the university is dragging its feet on the contract, and it's time to bring in the media to light a fire under the administration. The university, meanwhile, contends that it is Alan who is creating the bottleneck by not returning calls and reviewing documents. Whatever is happening, the uneasy relationship between Alan and Pete Swan, the two lawyers, has not improved. Jody is now well into her second month of working without a contract.

Alan gives Jody the okay to talk to Bob Rodman, the local sports reporter who has taken an interest in women's basketball. She gives Rodman a call, and a few days later, a story appears on the front page of the sports section. OREGON TRYING TO SIGN RUNGE TO PACT is the innocuous headline. The story reveals to the public for the first time that Jody has been working without a contract and that she has a lawyer negotiating for her. But it makes it sound as if the negotiations have been smooth, and the contract is about to be signed. Alan is quoted as saying that he "anticipates a written contract being executed shortly." Dan Williams expresses cautious optimism. Rich Brooks says nothing. He has resigned as AD to concentrate on football and, much to his liking, is out of the loop. Dan is now not only the vice president who oversees the athletic department but also the acting AD. No one in the article mentions dollar figures. No one mentions lawsuits. Everyone plays it close to the chest.

To the casual readers of the sports page, it looks like a nonstory. But it is a carefully timed, well-orchestrated communications effort that lays the foundation for later stories.

The six-figure salaries of two Pac-10 women's coaches are mentioned. The salary of the University of Oregon's men's basketball coach is mentioned. Jody's impressive first-season stats are mentioned. Alan's successful negotiations at the University of Georgia are mentioned. These are all discreet facts presented in the traditional deadpan journalistic style. The casual reader sees no red flags.

But for those few in the know, it is easy to pull together these facts into an interesting whole. When Alan is quoted as saying "Jody is asking for nothing more than what is equitable and fair" and then defines equitable and fair by invoking Title IX, administrators at the university get the point.

Meanwhile, there is still no contract. Alan is moving slowly, apparently distracted by other cases. The university is being deliberate too, with Pete Swan drafting the contract cautiously, clause by clause, paragraph by paragraph. It was barely a year ago that the university was hauled into court for breach of contract by the former men's basketball coach, who had been reassigned against his will to another sport. The suit was a messy—and expensive—business, costing the university almost four hundred thousand dollars in back pay and immeasurable goodwill. It was a public-relations nightmare, caused in part by the way the coach's contract had been written.

The university is not likely to make the same mistake twice. Pete is now crafting the most detailed-ever contract between the university's athletic department and a coach, a thirty-one-page epistle that specifies anything and everything that can possibly be specified. It will serve as the model for all future coaching contracts, so Pete is taking his time. It takes all of August and most of September for the two lawyers to hammer out the language.

There is much talk, and some bitterness, about Alan's insistence on the inclusion of a paragraph that states that Jody is signing the contract under protest and does not waive her right to sue. Pete contends the paragraph is unnecessary. There is nothing in the contract that would prevent Jody from suing.

But Alan is adamant. Jody will not sign the contract without the protest paragraph. He wants it in there not just to insure his client can mount a lawsuit, but also to send a clear message to the university that she is planning to mount a lawsuit. Incidentally, the paragraph will make good media copy.

As the lawyers bump chests, Jody tries not to think about how much control she's lost. She busies herself with recruiting phone calls. She goes on long runs by the river. She sits and worries about the new season.

On the big board in her office she has written the five starting positions on the team and listed the top candidate for each. Everyone says this will be a "rebuilding" season—a euphemism often employed in the world of sports, where predicting a "losing" season would be considered bad form and would, in any case, take a big bite out of ticket sales. But looking at the board, she can't help but say the word to herself: losing; a losing season. Last year's three top players, the center, the big forward and the point guard, the three who accounted for two-thirds of the team's points, two-thirds of its rebounds and 100 percent of its leadership, are gone. The hole they have left is so deep and so wide that Jody has no idea how she will fill it. She knows she won't be filling it with the newcomers. The freshman recruiting class is not strong.

She spends long minutes sitting at her desk, staring across the expanse of gray carpet at her scrawled lists on the board. Under number 1, the center, she's listed Sandie Edwards, a six-five sophomore from a small town in Washington State. Sandie is big—tall, that is; her build is slender—but the trouble is, she doesn't play big. She doesn't muscle inside for the ball or use her body aggressively to block out or fight for rebounds. It's not just that she's never learned how to use her body that way, it's that it's not her style, and Jody suspects it will never be. Sandie doesn't have that look in her eye. She doesn't have that killer instinct. She's a nice girl, sweet, friendly, innocent, the kind of girl you'd want as a big sister. Last year, as a freshman coming in from a B league high school, she got very little playing time and scored very few points. Jody knows Sandie is not yet strong enough or skilled enough or fast enough—and may never be tough enough—to start in the Pac-10. But Sandie is all she's got.

Jody sighs and shifts her attention to the number 2 spot, the power forward. There she has listed Arianne Boyer, the one they all call Red, a six-foot sophomore, the team's most talented player—and the one with the attitude. Red's world is books and basketball, and Jody thinks that if basketball came first, Red could be an all-American. She made the all-freshman Pac-10 team last year. She's got the fire. She's got the strength. What she doesn't have, Jody thinks as she stares at the board shaking her head, is a good work ethic. What she doesn't have is the ability to mesh with the others.

She's a loner, the youngest child of long-divorced parents, a kid who learned the lessons of self-sufficiency long ago and a little too well. But she's got guts. Last year, when the team needed her, when Jody needed her, she played an important game with a broken finger. The image is burned in Jody's brain like a brand: The big redhead cradling the ball with her casted left hand, dropping her shoulder and charging in for a reverse lay-up. The girl has all the moves.

At the number 3 position, the small forward, Jody has listed Jessica Schutt (pronounced, by happy coincidence, "shoot"), one of the two returning seniors. Jess is a quiet, intense kid from a large, close-knit farm family in Washington. Jody knows that Jess feels tremendous pressure about this coming season—pressure to perform and pressure to lead. Last year Jess had a terrific season, averaging eleven points a game and exploding for thirty-four points against USC late in the season. Last year Jess ranked fifth in the Pac-10 in three-point accuracy. Now, with the two top scorers on the team gone, she knows she'll be expected to contribute even more.

But she also suffered a second stress fracture to her tibia last season. She's healed; she's okay, but Jody is worried about the lingering psychological effects of this second injury. Will Jess play as hard, push herself as much? Will she allow herself to be as aggressive or will she hold back, hesitate just a bit, to keep herself from being reinjured? It's going to be tough for her, Jody figures, because waiting in the wings, waiting to challenge Jess for her position, is Betty Ann Boeving, a sophomore who's quite a bit bigger than Jess and showed a lot of promise last year. To have someone breathing down your neck in your senior year is not a happy prospect. Jody understands that. But maybe Betty Ann will keep Jess motivated.

Jody also knows that Jess is troubled about her role on the team this year. As the most effective returning starter, Jess knows she's expected to be the leader. But she doesn't know if she has it in her. She was team captain in high school for two years, but here at the university, she has kept mostly to herself, developing a deep and in many ways isolating friendship with another member of the team, Karen, the other senior. The two are inseparable, off and on the court, and their bond has created a distance between them and the others. Jess doesn't know if she can move out from that friendship to embrace the others. Jody doesn't know either, and she worries about the possibility of a leaderless team.

At number 4, the shooting-guard position, is Karen Healea, Jess's best friend and the only other senior on the team. Jody is torn about Karen. Karen is athletic, very smart, very conscientious, but Jody thinks she doesn't have that burning love of the game that would make her a great player. Jody doesn't know why Karen lacks self-confidence—she thinks it might have something to do with her relationships with men, starting with Karen's father—but she does know how that lack of self-confidence translates on the court. When it comes to clutch time, Karen is not the one who wants the ball. She doesn't want the responsibility. She's not ready to be someone others can depend on. This would concern any coach, but it worries Jody even more as she struggles to imagine who will solidify this team.

Finally there's number 5, the point guard. Jody shakes her head. Last year was tough on Cindie Edamura, the Japa-

nese Canadian whom the girls all call Eddie. Even though she
was a freshman, she had started at point guard, playing the
first thirteen games of the season before falling apart in a
game against Oregon State. Eddie seemed to feel from the
beginning of the year that she was playing way over her head,
a provincial girl from an ugly mill town playing in the big
leagues, a five-six freshman dwarfed by six-four seniors. The
Oregon State game proved it to her. Jody watched from the
sidelines as Eddie was banged and pushed, stolen from and
outplayed at every turn. After that, Jody never started her
again, which confirmed for Eddie all the fears and doubts she
had about her own abilities. This year, Jody has no choice:
She has to start Eddie, and she has to keep on playing her,
no matter what. There is no one else for the position. Eddie
knows this, and it scares the hell out of her. Jody doesn't feel
too sanguine about it either. If Eddie doesn't learn to be aggressive, if she doesn't take hold of the point-guard position,
the team cannot win.

Jody hasn't read all the new research on girls and sports
and self-esteem. She doesn't know about the study that found
that girls who play sports are less likely to be depressed or
dissatisfied with their bodies, less likely to do those things
kids with low self-esteem often do: use drugs, get pregnant,
stay in abusive relationships. She has never heard of the survey of women leaders in *Fortune* 500 companies, 80 percent
of whom report they were "jocks" growing up.

But she knows the territory personally. Sports gave her
her identity, her physical and psychological strength. Sports
carried her through adolescence when other girls began to
doubt themselves, to change from boisterous, risk-taking, self-
confident kids to hesitant, cautious self-doubters. But thanks
to sports, to the discipline it demanded and the leadership
qualities it bred, Jody was an Ophelia who did not need re-
viving. It was this experience—the power she felt growing up
with sports—that she knows she has to share somehow with
this year's team.

She is not a hand holder. She is not a touchy-feely, nurturing woman who has it in her to have long heart-to-hearts with her players about their inner selves. She is a jock from a family of jocks, articulate only in that special, odd way that coaches are articulate. She will have to show them strength and leadership by being who she is and demanding that they live up to her expectations. She knows she will have to teach by example, and that toughness and confidence are the most important lessons she has to impart. This is a team that will need both, and then some.

Jody looks at the board again, scans the roster and doesn't like what she sees. She knows the team is too young and too raw to make much of a showing this season. A bad year is bad for everyone, but for a second-year head coach on a one-year contract who is threatening to sue her employer, a bad year might mean a final year, maybe even a career-ending year. Jody tries not to dwell on it, but in the void created by Alan's silence and in the isolation created by the negotiations, she has little else to think of but her team's and her own tenuous future.

Into September, pieces of the contract are still being faxed from Atlanta to Eugene and back again. Jody doesn't understand what's going on, and she doesn't know why whatever is going on is taking so long. To her, this contract is a minor item, a document she doesn't like but has to sign so that she's employed when Alan files the suit. It's insurance against having her case thrown out of court like Marianne Stanley's. So why the delay? And why, she asks herself every day, isn't Alan calling her?

When she finally gets through to him again, he blames the university for holding up progress. But it's clear to Jody from the treatment she's been getting from Alan—the weeks of silence, the unreturned phone calls—that her own lawyer might be the problem. Not for the first time, she thinks about dropping him and finding someone else to represent her. She even makes a few phone calls. But in the end, she sticks with Alan. If her friend at the University of Georgia trusted him, she'll trust him too. But she won't be happy about it.

"I need more attention than you're giving me, Alan!" she yells at him over the phone one afternoon in mid-September. He has finally returned her almost daily calls. "I'm a high-maintenance person. You can't be treating me this way."

Alan mollifies her, or rather, Jody allows herself to be mollified. She feels she has no choice now. She's started something that she has to finish, and she needs Alan to do it. She needs someone to take care of this while she takes care of basketball.

Finally, at the end of September, she gets a call from Alan that he is about to fax her the contract. He always calls her a few minutes before he sends faxes so she can stand by the machine outside her office and grab the papers before someone else does. At this point, it is critical to keep the communication private. He tells her the contract is ready for her signature, and that it's the same deal they've been talking about since July, a one-year forty-eight-thousand-dollar base contract with an additional four thousand dollars in Nike money. It has the language Alan wants about preserving Jody's right to sue.

Jody watches the fax machine as the pages come through. She is relieved to finally get the damn thing, but mostly, standing there alone in the outer office, spine straight as a ruler, shoulders squared, long, slender fingers picking up each page, she is overcome with anger. She can't believe it has taken almost six months to get a contract she doesn't want. She's angry at Alan for taking so long and angry at herself for putting up with it. She's angry at the university for not giving her the respect she thinks she deserves.

Under the anger is a thin layer of dread: Signing this contract is just the beginning of a long, difficult process, the first step on a litigious path that could isolate her even more from her athletic department colleagues and cost her, even if she wins, her career. No university wants to hire a coach with a history of lawsuits, a troublemaker, a rocker of boats. But beneath the dread is the steely resolve, the hard, shiny core of Jody Runge, and it is from this place that she gathers her strength on this late September afternoon.

She brings the papers back to her office and shuts the door. She sits at her desk, her back to the big window. Outside it is a perfect fall afternoon. The sky is deep blue; the alders that line the river are flecked with gold. Inside, Jody sits reading, her face a mask. It's her game face, the tough look she puts on when she walks out on the court, the face that shows she won't take any shit. This is just like a competition, she is telling herself as she looks at the contract. This is a competition, and I want to win. The administration doesn't know how strong I am, she thinks. They don't think I have the guts for this. They don't think I have the guts to sue. They don't know me very well.

Quickly, she signs the contract and walks it across the building and down the hall to the athletic director's office. There are only two weeks until practice starts. She's got to start thinking about basketball.

PART TWO

PLAY
HARD

IN IT TO WIN IT!

FIFTEEN WOMEN IN BAGGY GREEN SHORTS SPRINT UP AND down the court, their hair damp and matted to their scalps, their Nikes squeaking on the polished floor. They are wearing identical oversized T-shirts with ferocious, basketball-dribbling Daisy Ducks printed on the front and, on the back, in three-inch-high green letters, their unofficial team motto: IN IT TO WIN IT!

"Good hustle!" yells Betty Ann Boeving, clapping her hands as one of her teammates finishes a set of sprints. Betty Ann, who everyone calls B, is a big, inveterately happy girl with a big, booming voice. Her high spirits are generally contagious. But not today, not at seven o'clock on a Saturday morning, the October sky leaden with rain, the air as dank and chill as a cellar. It is a morning made for sleeping or for sauntering around the house in fuzzy slippers with a mug of warm tea. But it is the first practice of the new season, and everyone is in Mac Court, taped up, stretched out, warmed up, and although not happy about it—with the exception of B—ready to go.

Jody stands off to the side of the court, groggy despite two cups of coffee, calling out the drills: dribble, bounce pass, chest pass. Four lines of players are going at once.

"Come on, ladies!" yells B, clapping loudly. "Let's go, Ducks." One of the freshmen in the line extends a palm for B to slap.

Jody watches intently, stepping in to offer instruction on the placement of thumbs or the position of elbows or the length of stride, stepping back to see the action. She is a believer in fundamentals, in technique. She has two basic strategies for the team this year: Get the girls in shape; teach them "the system"—the controlled, choreographed patterns and plays they will run in the game. Out on the court, her three assistants are directing the drills, each at the head of a line of players. There's Stephanie Osburn, a pretty, dark-haired woman with a powerful body, who used to play for Arizona State. Now twenty-eight and a veteran of the coaching staffs of the University of Hawaii and the University of British Columbia, she is the assistant with the longest tenure in the program—two years. She is serious and focused, assertive, occasionally hot-tempered. Next to her, yelling out instructions to a line of players, is Joe Jackson, the assistant Jody hired last year, hoping that his basketball connections in Southern California would help her recruiting efforts. Joe, who is thirty-two, has been coaching L.A.-area junior college and high school basketball for thirteen years. He is a tall, good-looking black man with an easygoing disposition and the gift of gab. Down under the basket is Kelly Kebe, the third assistant. Loose-limbed and agile, she looks more like the college player she used to be just a year ago than the coach she is trying to become.

Every time the girls think they're finished, Jody calls another drill. Up and back they run, up and back. The drills are endless, repetitive, uninteresting, like playing scales over and over again.

"You're getting bored out there. You're getting sloppy!" Jody yells. She gets them started on a shooting drill,

looks for a moment, then does an about-face and walks toward
the sideline where Karen Healea is riding a stationary bicycle.
Karen is pumping away, unsmiling, just beginning to
break a sweat. She is not tall for a basketball player, only
five-foot-nine, but her leanness makes her look elongated, like
a stretched rubber band. Even in a bulky warm-up suit, sitting
hunched over the handlebars, she looks skinny. Her eyes are
huge in her slender face, dark, serious, determined and, this
morning, sad. Karen is a senior, a three-year veteran, a player
Jody had counted on in the starting lineup for this season. But
right now, Karen is in too much pain to even go through
simple drills. "If it were me," a doctor told her last week,
"I would forget about playing altogether."

Karen knew something was wrong years ago back in
high school. She was a star on her suburban Portland high
school basketball team, team captain, season high scorer,
named to the AAAA all-state tournament squad—but playing
with pain. Her leg hurt as if the muscles were strung too
tightly from hip to knee. Sometimes her hip hurt with a deep,
bone ache. She didn't tell anyone. She didn't see a doctor.
She didn't want to know what was wrong; she just wanted to
keep on playing ball. The pain in her legs came and went;
she ignored it. Finally, it seemed to go away.

But a few months ago, back home for the summer, she
was out on her daily run when her knee started to bother her.
The next morning, she could barely walk. Okay, she said to
herself, I'll just stop running for a while, and it will get better.
But it didn't. She was in serious and constant pain.

She thought about telling her parents, but she just
couldn't bring herself to do it. Her father especially had so
much invested in Karen's athletic career that she felt any hint
of a serious injury could devastate him. Gary Healea was a
sports fan in the original sense of the word: a fanatic. His own
ball playing was limited to two years at a junior college, but
he coached kids' sports for years and couldn't wait to coach
and train his own son, who he felt sure would have the high-
powered collegiate sports career Gary didn't. These plans

were only slightly modified when he and Joanne, his high school sweetheart, had two girls.

Karen and her older sister never had much choice: Sports is what they did, defining the seasons not by the calendar but by the practice schedule, by the game to be played: fall, volleyball; winter, basketball; spring, softball. Fortunately for the girls, they liked sports and did well. Gary coached his daughters not only during practices and games in elementary and middle school, where he served as the official coach for every team they played on, but at home, every night and on weekends, his comments and criticisms a continuous undercurrent in their lives.

When first her sister and then Karen reached ninth grade, and the high school coaches took over, Gary could not let go. At home, before the game, he would tell them what to do. During the game, he would shout from the stands. "What are you doing out there?" "Take the shot! Take the shot!" Of course, many people yelled and cheered from the stands. But Karen's father was the loudest and most insistent. It got so bad that her mother refused to sit next to him. It got so bad that Karen's sister quit the basketball team her senior year.

That gave Gary more time to concentrate on Karen. The before-the-game talks, the yelling from the stands, the after-the-game debriefing—Karen felt trapped by her father's expectations, drowning in his reproaches, smothered by his attention. One basketball game during her junior year, Gary was so loud from the stands, so over-the-top, that Karen couldn't take it anymore. When they got home, she issued an ultimatum: Either he stopped going to her games altogether or he learned to keep his mouth shut. That's just how she put it, that bluntly, a skinny seventeen-year-old going mano a mano with her father. It was scary, but it felt good. Then Karen played her trump card: She told Gary that if he couldn't stay away or be quiet, she would quit playing.

Not coming to the games was out of the question for Gary, as was the idea of Karen following in her sister's footsteps and quitting. So he had only one choice: He had to keep

his mouth shut. Joanne moved back to her spot in the bleachers beside her husband so she could monitor him, sometimes
actually putting her hand over his mouth when she saw he
was about to erupt. Slowly, very slowly, he got better. But he
never entirely cured himself.

That year, when the college scholarship offers started
coming in, Karen seriously considered going far enough away
for college so her parents couldn't come to the games. But
there was enough of the good girl in her that she couldn't do
that to her father. He might not understand her, but she sure
understood him. She knew how much her collegiate career
meant to him. She couldn't deny him what he seemed to need
so badly. She chose the University of Oregon, an easy two-
hour freeway drive from home. That meant he and Joanne
came to most every home game. In Mac Court, Karen could
sometimes hear him from the stands.

She couldn't tell her father that she was in so much pain
that even walking hurt. He was counting on her to have
a great senior year, not just her final year of play but his
final year as well. She didn't tell Jody either, or the team
trainer. Instead, she quietly went to her local doctor for anti-
inflammatory drugs. They didn't help. She went back to daily
workouts, thinking she could run through the pain. She
couldn't. Three weeks before fall term was to begin, which
meant five weeks before practice was to begin, Karen finally
admitted to herself that something was very wrong and that
she better find out what. She called Kim, the trainer, on the
phone and, in between uncontrollable sobs, told her what was
happening.

Kim immediately set up doctors' appointments for her
in Eugene—a sports medicine Mecca, thanks, in part, to
the university—and Karen made the two-hour drive to get
x-rayed, ultrasounded, examined, medicated and massaged.
She was hoping for a course of physical therapy. She would
stay with it, however difficult it was. She would get better. It
meant everything to her to be able to play her senior year.
She and Jess, her roommate and best friend, had been plan-

ning for it, dreaming of it since they played their first game in the Pac-10 three years ago.

But looking at the X rays, the doctor had other ideas. He saw Karen's problem clearly, and it was not something that could be solved by physical therapy. Karen had been born with unusually shallow hip sockets. To compensate for this, to keep her thighbones from rotating too much, the muscles and tendons around her hip joints had tightened. They would stay tight—they had to stay tight—unless or until Karen had major surgery to dig deeper bowls in her hip. This would be career-ending surgery.

Karen listened to the doctor, but she didn't hear him. Sports psychologists say that an athlete who suffers a major injury reacts much the same way as a person who faces a fatal diagnosis: First, and perhaps for a long time, there is denial. Karen was the queen of denial. She refused to think about anything short of curing herself. She did not hear that curing herself was not possible.

At home again, after the diagnosis, she was talking to a friend on the phone and she broke down. Her parents heard her crying. That's how they found out. She told them then about the shallow hip sockets and the tightening tendons and the surgery. She told them the doctor said not to play. Her mother held her and cried. Her father was silent for a long time. Finally, he said—almost grudgingly, Karen thought— "Well, if playing this year is going to hurt you for your whole life, you know the best thing to do."

She wasn't exactly sure what he meant by that. But Karen was interested in playing for herself, not just to satisfy her father. She truly loved the game, and she was good at it. In the time she had before school began in the fall, Karen forced herself to work out six days a week, alternating stationary bike with StairMaster, adding swimming, taking hour-long walks. Everything she did caused her pain. But as her muscles warmed, as she forced them to stretch day after day, she felt the pain lessen. The doctor shook his head. In this town known as the Jogging Capital of the World, home to

Steve Prefontaine, Mary Decker Slaney, Alberto Salazar and a raft of former and would-be Olympians, the doctor understood this kind of persistence. Okay, he said, that's great. But you must be pain-free for two weeks before you can start running again. Karen knew she had to be able to run before she could practice with the team.

Today, the first day of practice, Karen is not pain-free but she is pretending to be.

"How do you feel?" Jody asks her, laying a hand on her back.

Karen looks up at her, her legs pumping hard, and forces a wide grin. "I feel good. I feel fine."

Kim, the trainer, who has had her eye on Karen all during her warm-up on the exercise bike, walks over from the bleachers. "Okay, Karen? How's the knee?"

Karen gives her a version of the same smile, slightly frayed. She is tired of being asked. She is tired of being injured. "Yeah. Okay. Fine."

Jody and Kim exchange a brief look, which Karen doesn't see. Jody's look to Kim asks: Is she really okay? Is she going to be able to play? Kim's look says: Don't count on it.

Jody doesn't know what she'll do if Karen isn't in the starting lineup. It's not that Karen is a star—she averaged only six points a game last season—but she contributes. She led the team in steals. She's a good three-point shooter. She understands the system. If Karen can't play, Jody's options are very limited. The team needs stability and maturity, which Jody figured were going to come from Karen and Jess, the two seniors. If Karen can't play, the team will be in trouble.

Karen is pumping away in earnest, her long, dark ponytail sashaying from side to side, sweat running down her temples. Jody nods at her, then walks back to the court, head down. She is busy turning over the possibilities: If Karen can't play, who can she put in the shooting-guard position? Who can contribute from the bench? How will she reconfigure the starting lineup to make this all work? There are no easy answers. Jody files away the problem and redirects her attention. Out on the court, the players are practicing free throws in groups of four. She scans the groups until she sees a six-foot-three player slouching under a far basket. At least there's Roy, she thinks, looking at the girl. At least there's Roy.

Roy is Renae Fegent's nickname. And Roy is a godsend, a windfall, an unexpected, unplanned-for bonanza. All summer Jody had been quietly worried about who would play center this season. Sandie Edwards, at six-foot-five, was the natural, and the only, choice. But she was timid on the court, a sophomore who had not gotten much playing time the year before, a tall girl who didn't yet know how to play big. Jody knew Sandie wasn't ready physically or mentally and would have a tough time handling the pressure of being a starter. But Sandie was all she had—until Roy appeared.

Roy was a twenty-two-year-old Australian who had been playing basketball since she was eight. By age sixteen she was playing for the prestigious Australian Institute of Sports. At eighteen, she was touring Europe and the United States with the Canberra Capitals of the Women's National Basketball League, averaging thirteen points and nine rebounds a season. Basketball was not just the center of her life. It was her entire life. She worked for the institute. She practiced. She played. But after three seasons in the national league and thirteen years of uninterrupted competition, Roy hit the wall. Her body—strong, big-boned, muscular—could take the punishment, but she was mentally exhausted, emotionally spent. She needed to get away from the game, maybe forever, and clear her head, find out who she was and what she wanted. In the Australian tradition, she decided to go on a walkabout, to have an unplanned adventure in an uncharted land. She bought a one-way plane ticket to terra incognita: the United States.

Las Vegas was her destination. There she met up with an old basketball-playing friend from Australia and camped in her apartment for a month and a half, sleeping late, partying late, taking one day at a time and giving no thought to basketball. When summer came, the two decided to tour the

States together, and Roy went out to buy a truck for that purpose. The guy at the used-car lot turned out to be a former University of Nevada at Las Vegas assistant women's basketball coach. He took one look at Roy, at her big hands and her long arms, at her solid six-foot-three frame, and he called an old friend of his who he knew was desperate for good, tall players. The friend's name was Jody Runge.

Jody understood, after talking to Roy, that she was not particularly interested in playing basketball for the University of Oregon, or anyplace for that matter. But Jody thought: Maybe if I can get her out here, maybe if she sees the team, the town . . . maybe she might change her mind. Jody got Roy to come to Oregon on an unofficial visit, but the lure wasn't basketball. It was the state's inexpensive automotive vehicle registration fee. In Nevada, registering her truck would cost several hundred dollars. Come to Oregon, Jody coaxed on the phone. The registration is cheap, and you can see what we've got out here. Jody figured it was a real long shot, but she had nothing else going. And the team needed a big girl.

As it turned out, Roy loved the team, and the team loved Roy. To her, the Oregon players seemed so much more friendly, more openhearted, more naturally inclusive than the girls she had played with back home. For their part, the Oregon players found Roy relaxed and funny and unassuming, talented but egoless; in short, a terrific teammate. She looked around campus—she had never gone to college or much considered it—and a thought struck her: It might be interesting to experience American college life. She didn't think about classes or a major or a career direction, but rather soaking up the ambiance, immersing herself in a subculture she knew nothing about. Jody offered her the means to do it, a two-year scholarship that would pay for everything Roy needed, from tuition, fees and books to an apartment and food on the table. She would have instant friends, instant camaraderie and the chance to travel.

The idea of staying in Oregon was beginning to appeal

to her, but Roy was nonchalant about it. She would have to take the SATs and score at least 700 to be admitted as a student and qualify as an NCAA athlete. A 700 score wasn't much, but she had been out of high school for five years and had never been much of a student even back then. She doubted she'd make the grade but adopted a Zen-like attitude toward the process: She would take the test. If she scored high enough, she would come to the university and play ball. If she didn't score high enough, she would continue her wanderings. Jody was much less sanguine. She wanted Roy to pass. She needed Roy to pass.

Roy took the test in July and, while Jody quietly agonized, hoping for a miracle, Roy loaded up her truck and traveled to Seattle, Calgary, Toronto, Cleveland and Montreal, seeing some of the country she had come to see. She returned in August, dead broke, to discover she had gotten the necessary SAT score. So now Roy is out there on the court practicing with the team, a big, strong, experienced player who Jody hadn't known existed three months ago, a starter, perhaps even a star, whom she had not spent a second recruiting; a gift.

More than anyone, Jody understands how lucky she is that Roy is here. She watches the big girl maneuver under the basket for a layup. The team is going through yet another drill. Roy needs to get in shape, but Jody can see what a good player she will be, how smart she is about the game. If she were not so preoccupied with her equity case, Jody might even be happy right now.

As it is, she feels very much on edge. The article announcing that she signed her contract under protest appeared in the local paper a few days ago, and life has gotten progressively less pleasant since then. First it was just the cool stares of her colleagues; now it is a wider reaction. The sports columnist for the *Register-Guard* writes a strongly worded piece stating unequivocally that men's and women's basketball are not equal, that the coaching jobs are not equal, and that the pay should not be equal. If this kind of thinking makes Rich Brooks a dinosaur, the columnist writes, then I'm a dinosaur too. Two days later, he writes another column. The subject of this one is how well funded football and men's basketball are, how women's sports don't attract big-money donors and how that's too bad but that's the way it is. Jody figures the columnist and Rich Brooks are having a good time talking to each other.

What upsets her much more than the two columns is a stinging letter to the editor published in the sports pages. The editor has appropriately titled the letter FIRE HER. It begins this way: "Jody Runge is a lawsuit looking for an excuse to happen. She's a cancer looking for a body. She is an egocentric, angry, combative woman spoiling for a fight. Get rid of her."

And that's the nice part. The letter writer, a choleric male from a small coastal town a hundred miles from Eugene, considers Jody hostile, caustic, embittered, a one-woman plague, and ungrateful to boot. She was a "no-name assistant" when the university offered her the chance for "relative fame, lots of fun and relative fortune," he writes. She should have shut up and enjoyed it. "Whatever it takes to get her out of there," he writes in his final paragraph, "do it."

Jody has never before felt so publicly vulnerable. It is dawning on her that reactions like this may become commonplace if she actually mounts the lawsuit. She's not prepared for the unpleasantness and doesn't think she will ever be. But she is convinced of her cause and feels there is no turning back. She will just have to grow a thicker skin.

Rather than intimidating or subduing her, the letter impels her to action. If there is going to be unpleasantness, she wants it to happen now. If there is going to be a lawsuit, she wants Alan out here filing it immediately. She tells him so on the phone the day after the first practice. Alan promises to get moving, but Jody hears nothing for several days. Then, after two more prompting phone calls, she gets a copy of a fax Alan has sent to Dan Williams, the acting AD.

The letter begins by calmly stating that Jody's salary and "several aspects of the treatment of women basketball players" do not comply with Title IX and reminding Dan that Jody signed her one-year contract under protest. It is now time, writes Alan, to address the issues of inequity that led to the statement of protest in the contract. After several paragraphs comparing the men's and women's programs and their coaches, making the point that Jody has far outperformed her male counterpart, Alan comes to the point: His client wants a seventy-thousand-dollar-a-year contract, and she wants equal access to practice times and "to the same opportunities as the men's basketball players and program."

"My client does not wish to have this matter escalate to the point of litigation," he writes, "but is prepared to do so if absolutely necessary as a last resort." Alan gives Dan a deadline of 5 P.M. the following day to respond. He says he is faxing Pete Swan, the university's legal counsel, "a draft copy of a suit that may be filed by Jody next week."

The letter to Dan arrives just after noon on a Thursday in late October. At 3:30 P.M., university president Dave Frohnmayer, the vice president for public affairs and the university's communications director meet in emergency session in the president's office. Until a few hours ago, university officials were not at all convinced that Jody and her lawyer would be doing anything other than making noise. Now, they are taking the threat of a lawsuit seriously—especially the communications guy, who sees nothing but trouble ahead. He has already given much thought to the situation and, since the publication of the newspaper story about her contract signed under protest, he has been holding his breath. The fax today scares him. He smells disaster.

He tells the president that, regardless of the merits of the case, if it goes to court there will be negative public relations for the university, not just locally but regionally and nationally. Everywhere the team plays, the story will be on the sports pages. It will be picked up by the national media. He speaks with a calmness he doesn't feel. He chooses his next words very carefully: "No matter what we do, we are going to be viewed by certain members of the public as a big, cold institution fighting a solitary woman who wants nothing more than equity." He lets that idea sink in.

The president listens carefully, but his reaction is lawyerly. He attacks the letter from Alan; he finds holes in the argument.

"It doesn't matter if the case is good or not," says the communications guy. "The public-relations problem is the same."

Dan Williams arrives late from another meeting. He takes a hard line. Jody just signed a contract, he tells the group, and now is not the time to start negotiating new terms. The time to negotiate, if we want to, is next year, when the contract expires. That's the end of it, as far as Dan can see. There's nothing more to talk about.

No one else in the room is that sure. The threat of the lawsuit continues to drive the conversation. The president is beginning to see that something will have to be done for women's basketball, if not now, then soon. Coaches' salaries and other expenses for the football and men's basketball programs are boosted by outside donors. He thinks he might be able to do the same for women's basketball, if given the time. He tells the men around the table that he might have a line on a donor who could help support the women's program but that she would most probably be driven away if there is a lawsuit. He doesn't say who she is. In fact, he asks everyone at the meeting to keep the donor idea under wraps.

Alan's fax gave Dan a twenty-four-hour deadline to respond. But the men in the president's office don't take that too seriously. It's just posturing, just a lawyer flexing his muscles, they figure. At any rate, it is an unreasonable deadline, and they have no intention of trying to meet it. There is noth-

ing they can say to Alan tomorrow. There is no new offer
they are going to make to Jody in twenty-four hours.

Alan waits for a response all day Friday. Jody calls him
twice. At 5 P.M. Oregon time, 8 P.M. in Atlanta, Alan fires off
another fax. Your lack of response is just another example of
your lack of concern about these issues, he writes to Dan.
Neither Jody nor her lawyer know that the president and his
advisers have met to discuss Alan's letter. Jody figures she's
being completely ignored. She wonders if Dan even got the
fax, if he read it, if he showed it to anyone. Alan tells Jody
they will wait for a response until Monday afternoon before
they consider their next step.
    On Saturday, at 8 A.M., Jody is in Mac Court running a
tough practice. On Sunday, she is nursing a bad cold. Alan
calls her three times Monday. If there's no response by this
afternoon, he tells Jody, I'm going to the press.
    "Shouldn't you call the university first?" Jody asks him.
"Maybe find out why there hasn't been a response." Jody is
reluctant to air this in the media right now. She is still reeling
from that nasty letter to the editor. She is at home in bed. Her
cold is worse. She is swigging Benadryl for a bad case of
stress-induced hives.
    "Listen," Alan tells her. "We sent two letters. They
should respond. It's clear they're not taking this seriously. So
we've got to force them to take it seriously." Alan hangs up
the phone, waits another hour, then puts a call through to Bob
Rodman at the *Register-Guard.*
    The next morning, Jody wakes up in the dark at six with-
out the usual urgings of the alarm clock. At 6:15, she goes
out to the mailbox to get the morning paper. She doesn't know
if the story will run today. Alan spoke to the reporter late in
the afternoon, and there may not have been time to get reaction from the university. She picks up the paper and is about
to turn to the sports section when she sees her picture on
the front page next to a story headlined COACH PROBABLY
WILL SUE THE UO. There, in the second paragraph, is Alan's

headline-making quote: "I anticipate a lawsuit will be filed shortly."

Jody sees that the reporter did manage to get through to Dan Williams for a comment. He says publicly what he said privately at the meeting in the president's office, that the time to talk about contract terms is next spring, not now. "We would be disappointed if this ends up in court," Dan tells Bob Rodman. "We would not knowingly be in violation of Title IX."

Jody reads the story again as she waits in line at Starbucks for her morning coffee. She is thinking about what she will tell the team in practice this morning. As it turns out, it is easier than she imagines.

When she gets to Mac Court, the girls are on the floor in their usual prepractice circle, stretching out and joking quietly among themselves. No one takes much notice of Jody as she stops for a moment to talk to her assistant coaches and then strides across the court—no one, that is, except Red. Red keeps sneaking sidelong looks at Jody, which Jody pretends not to notice.

"How many of you read the newspaper this morning?" Jody asks, looking around the circle. Red says she has. The others are silent. "Well, there's a story in there about me." Jody looks around the circle from girl to girl. Their faces are blank with sleepiness. "I just wanted you to know before I say anything else that I am your coach, and I am going to be your coach this year and I hope for a long time. I have a contract this year, and I signed it so that I can negotiate better things for us."

Red is staring hard at Jody. The others are in various states of distraction: Eddie is shifting from foot to foot; Roy is retying a shoelace; B is finishing her stretches. They are listening because Jody is the coach, and you listen to the coach. A few have read last week's sports column, the one challenging the notion that the men's and women's basketball coaches do the same job. But most of them don't read the paper. And most of them, although they are the direct beneficiaries of Title IX, don't think about their life in sports as having anything to do with politics or the law.

"I'm trying to fight for what we need to be a successful program," Jody tells them. "We got the locker room mostly taken care of, but there are other things, lots of things." Jody is talking fast now. She sees that the girls aren't much interested. She's uncomfortable too, not knowing what to tell them, not knowing how much to tell them. "I've spent the last seven months trying to express these concerns to the university, and now it's come down to making them take me seriously." She pauses, not wanting to say anything bad about the university, not wanting to say anything concrete about her legal affairs. Red is still staring at her.

"I don't want you to think about this," she says, finally. "I'm here. I'm your coach. Whatever happens I'll be your coach this year." That's all she's going to say. This is her fight, and although she feels she is fighting it for them, for the team, for the program, she thinks it's best that they all concentrate on basketball. "Does anyone have any questions?"

There is a long pause. Then one of the girls asks, "What do we say about this if someone asks us?"

"Just tell them you don't know much about it," Jody says. The girls seem relieved.

"Okay, let's go," says Jody, clapping her hands. The circle contracts. The girls raise their hands high, touching fingers.

"Practice hard. Stay focused," they chant like marines in boot camp. Then they move out onto the court.

It is not as easy for Jody to stay focused. She is worried about Karen, who has not yet been able to practice with the team, who even when she does start to play, probably won't play well. The first game of the season is a month away, and Jody doesn't know what she's going to do for a shooting guard. She is worried, more generally, about the lack of depth on the team. It's not just that there's no replacement for

Karen, it's that Jody figures there are only maybe two people on the bench capable of Pac-10-level play, B and Sandie. A junior college recruit she had great hopes for is not coming along fast enough. One of her freshman recruits is already injured. Another seems incapable of hard work. A junior who is tired of sitting on the bench is creating morale problems. As disquieting as all this is, Jody finds it easier to think about than her legal situation. She understands basketball. Lawsuits are another matter entirely.

In the days after the COACH PROBABLY WILL SUE front-page story, public reaction escalates. Jody is heartened by four letters to the editor in the *Register-Guard,* all written by women supporting her fight for equity. "Jody tells her players that they should fight for what they believe in, and never to settle for anything less. Is she not supposed to practice what she preaches?" writes one woman. Another letter writer calls her "an excellent example of a role model." One of the local radio stations, the only one with a female sports reporter, does an on-air telephone interview with legendary Stanford coach Tara VanDerveer, asking her about Jody's case. Although Tara, one of the few female coaches in the country who is paid the same as her male counterpart, declines to comment directly, she offers a rousing minilecture on equal pay for equal work.

The local newspaper sends out a reporter to roam the University of Oregon campus looking for reactions to Jody's threatened suit. His front-page story quotes two male students who don't think the men's and women's basketball coaching jobs are equal and two women who are not sure. The sports reporter, Bob Rodman, spends time at the Cas Center interviewing Jody's coaching colleagues. "This is upsetting to everyone," the wrestling coach, a fourteen-year Oregon veteran, is quoted as saying. He makes $41,000 a year. "Jody is a person with strong opinions," says the men's volleyball coach, in his ninth season with a base salary of $41,400, "and whether you agree or disagree, you have to respect her for taking a stand." The softball coach, one of only three women coaches in the athletic department (Jody and the women's golf coach are the other two), won't comment. "I don't want to get involved in it," she tells the reporter, "because it is such a tough issue." She makes $33,900 and has been coaching at Oregon for five years.

Jody reads the paper and winces. She is not the only one. The local promotions person for Burger King, who had promised $500 to help pay for a women's basketball poster, reneges. She's read about the possibility of the suit. She's read the reaction stories. She doesn't want any part of it. Jody curses under her breath and makes some quick calls to Portland to line up another sponsor.

Rich Brooks, no longer Jody's boss but still playing the father role, catches her in the office the next day. "Just speaking colleague to colleague," he tells her, "don't do it. Don't sue the university. You can't get things done here at Oregon unless everyone helps you. You need everyone on your side." Jody doesn't know what to do with that advice. Part of her wants to believe that Oregon has her best interests in mind, that she is part of one big, happy family, that she and the president can sit down together and work out an amicable solution. But another part of her, a bigger part, is angry and offended and embattled, tired of trying to buck the system alone. That part is waiting impatiently for Alan to call to say he's hopping a plane to Oregon to file the lawsuit. It is now almost a week past the deadline in Alan's fax. She has not heard from her lawyer or from anyone in the administration.

Finally, the president's secretary calls Jody to set up a meeting. But Jody won't meet privately with Dave. It's not just that Alan has told her not to, it's also that Jody is smart enough to know that she is not smart enough to go one-on-one with Dave. I'm not a lawyer, she says to herself. I'm not fast on my feet. I'm just a basketball coach. I need Alan. She calls him.

He agrees to a conference call with the president and Pete Swan, but he is not in a conciliatory mood. "Either they make an offer tomorrow on the phone or we go to court,"

Alan tells Jody. "This may be a five-second call. I'll say: 'Gentlemen, what is your offer?' If they don't have one, then it's, 'Okay, I'll be flying out to file this lawsuit. Good-bye.' "

At 4 P.M. the following day, the appointed and agreed-upon time, Dave and Pete wait in the president's office for the call to come through. Five minutes go by, then ten, then twenty. At 4:40, when Alan finally calls, Dave and Pete are long gone. If they harbored any professional respect for Alan, it went with them. Jody, oblivious of what has happened, waits for Alan's call at home, fully expecting to hear that he'll be flying out this weekend. Instead, she hears that the conference call never happened. She is angrier at her own lawyer than she is at the university. At practice the next morning, pasty-faced and exhausted even after nine hours of sleep, she barks out drills from the sidelines. The conference call has been rearranged for later in the week. She doesn't know how much more of this she can stand.

The following evening, the team is practicing for the benefit of the local media. Jody pulls herself together, gets a shampoo and set at David's salon, puts on enough makeup to give her pale face some color and dons a new University of Oregon warm-up suit. She is one of the few women alive who can look elegant in sweatpants and a warm-up jacket. The preseason event, orchestrated by the sports information office, is meant to showcase the new team, introduce the players to the reporters and, three weeks before the first game, generate some excitement. For Jody it is the occasion to announce the starting lineup, both publicly and to her own players. She hasn't done so already, even though she's known who most of the starters will be for months. She thinks the girls practice harder if they aren't so sure of themselves. Besides, she has been puzzling over how to create a lineup without Karen.

In the pocket of her dark green sweatpants is a list of the starters. She watches from the sidelines as the girls run through their drills. For almost an hour, they run and shoot and dribble and pass. Then she calls them in. She takes the paper from her pocket, looks at it for a second and starts calling out the names of the players on the two teams that will be scrimmaging for the benefit of the press.

"I want Eddie, Jess, B, Red and Roy over here," Jody yells. She offers no explanation or announcement, but everyone knows that scrimmage team number one constitutes the team's starting lineup. The list comes as no surprise to Eddie and Red, who have long known that their positions are secure. Roy, the Australian, has known she'll be starting since she passed the SATs in August. Jess, as a senior, has felt she's had a lock on her position, even if, privately, Jody has not been as sure. The only surprise is B, the genial sophomore who, because she plays the same position as Jess, never thought she'd get a chance to start this year. She smiles broadly when her name is called. Jody has worked around Karen's injury by moving Jess to Karen's old position and bringing B in to take up the slack. B is sorry she's getting her chance because of Karen's health problems, but she's not sorry she's getting her chance. Jody glances down at the paper again, then announces five more names, the second team, the women who will spend much of the following four months on the bench. Among them is Sandie, the six-foot-five center who was in the starting lineup until Roy suddenly appeared. Another player might be hurt or angry or even bitter. Sandie is relieved. She knows the time is not right for her.

After the scrimmage, which is spirited but ragged around the edges, the girls grab paper cups full of water and head down to the locker room. On this early November evening it is eighty-five degrees down there. Ventilation is still on the to-do list. The girls are sitting on folding chairs facing the front of the windowless, low-ceilinged room. Jody is pacing, arms crossed tightly over her chest, waiting for everyone to settle in. In a minute, the sports information guy will come to escort two or three players to the media room, where they will be introduced to the local reporters. Jody waits for quiet.

"Tonight the media may ask you about the lawsuit," she tells the players. "Well, there is no lawsuit." She says this emphatically and a little too loud. Technically it's true, of course. Alan has not filed the suit. But Jody makes it sound as if a lawsuit is not even a remote possibility, as if it might be the furthest thing from her mind. "There is no lawsuit," she repeats. The room is silent. "If they ask you how you feel about the university's treatment of women athletes, tell them you thought you were here to talk about basketball."

Jess and Red are called to the media room. Jody's admonitions turn out to be unnecessary. None of the members of the press ask them about anything other than basketball.

"What kind of year do you think you'll have without Sara, Deb and Missy?" one reporter asks. Sara, Deb and Missy, last year's seniors, were the triumvirate primarily responsible for the winning season, scoring three-quarters of the points and pulling down two-thirds of the rebounds.

Jess and Red exchange looks. Red is the talker, but Jess is the senior, the ranking member of the team.

"Of course we'll miss them," Jess says, "but we have a good team this year. We're looking forward to a good year." Jess shifts uncomfortably in her chair. She doesn't like these media outings.

"So who's going to be the new Missy?" another reporter asks. Missy was the fiery point guard, the spark plug of the team.

"It's a different team this year," says Red, getting the jump on Jess. "You'll just have to see us play."

"What kind of hole did Sara, Deb and Missy leave?" someone else asks a few minutes later.

Red and Jess sit behind the big table at the front of the room waiting for questions about them, about their hopes, about how they expect to play. Jess is particularly sensitive to all these queries about last year's stars. This is finally *her* year, and although she doesn't think of herself as having a

big ego, she knows she wants some recognition, some measure of respect. She was in the shadow of the triumvirate last
year. She didn't count on being in their shadow after they
were gone.

"So about that offense, how are you going to manage
without Sara and Deb?"

Jess and Red exchange another look. Jess is just about
to say something when Jody arrives. They are delighted to
leave. The reporters pepper Jody with the questions that reporters have been peppering coaches with for as long as there
have been reporters and coaches. "Who's gonna play the key
roles this season?" "What's the defense gonna look like?"
"What do you expect from the newcomers?" Jody fields the
questions like a pro, her answers studded with sportisms and
comforting clichés.

"We're young," she says. "We're a little raw, but we're
gonna work hard, take it to the hoop, step up on defense and
play smart."

She is good at this. There is an ageless, genderless, re-
gionless way that coaches talk to reporters. The interchange
is so predictable that it is almost a ritual. At the end of the
session, the one female reporter in the room, the same woman
who interviewed Tara VanDerveer on the air last week, asks
quietly, almost apologetically: "Is there anything new on the
legal front?"

"I'll be talking with the president tomorrow," Jody answers, referring to the rearranged conference call, "and I hope
good things will come of it." She is going to leave it at that,
but then she adds, "This is not a distraction for the team. I'm
handling it. It is my business." There are no follow-up questions.

The next afternoon at three, the conference call goes
through. Jody takes it in her office. The president, the university's lawyer and the acting AD are in the president's office. Alan has told Jody his strategy. She expects him to come
out swinging. The president begins by diplomatically but

pointedly commenting on how difficult this call has been to arrange. This gives Alan an opportunity to apologize for messing up on the previous call, which he does, and everyone feels a little better.

"Let's talk about some of the issues you are raising," the president says to the lawyer.

"There is only one issue," Alan says. "What are you going to pay my client?"

The president tries again to steer the conversation onto a broader plane, mentioning the practice-time problem, the facilities, promotion of the program and other concerns Jody and Alan have raised in the past.

"Those issues are trivial compared to the main issue," Alan says, beginning to get testy. "We want to hear what you have to propose. Are you willing to offer my client what she wants?"

Jody is sitting at her desk, phone pressed to her ear, spine forming a sharp right angle with the seat of her chair. She has not said a word and hopes she will not have to. She thinks of herself as pretty tough, a person who knows what she wants and gets right to the point. But listening to Alan is an education. Hearing him in action restores her confidence in his abilities.

The president is now talking about how ugly litigation can get. He's been in court many times, he says, and no one comes out a winner. "There are always lots of casualties," he tells Alan. Before Alan, who spends most of his days in court embroiled in litigation, can respond, the president takes a new tack. He says that he has in mind a particular person who might be interested in endowing Jody's salary. This is the potential benefactor he mentioned privately at last week's meeting with his advisers.

"I want some specifics," says Alan.

The president says that he has in mind a $1 million endowment, which would generate about $50,000 a year.

"What exactly would be your intentions for this money if you get it? How much of it would be put toward Jody's

salary? How much for promotions and marketing? How much
to fix up the facilities?"

Dave explains that, of course, all this needs to be worked
out carefully but that first the donor has to be brought on
board. He seems to be suggesting the endowment as a quick
solution to an immediate problem, but he knows better. Courting big-money donors takes time, sometimes years from the
first contact to the delivered check. But Jody doesn't know
that, and neither apparently does Alan. They are thinking that
Dave is going to dash out tomorrow, grab a million dollars
and, in short order, supplement Jody's salary.

"One thing," Dave says. "I can't go out looking for
money with the threat of a lawsuit hanging over the university."

Alan agrees to put the suit on hold and to stay away
from the media while Dave pursues the potential donor. Alan
says he will call university counsel Pete Swan in the next few
days to talk more specifically about how the money might be
used.

No one is saying who the donor might be, but Jody has
her own sources, namely her hairdresser, David, who seems
to know or know of just about everyone who is anyone in
Eugene, Oregon—admittedly a short list. The list of those
able to write million-dollar checks is shorter; the list of
wealthy women—David is immediately convinced that the
mystery benefactor has to be a woman—is shorter still. As it
turns out, David guesses right. A few days after the conference call, Jody is sitting in his salon getting her hair cut and,
as women have always done with their hairdressers, telling
him her troubles. David quickly thinks through the donor possibilities and mentions the name of a middle-aged woman
worth, he thinks, in excess of $400 million. One of David's
friends has just finished constructing a $100,000 staircase for
her new home. Jody listens intently. There is not much she
can do with this bit of intelligence. She has no way of knowing whether David is even right. But it makes the whole idea
of the endowment more real to attach a name to the donor. It

makes it all seem possible, even probable. Jody is suddenly, unexpectedly optimistic.

It doesn't last long. A long week goes by without word from Alan. She was expecting a phone call from him within days. She was expecting Alan to tell her what concrete plans he and Pete had worked out for this $1 million endowment. But Alan doesn't call, and he doesn't return her calls. Now two weeks have gone by, and Jody has worked herself into a lather, calling Alan's office two or three times a day, cursing him to anyone who will listen, including his secretary. She is also back to making calls to see if she can find a different lawyer, and she's giving serious thought to dropping Alan entirely and just dealing personally with the president.

She admires Dave Frohnmayer. She thinks he's a fair and honest man, and she'd love nothing better than to cut through all this crap, pick up the phone and talk to him. But she stops herself. Without a lawyer, without the threat of a lawsuit, she is sure the university will lose its incentive to work on her concerns. She has already figured out that it is in the university's best interest to stall her as long as possible. So she curses Alan, but she keeps him. She curses Alan, and she waits.

It's not that she doesn't have other things to occupy her time. Between six-day-a-week early morning practices and a string of visits by high school recruits, Jody is at full throttle. Between battling her own lawyer and a cold that she can't seem to get the better of, Jody has bought a house, painted and decorated it and had all of her sturdy Midwestern antique oak furniture moved from the cramped rental she's been living in for a year and a half to the new place, a pretty three-bedroom ranch-style house on a quiet, winding, tree-lined street. The house comforts her as much as she will allow herself to be comforted. It absorbs some of her fury.

November is slipping by. All of a sudden it is the last week of practice before the first game, a two-day invitational tournament scheduled for the Friday and Saturday of Thanks-

giving weekend. At practice early that week, the team concentrates on half-hour scrimmages with the starters playing
together on one team and the bench, wearing green jerseys
over their IN IT TO WIN IT! T-shirts, on the other.

Karen is finally out on the floor playing with the starters.
Jess is at her old position, and B is back with the second
string. Jody doesn't know if this is going to work, but Karen
has impressed her so much these past few weeks with her
determination and persistence, with her tenacious workouts
and her stubborn refusal to give in to her hip problem, that
she has to give the girl a chance. Jody watches as the white
team, the starters, runs all over the greens. Jess is making
three-pointers at will. Then Karen misses two easy shots. Jody
shakes her head. Karen is not being pressured by the greens;
she's playing tentatively, stiffly, with no rhythm to her moves,
no timing to her shots. She misses another from fifteen feet
out. Jess rushes crosscourt and touches Karen on the arm.
"Nice try," she tells her. Karen grimaces but smiles back.

This fall has been difficult for the two of them, roommates since their freshman year, best friends and confidantes.
Jess had been holding back, not able to share her excitement
about this senior year, not able to joke with her friend after
practice, to debrief, to gossip. With Karen not knowing if
she'd play again, Jess wanted to tread softly. Basketball, the
overwhelming, all-consuming thing these girls have in common, was all of a sudden not a safe topic for conversation.
Now, with Karen out there, regardless of how she's playing,
their friendship has returned to familiar turf.

Jess is wide open on the right side. Jody watches from
underneath the basket as the green defense does nothing to
stop her. She sinks another one.

"If you're gonna play halfway or half-assed or however
ya wanna say it, we're gonna lose this weekend, and we're
gonna lose big," Jody says. She is yelling, but the head cold
is making her voice high and whiny. "Now let's play. Let's
see something out there."

Jody shifts her attention to Cicely, the six-foot-two junior college recruit from Los Angeles, the new player her assistant Joe Jackson has recruited. She has high hopes for Cicely, but Cicely is not playing well. She's very quick, but she can't seem to shoot, and she rattles easily. It has taken her a long time to learn the plays, and she still looks uncomfortable out there. Part of the discomfort is real—she is having a great deal of trouble with the structure Jody imposes on the game— but part is perception. Cicely has a springy, edgy way of moving, halfway between a frightened deer and a 440 hurdler. She runs down the court, almost prancing, knees high, in big, bounding steps that elevate her Nikes a foot and a half off the floor. When she dribbles and stops, she takes the last step as a two-foot jump, pounding the floor and surprising herself with the noise she makes. When she gets the ball, she looks as if she can't wait to get rid of it.

Jody wants Cicely to be able to come off the bench and do something this year. She needs Cicely to be ready, to succeed, not just because she is in desperate need of strong bench players, but because Cicely represents one of the very few recruiting successes the Oregon women's basketball program has had among black athletes. If Cicely plays well, if she becomes a presence on the team, moving from the bench this season to a starting position next season, other African-American players may consider Oregon more seriously.

Jody is particularly sensitive to this right now because her top recruit this fall, a big, smart black player from Inglewood, California, a girl not just physically talented but mentally savvy about the game—in short, a potential all-American—has just announced that she will be taking up the University of North Carolina on its full-ride scholarship offer, not the University of Oregon. It's not just because UNC is the current national champion, the girl tells Jody, it's because of a wonderful meeting she had with black faculty members in North Carolina. It's because she will feel "more at home" there.

Jody understands the code. In a state almost blindingly white, at a university with a minuscule black student population of mostly football players and a faculty that numbers 5 African-Americans out of 1,100, it is no surprise that Jody and her predecessors have not had much luck enticing African-American players. Cicely is Jody's great black hope. But right now, watching her bolt across the court, bang into Sandie and throw off the offense by being out of position, Jody doesn't feel too hopeful.

At practice the next morning, Jody's cold is worse but her mood is better. She has finally gotten through to Alan, who has set up another conference call with the president and the university's lawyer. Alan has told her that he'll demand to see a specific plan for how the university will meet Jody's seventy-thousand-dollar contract demand, devote money to promoting women's basketball and find the funds to finish the women's locker room. Alan tells her that he'll give the university ten days to present the plan; otherwise he'll be on a plane heading west to file the lawsuit.

Jody is encouraged by the conversation with her lawyer. For starters, he actually called her. And he does seem to know what he's doing, she tells herself. This will work out. But she is even more heartened by the announcement that the University of Oregon football team, under Rich Brooks's direction, will be going to the Rose Bowl in January for the first time in thirty-seven years. Jody likes football well enough, and she's happy that the school will be in the national limelight, but that's not the reason she's buoyed by the Rose Bowl announcement. The reason is that the athletic department will be getting millions from the Rose Bowl—TV money, merchandising deals, who knows what else—and that means extra money in the departmental coffers, funds that can be spent on women's basketball. Now the university can't plead poverty, she figures. If they don't devote some money to her program it won't be because they can't do it. It will be because they choose not to do it. Either way, Jody figures she comes out ahead. If they use some of the Rose Bowl money for her, she wins. If they refuse, she has a stronger case against them.

That afternoon she leaves her office early, determined to shake this almost two-month-long cold by spending some time in bed. She is not used to being ill. In fact, she cannot remember ever being this sick for this long in her life. She has not been smart about her health. The previous weekend, on a raw, rainy Saturday, she watched the University of Oregon–Oregon State football game from the exposed bleachers. Since then, her head has felt like a concrete block.

At 4:30 in the afternoon, the call comes through to her home. Alan, Dave and Pete are on the line. Jody tells Dave that she's at home with a cold worsened by last weekend's game.

"Don't tell me you actually went to that game in the rain?" the president says, teasing her. Of course he knows she went to the game. It was Oregon's biggest football game in decades, the game that clinched the bid to the Rose Bowl.

"I wouldn't have missed it," Jody says, laughing. This is the first time in many months that Jody and Dave have traded lighthearted conversation. It feels good to Jody, but she is caught off guard. Then Alan doesn't take the tack Jody expects.

"We're calling to see what luck you've had with that endowment prospect," Alan says, his voice casual. Jody thought Alan would be taking a hard line right about now, demanding to see a plan, delivering an ultimatum.

"We were waiting to hear from you," Pete says, remembering that Alan was supposed to call weeks ago to discuss details.

"Well, we were waiting to hear from you," Alan answers quickly. The best defense is a good offense, Jody figures. She keeps her mouth shut. Let the lawyers bump chests.

Dave gets the conversation going again, explaining how courting and nailing down a prospect take some time. He is now giving Alan and Jody a realistic picture of what it takes to bring in a sizable endowment. Jody listens for hints. She can't tell from Dave's remarks whether the university has had any contact at all with the prospect since the last conference call.

Apparently Alan has his doubts. "Listen," he says, "we need to know that you're actually working on this. We want to know within ten days that you have set up an appointment with this person. We want to know the date of the meeting and what your game plan is."

Dave balks, explaining again about the time and patience it takes to bring a person to the point of signing her name on a $1 million check. He has another idea. He tells Alan that the prospect will be going to the Rose Bowl with the president's party, an elite group of powerful and would-be friends of the university. "This would be an ideal time to work on this," he says.

Jody stifles a groan. The Rose Bowl? That's almost six weeks away. She can't believe she's going to be in limbo for another month and a half. She thought this would all be resolved—either the university would meet her demands or the lawsuit would be filed—before the season started. It's now four days to the first game.

Alan seems to be going for the Rose Bowl idea and backing away slightly from the demand for a progress report in ten days. Somehow, without Jody knowing when, the conversation segues into banter about Oregon's chances in the Rose Bowl. Just as sports talk bridges the gap between men of different backgrounds in barbershops and bars, it has temporarily bridged a gap here. This afternoon, for a minute or two, Alan and Dave are not squaring off as litigious lawyer and potential defendant. They are just two guys talking football. Jody listens, an outsider, and hopes there's something in it for her.

IT WOULDN'T HURT FOR YOU TO SMILE

IT IS TEN MINUTES TO GAME TIME. THE GIRLS ARE SPRAWLED on the couches and chairs in the locker room, jittery, restless, already sweaty from their twenty-minute warm-up. Tonight is the Mac Court Classic, a four-team invitational tournament, the first of the preconference games the team will play in November and December. These next nine games count—the wins and losses will be duly recorded and will figure into national rankings and later, in the spring, will help determine the seeding for the NCAA tournament—but they are also considered warm-ups for the main event, the eighteen Pac-10 contests that will follow in January, February and March.

The Pac-10, today one of the toughest conferences in the country, traces its roots to a 1915 meeting at the Oregon Hotel in downtown Portland. There, representatives from the University of Oregon, Oregon State College (as Oregon State University was then called), the University of Washington and the University of California, Berkeley, created the four-member Pacific Coast League. The conference would expand several times during the next seven decades, dissolve, reform, change its name and change its name again, but one thing would remain constant: its male-only membership. Although the women of Stanford and Berkeley had been the first in the nation to play intercollegiate basketball back in 1896, women's teams were not a part of the conference until almost a century later.

Across the country, women competed within their own separate but not equal female-only leagues with no central leadership until the formation of the Association for Intercollegiate Athletics for Women (a female version of the then-male-only NCAA) in the early 1970s, just about the time Title IX was taking effect. But the AIAW had little clout. The women's teams were un- or underfunded. They offered no scholarships. They attracted no media attention. On a good night, fans numbered in the low hundreds. Yet it was also a time when women were left alone to control their own athletic destinies. More than 90 percent of women's collegiate teams were coached by women in those days, with female women's athletic directors running their own shows at universities, and the whole system administered by the women-only AIAW.

But when the NCAA began offering televised women's championships, the AIAW could not hold its members, and in the early 1980s, the NCAA took over women's intercollegiate sports. A few years later, the Pac-10 swallowed up two women's western leagues and, as conference publicists put it, "took on a new look": the women arrived. But there was a trade-off for all this inclusiveness. Women's once independent athletic departments were subsumed under men's, and by the early 1990s, almost 85 percent of women's intercollegiate programs were headed by men. Twenty years before, men had coached fewer than 10 percent of the women's teams; now they coached more than half of them. Male-dominated organizations administered women's sports on the conference and national levels. Women's athletics had won a tentative place at the table—some scholarships, modest but increased budgets, a modicum of press coverage—but in doing so, it had lost its autonomy.

Few of the current generation of women's coaches like Jody mourn the old days. They came of age with the new system and do not question it. Jody feels nothing but pride about coaching in the Pac-10. The league is proud of itself too, billing itself as the "conference of champions" and "the nation's premier athletic conference." It does so with justification. In the mid-1990s, the National Association of Collegiate Directors of Athletics ranked the conference number one in the nation, based on how men's and women's teams at all ten schools performed in twenty-two different sports. Five Pac-10 schools ranked among the top ten in the nation during the 1993–94 season. On the women's side, Pac-10 schools have won more national team championships than the schools in any other conference, including ten of the last thirteen softball championships, ten of the last thirteen tennis crowns and three of the last four volleyball titles. In women's basketball, where Southeastern Conference teams like Vanderbilt and Tennessee have long held power, Pac-10 teams have made their mark, with USC a national force in the 1980s, and Stanford dominating in the 1990s. The University of Washington, perennially in the national rankings, has been a tournament-goer almost every year.

Jody knows what she's up against when the Pac-10 season begins. She knows Oregon is one of the weak sisters in the conference. That's why it's so important to use these pre-conference games to their best advantage, to get the team functioning as a team, to build confidence, to rev up for two and a half months of grueling conference play. Jody has some control of these first nine games. She negotiates with the coaches of other teams to set up the most propitious schedule. It's a balancing act: She wants to include some teams that can challenge Oregon, the operative theory being that a team plays better against a better team. But she needs to choose some teams she knows Oregon can beat, for the sake of both confidence building and the national win-loss scoreboard. This year, she's scheduled games against marginal teams like Idaho State, Brigham Young and St. Mary's, and tougher contests against Santa Clara, the team Oregon played in last year's first-round NCAA, and powerhouse Vanderbilt. For the Mac Court Classic, she has invited the University of Illinois and Boise State, two eminently beatable opponents, and Drake, a tough Iowa school. The game tonight is Oregon versus Illinois.

Jody stands at the front of the locker room waiting for the girls to settle down. Roy is having two fingers taped— not an injury but a precaution; Eddie is having her shoulder iced; Red is tying and retying her ankle supports. B calls for a cup of water; Sandie calls for a stick of gum. Stacy, the equipment manager, solemnly handles the requests. The girls are fidgety, unfocused, apprehensive. Jody, nervous too but taking pains not to appear so, is elegant in a cream-colored skirt and tunic with cream-colored hose and matching three-inch heels. She looks like a swan. Her hair is perfect; her makeup is perfect. Any minute she could be gliding down a runway at a Saks fashion show. Instead, she opens her mouth, and what comes out is pure coach.

"Hey, this girl is *so bad* we didn't even recruit her when I was at Missouri," Jody is saying. Her perfectly manicured finger points to a name on the Illinois roster. She has written the names of the opposing starters and some of their pertinent statistics on the board behind her. "And *this girl*"—she pivots neatly and points again—"I mean *this girl* just can't shoot." Jody is bantering. She is talking a little trash in an effort to break the tension in the room.

It's not working for Sandie, who is sitting on the couch chewing gum so hard that she's going to need her jaw iced after the game. Since the pregame dinner at three, Sandie has told everyone who will listen just how scared she is. Her father is in the stands tonight. She knows where he's sitting, and she knows he'll yell at her when she's on the court. "Shoot the ball! Shoot the ball!" She can hear it inside her head right now. The skin around her mouth feels tight and prickly. "I'm gonna throw up," she whispers. "I know I'm gonna throw up."

Sandie's father is only imperceptibly mellower than Karen's father. Both set sports goals for their daughters before their daughters knew what goals were. Or sports. The difference is that Karen learned to talk back, and Sandie didn't. Sandie never had the confidence. Maybe it had something to do with reaching her full height of six-foot-five at age fourteen, a teenager's natural discomfort intensified, a teenager's yearning to fit in unrequited. She was a very pretty girl with opalescent skin, dark, shiny hair and big brown doe eyes, slender, shapely—and incredibly tall. At fourteen, she was too young to know how to handle it but old enough to understand that it would forever define her.

Height is not something you can hide from. It isn't like having a bad hair day. It isn't something you can fix, like a bumpy nose, or grow out of, like pimples, or learn to compensate for with clothing, like wide hips. Height is inarguable, an absolute. While a five-foot-nine or -ten or even -eleven woman might be thought of as willowy—or later, stately—and might be admired for how well she wears clothes, a six-foot-five woman is clearly over-the-top. Even in basketball, a refuge for very tall women, Sandie was at fourteen as she is at twenty, the very tallest on the team. In high school, she was known as "the Big Girl" (as in "Who's going to guard the big girl?"), and she's struggled with the adjective, as she has with what it describes, ever since.

Towering over both teammates and opponents, Sandie averaged twenty points a game in high school and once posted a forty-eight-point game. Other kids would get puffed up about something like that; other kids would start believing they were pretty good to score all those points. But Sandie never lost sight of where she was—a tiny high school with a senior class of seventeen where every girl (there were seven in her class) played every sport, out of necessity, with or without talent. There was no competition to make the team and not much competition during the season. The school was at the bottom of the heap, a B league school, with the bigger, more powerful AAA, AA and A leagues preceding it. So her

personal statistics never infused her with confidence. If anything, they made her even less sure of herself. I'm able to
play like this because of the league I'm in, not because I'm
any good, she would tell herself. Her father, yelling from the
bleachers, only deepened her uncertainty. Tonight is the beginning of her second year on the team, the year she knows
she'll get plenty of playing time. The idea paralyzes her.

Jody knows Sandie is barely holding it together. She can
see it on the big girl's face tonight. She can read it in her
body language. Sandie is sitting on the edge of the couch,
bent from the waist, almost doubled over, chin on knees, staring at the carpet and chewing gum with such ferocity that her
ponytail is moving up and down from the effort. But Jody
figures the only cure for Sandie is to play. No pep talk is
going to be as meaningful as sinking a basket or two. Still, it
is that moment right before the game especially reserved for
locker-room pep talks, so Jody goes for it.

"Tonight is a good opportunity to show the people out
there that this team is gonna have a great year," Jody says.
She begins quietly, purposefully low-key. The girls are tense
enough as it is. They hear her voice, soft, calm, reasonable,
and stop fidgeting. Sandie forces herself to sit up straight. She
looks almost woozy with fear. "Let's show them that although
we lost all these"—she pauses for effect and drops her voice
a few notes—"*miraculous players*, we right here in this room
are a strong team." She is deliberately tapping into the team's
anger over early media coverage of the season, the sports
stories that lament the loss of last year's seniors, the Deb-
Sara-Missy triumvirate, the sportswriters who focus on what
once was rather than what might be. She knows talk like this
will really get to Jess and Karen, the seniors who want so
much to make this year their own. Karen is starting tonight,
but both she and Jody know how tenuous that position is.
Karen has been practicing with the team for a few weeks now,
but her hip keeps her from going full bore, from hitting her
stride.

"Listen," Jody tells the girls, ratcheting it up a notch,

"Illinois plays in the Big Ten, and they think they're pretty good. Well, ladies, you play in the *Pac*-10." She lowers her chin and gives them a hard stare. "Jump on 'em and show 'em who lives here."

There are 1,500 people in the bleachers, three times the crowd that came to the Ducks' opening game last year, but less than a quarter of the fans the men's program attracts in a losing year on a bad night. Still, the arena is cozy enough and the crowd enthusiastic enough that Jody is pleased. Fifteen hundred is not a shabby way to begin. The girls pick up on the excitement of the crowd and come out strong. In the first ten seconds of play, Roy attracts a foul and sinks a free throw. Illinois gets the ball and Eddie promptly steals it. When Illinois gets the ball again, Red steals it and muscles under the basket to make a reverse layup. Then Jess plants herself in front of the Illinois player with the ball, her face an inch away, arms flailing, grimacing, yelling "Ball, ball!" in her face, and the girl can't get off a pass. This is just what Jody loves to see: physical, aggressive play, every opportunity seized, all pistons firing.

A few minutes into the half, with things going well, Jody substitutes Sandie for Roy. She knows Sandie is not ready, but she never will be ready if she doesn't get out there and play. Sandie gets a pass under the basket. She wishes she could pass it away. She wishes she were still sitting on the bench. She thinks she hears her father yelling, but she doesn't know if it's really him or just his voice inside her head. She knows she has to take the shot. She's got one. It's a little jumper from a few feet out, an easy shot for a tall girl. Her hands are shaking as she puts it up.

It goes in—not cleanly, not with panache, but through the hoop nonetheless. She can hardly believe it. She lopes down the court, a bit of color returning to her face. But, despite the promising start, this is not going to be her night. She goes on to miss three free throws. Then she travels with the ball. Then she makes a bad pass. Then she commits a stupid foul. Stephanie, one of the assistant coaches, slams her clipboard against the back of the bench. "Jeez, Sandie!" she yells.

At halftime the score is 32–24 Oregon, but Jody isn't happy. There has been no intensity on the court since the early moments of the half. Oregon has played well enough to maintain a small lead but not well enough to pull away. Jody thinks the girls are coasting. The idea that they're out there playing but not giving it everything they've got makes her angrier than if the team were losing. She comes into the locker room steaming.

"You better take care of business out there or you're gonna get your asses whupped!" she yells at them. It doesn't take much volume to fill the low-ceilinged room. The girls are sweating and sucking on sections of orange. They are taken aback by Jody's tone, her vehemence. It's their first game; they are eight points up at the half, and things are looking pretty good as far as they can see. Jody sees it differently. "If you think they're gonna play as bad in the second half as they did in the first, you're mistaken. They think they can beat you now. They think they can take you. Go out there and show them they're wrong."

There will be a lot riding on every game this season for Jody: The better the team does, the more community support she has, the more secure her job, the better her case looks. But this game, even though it's not a Pac-10 game, even though it's not against some longtime rival or a well-known or particularly worthy opponent, this game is the first. It sets the tone for the fans. It sets the tone for the media. Most important, it establishes the coach's expectations for her players. Jody wants them to know, in no uncertain terms, that she is interested in one thing this year: winning—both on the court and, if necessary, in the courts.

The second half is more to her liking. Whether it is due to her halftime scolding or the fifteen-minute rest she doesn't know, but the team is back on track, working hard and playing as if they care. Jody paces the sidelines just in front of the bench, four long strides right, four long strides left, eyes never leaving the court. As the gap slowly widens between the two teams, as Oregon pulls away, she allows herself a few deep breaths and takes a second to look back in the stands.

Her parents are up there. They flew in last night, along with Jody's brother, sister-in-law and twelve-week-old niece, to spend a long Thanksgiving weekend at her new house. They knew she needed their support. They knew she was lonely. And she's glad they're here, even if it meant spending the entire day before her first game in the kitchen cooking a full-trimmings turkey dinner. Right now, Jody's just happy that they're going to see her win.

Oregon is finally pulling away, fifteen, now eighteen points ahead of the opponent. Mostly it's because of Red. She's shooting inside with grace and agility. She's using her body, dropping her shoulder and pushing in, attracting fouls. She's grabbing rebounds. She's making steals. She is the most physical player out there, the most powerful woman on the court, the one the fans are watching, and she's clearly having a good time. With nine minutes left in the game, Jody takes her out. As long as Oregon is this far ahead, she needs to rest the starters for tomorrow night's game.

The crowd roars as Red leaves the court. In Mac Court, the bleachers are packed close to the court, rising steeply on all sides. In a sprawling arena like UCLA's Pauley Pavilion, 1,500 people would rattle around. Here they make serious noise. All the players on the Oregon bench are standing, clapping, extending their hands to Red for high fives.

Red lopes past Jody, who is standing by the sidelines with her arms crossed tightly against her chest. She is momentarily motionless, statuesque, queenly. She doesn't seem to hear the crowd or notice anything but the action on the court. If she sees Red walk past her, she doesn't show it. Jody rarely acknowledges the players as they come and go out of the game. Other coaches might slap a back or give a nod, but that's not her style. Her focus remains on the game. Her eyes stay on the basketball.

Red walks three or four paces past Jody, then turns back, stands in front of her and extends her hand for a high five.

She's leaving the game with seventeen points and seven rebounds, the team's high scorer in both. She wants Jody to
recognize her for that. The bench can't believe what's happening. You don't confront Jody like that. You don't get in
her face. She's the coach. She makes the rules. She sets the
tone. You fit yourself in. The players on the bench stop clapping and stare at Red standing there, completely composed,
just the hint of a smirk on her face, waiting. It seems to take
Jody a long time to see Red. Finally, the coach looks down.
With the heels, she's six-feet-six to Red's mere six feet. Jody
hesitates, then slaps Red's hand. Red cracks a smile and
moves on to get her due from the bench. It's Oregon's game,
72–55.

The next night, the game against Drake doesn't go as
well. To begin with, Jess is out of the starting lineup. There's
something wrong with her knee, some instability in the tendons around the kneecap. It probably isn't serious, but this
early in the season, with all the games yet to be played, neither
Jody nor Jess wants to take any unnecessary chances. Then
there's Red. She is in the starting lineup, but she has been
sick since the midafternoon pregame meal at a local Italian
restaurant. Red has a tendency to eat big. She is the team's
top carnivore and proud of it. Two hours before game time,
she was curled up on her living-room floor clutching her stom-
ach. When she came in to be taped, the first thing she asked
for were two Mylantas. Now, out on the court, she is moving
as if she has weights on her legs, as if she is stuck in one of
those dreams where you try to run but everything is in slow
motion, and the air is suddenly so thick you can't move
through it. Karen is playing, but her timing is way off. Eight
times she puts the ball up from beyond the three-point line.
This is her shot. In the history of the Oregon program, Karen
has the sixth highest three-point goal percentage. Tonight, she
misses seven out of eight.

At halftime in the locker room, the only sound is the
whirring of the two fans that are unsuccessfully laboring to

ventilate the place. No one is talking. Jody walks in slowly.
She takes her jacket off slowly, placing it on the arm of the
couch. She faces her back to the players and slowly erases
her pregame notes from the board. Everyone is staring at her
back. They are all waiting for her to say something. Carefully,
she prints on the board, in six-inch-high letters, BIG HEAD.
Then she whips around and starts in on them.

"Just because you beat Illinois by almost twenty points,
you think you're so damned good," she says. "Well, you look
like shit out there." Jody is not so much yelling as she is
spitting out the words. She does not usually say words like
"shit," so she lets it sink in for a moment. She stares them
down, disgusted. "You're not playing hard. You're playing
stupid."

The second half is more of the same. They are running
back late on defense, allowing layups, allowing a demoralizing string of three-pointers from a little guard on the Drake
team. Their shots are simply not going in.

Jody paces the sidelines, watching her team lose. Oregon
is down by ten and can't close the gap. Everyone is getting
frustrated. Karen gets fouled badly right in front of the Oregon
bench, and the ref doesn't call it.

Joe, one of the assistant coaches, yells in to the ref,
"Hey, what's going on? Dincha see that foul? Hey, can you
see out there?"

It's typical trash talking from the bench. Coaches are
always yelling at referees, remarking on their visual impair-
ments and attention deficit disorders. But this ref is having
none of it. She calls him for a technical. The little three-point
shooter takes the shots and sinks both of them so neatly that
the net barely moves.

Jody puts Jess in, hoping her intensity will spark something. Jess's knee is taped, but she seems to be okay. She runs
down the court on defense, sees the little three-point shooter
get in her sweet spot and plants herself between the girl and
the basket. She's right in her face, not letting her move an
inch. The bench is calling in encouragement: "Stay on 'er,

Jess!" "Go, Jess, go!" The little guard is trapped. She lunges forward, trying to clear a way for herself. Jess is right there. The ref calls the foul on Jess.

"That was an offensive foul!" Jess yells at the ref, moving her hands to illustrate how the Drake player pushed into her. As she gestures, she clips the forearm of the little guard. From across the court, one of the other refs sees this out of the corner of her eye, and it looks to her as if Jess is trying to start something. She races crosscourt and calls a technical on Jess, who has already turned her back on the scene and is walking over to line up on the free throw line. A technical? Jess can't believe it. She knows she didn't do anything wrong, but there is no recourse. She walks off the court, red-faced and limping, then grabs a towel, sits down quickly and buries her head in it. She doesn't see that the little guard sinks both of the free throws and both of the technicals. By the time Roy pours it on, sinking three baskets in a row—she's scored thirty-one points, almost half of the total for Oregon—it is too late to win.

In the locker room Red is sitting on a chair with her head down. Eddie is slumped over on the couch. The stack of pizzas at the back of the room, a standard postgame treat donated by a local restaurant, is getting cold. Jody lets them sit there by themselves for ten minutes while she stands alone in the hallway, silent, stone-faced, so angry that she looks menacing. Her assistants leave her alone. Finally, she opens the locker-room door and walks in.

"I hate losing," she tells them. Her voice is hoarse from yelling. "I . . . hate . . . losing." She says it again, slowly, emphasizing each word. She is so angry she is almost shaking. If she eases up on herself for a moment, if she lets herself go, it looks as if she might stomp across the room and wring Red's neck or take Sandie by the shoulders and shake her until her head snaps. "Well, ladies, you are *all* gonna hate to lose. You're gonna practice so hard that you're gonna *beg* to have a game so you can win."

She takes a breath and labors to get her anger in check. "You just got a dose of reality out there. This is gonna be a long season, ladies, unless you start stepping up." She pauses for a second and decides to try another strategy, her ace in the hole. "You know, everyone hates to hear about last year and last year's team and last year's players, but out there tonight it looked like you were all waiting for someone else to take over. Well, you know what? It's just you, ladies. It's just you." She turns quickly and walks out the door. If she could slam it, she probably would. But it's one of those pneumatic doors that close with a hiss.

The next afternoon, Sunday, Jody makes good on her promise. Practice is grueling. It begins in the locker room with the videotape of last night's game. Jody screened it that morning at home, hunched in a chair planted six inches in front of her TV, shaking her head, muttering to herself, sighing audibly. If any of the anger of last night has dissipated, Jody replenishes it as she watches. By the time the girls gather in the locker room at three, Jody is seething again. She stalks in and puts in the tape. The girls sit and watch in silence. Every few seconds, Jody hits the pause button, freezing a frame to show them how out of position they are. They all watch as Red loses control of a pass.

"Look at that," Jody says disgustedly. She rewinds the tape and plays it back. "You're just lazy here," she says a few minutes later, watching their botched defense. "You're not out there taking care of business." She rewinds the tape and plays it again. It takes an hour and a half to watch the game. Then they go upstairs for an hour of drills.

On Monday, after a two-hour practice, Jody still isn't seeing the intensity she wants to see. She has the girls go home and write essays: Why did we play so badly? Why aren't we working hard? Essays worked for last year's team. It was just at this point, early in the season after a loss they shouldn't have suffered, that last year's players got the same assignment. It forced them to examine their motivations. It forced them to think through what they were doing, and it gave Jody some insights into their character.

But when the essays come back the next day, Jody sees that most of the girls on this year's team just parrot what she has said in practice: "We just didn't step up." "It was like we were all waiting for someone to take the lead and no one did." Reading the essays in her office, she is not fooled by those who mimic her, either because they want to curry favor or because they haven't taken the time to think for themselves.

She's impressed with Roy, though. Her essay is a sophisticated analysis of how the team moved the ball, the advantages and disadvantages of the zone defense, how each player played her spot. It reads like a coach's notes. From her years of playing in Australia, Roy understands basketball better than any of the other players. She has a basketball mind. Although being at Oregon is really an accident, and playing basketball this year is not what she had in mind when she set out on her American adventure, she has thrown herself into the game. "I want to go to the NCAA," Roy writes at the end of her essay. "I just hope enough other players want to go with me." This is music to Jody's ears. She likes the sound of these two sentences so much that she reads them again, aloud.

Eddie's essay interests her also. "I hate to lose," she writes. "If I'm not playing hard, single me out and tell me." It's so like Eddie to immediately doubt herself, Jody thinks. She wishes there were a way to be hard on the team without being hard on Eddie because Eddie is already too hard on herself. She's a perfectionist, an overachiever, the most conscientious player on the team, the player with the best work ethic. She takes her workouts seriously, performs each drill as if it mattered and scrimmages hard. Eddie writes that maybe she's not in good enough shape. Jody laughs out loud. Eddie is in better shape than anyone else on the team. What she lacks is not physical, it's mental. Eddie's a good point guard, Jody says to herself, and Eddie can be a great point guard if and when she decides she's great. It's attitude now, not ability.

Jody flips through a few more essays and stops at Red's. She reads it quickly, shaking her head. Red writes about feeling tired before the game, about feeling sick. She didn't play well not because she had a big head, as Jody said, and not because she didn't want to win. She just didn't play well. "Isn't it possible to just have a bad game every once in a while?" Red writes. Jody doesn't like her tone. She can hear it under the words, or thinks she can, and it sounds defiant, confrontational.

She reads on, frowning. Jody sees Red as a great player who is settling for being a merely good player. But she doesn't know how to reach the girl. Red isn't open and vulnerable like the others; she doesn't need Jody's approval. Red doesn't seem to need basketball the way some of the others do. Maybe that makes Red uncoachable. This is not the first time that idea has passed through Jody's mind. She reads to the end, the frown deepening on her face. It's the final comment that really gets to her. Red has written: "It wouldn't hurt for you to smile once in a while."

Red is the only one on the team who would write something like this. To the others, Jody is the all-powerful coach, the authority figure who sets the rules and issues the edicts, the one for whom they perform, the one they want and need to please, the one who controls their collegiate future. They do not—and do not want to—look at their coach as a fallible human being, someone with a life outside the basketball court, someone with troubles, with moods. The others see Jody the way elementary school kids see their teacher, as someone who never eats, never sleeps, never goes to the bathroom, who is purely and simply there in the classroom, unknowable, a symbol more than a person.

But Red is not intimidated. She is not even particularly politic. The audacity that makes her so powerful on the court makes her difficult off it. The worst of it is Jody knows she's right: She hasn't been smiling; she has been increasingly short-tempered with the team as her contract negotiations have dragged on. But it's not what she wants to hear from one of her players. Red, though, is something else. Red is different.

She even looks different. The other girls—whether they're six-foot-five like Sandie or five-foot-six like Eddie, big-boned like Roy or delicate like Karen, brown- or blue-eyed, white or black or Asian—the other girls have something young and innocent in their faces, a certain vulnerability, a playfulness. Their faces show emotion easily, on the surface, like children's. Red has a Meryl Streep face, broad and Slavic yet also refined and aloof, with high angular cheekbones, a strong jaw and a long, interesting nose. She has curly, upswept hair the color of autumn oak leaves, the translucent skin of a redhead and chilly blue eyes that don't give away much. It is a face that masks emotion rather than displays it, a composed face, insular, a little haughty.

Red is the only one on the team who lives alone. The others room with each other—every player has a player roommate or two—and live in dorms or the kind of well-worn student housing that surrounds every campus. Red lives miles away. She likes it that way. She's used to being solitary, to taking care of herself. When she was seven years old, her parents divorced, an experience that affected them in very different ways: Mike Boyer quickly remarried; Carol Boyer cried. When she got finished crying, which took a long time, she went back to school to train as a nurse. Through her period of readjustment, through the years of schooling, through her working single-motherhood, Carol pretty much left Red alone, not as much by choice as by necessity. It turned out to be a workable system: Carol didn't tell her daughter what to do, and Red didn't ask. She grew up lonely, but she grew up trusting herself.

By middle school she was so self-contained and so self-sufficient, so seemingly sure of herself, that she had little in common with her peers. They took her maturity—and her loneliness—as arrogance, and they stayed away. Red wanted friends, but either she didn't know how to reach out or she was too proud to show she needed anyone.

Instead of family, instead of friends, she had sports. She learned to shoot baskets from her much older brothers in the driveway of their Vancouver, Washington, home. She was good at it almost immediately, and her body cooperated, growing tall and strong, a no-nonsense, muscular body, neither slender nor bulky, but tough, agile and androgynous, a body custom-built for athletics. At her big, competitive high school, she made the three varsity girls' teams, softball, volleyball and basketball, in her freshman year, and would have graduated with twelve varsity letters—three sports for all four years—had she not given up volleyball in her senior year to train extra hours with her basketball coach. That year she led the team to the state tournament, averaged twenty-nine points and twelve rebounds a game and was named a high school all-American by *USA Today*.

All those achievements, not to mention the outstanding grades that gained her induction into the National Honor Society, served to distance her even more from her classmates. Throughout high school, and even now, in college, Red has had only one friend, Linda. Linda first saw Red at a middle school volleyball game. Then a thirty-year-old coach at a rival school, she watched Red on the court. The kid was very good, and the kid never, ever smiled. "Who's the big redhead with the attitude?" Linda asked someone standing next to her.

She found out two years later when she started to coach Red's high school volleyball team. The team was in a tournament playoff game, three points away from a win, with Red, a fourteen-year-old sophomore, at the serving line. Linda walked up to her. "If you make these next three points, I'll be your best friend," Linda told her. Red, who even then didn't engage in light banter or even understand it, nodded. Then she threw the ball up and slammed it over, serving an ace. She stood there for a moment, very still and looked over at Linda. Then she raised one finger in the air. *One.* And Linda thought, wow, what kind of kid is this? Red served another, smashing it across for a second ace. She looked over at Linda, deadpan, and raised two fingers. *Two.* Her third serve rocketed over the net, an ace. Three fingers. No smile. *Three.* Red's team won the game, but Red figured she won much more. "Okay," she said to the tall, pretty woman who was seventeen years her senior, "now you're my best friend."

And oddly, that's what Linda became, the confidante she never had, the staunch supporter her mother didn't have time to be, the older sister who could put things in perspective. Now, five years later, the friendship is even stronger and it is still the only one in Red's life. When she drives home after a tough morning practice and a full day of courses—premed, no less—Red microwaves a dinner, roughhouses with her cat and talks to Linda on the phone for hours. Jody thinks it's an unhealthy relationship, that it's distancing Red from people her own age and creating tension between her and her mother. Especially now, with Linda in the middle of a divorce, Jody thinks Red is getting too cynical too fast about men.

Jody puts Red's essay facedown on her desk. She wishes her knowledge of the girl's personal life translated into knowing how to deal with her. But it doesn't.

The next morning, at 7 A.M., Jody comes to practice with a new plan. It is one part motivation, two parts punishment. She is determined to make the girls hate losing, or failing that, hate the consequences of losing. This morning the team will be scrimmaging but with a difference. Jody instructs her assistants, Steph, Joe and Kelly, to take up positions along the sidelines. They are to watch every play, scrutinize every move. If a player doesn't post up, if someone mishandles the ball, if she doesn't set a screen, whatever the transgression, they are to call out the player's name. Meanwhile, Stacy, the equipment manager, sits on a bottom bleacher with a book in her lap. Each mistake called aloud is a slash mark next to the player's name. Every five slash marks translate into one "suicide"—a sprint up and down the court in twelve seconds or less. That morning Cicely does fifteen sprints. When the scrimmage is over, the girls line up in groups of three to shoot free throws. If anyone on the line misses, the whole line has to do a sprint. It is not a popular drill. The girls are getting the idea.

Two days later, they are suited up and sitting in the locker room. The game tonight, their first since the Drake defeat last week, is an exhibition game against an amateur team of women who used to play top-notch collegiate basketball, including a Stanford graduate who played on the 1992 NCAA championship team. Outstanding male collegiate basketball players go on to multimillion-dollar contracts in the NBA. Outstanding female players, until 1996, had only two choices if they wanted to continue playing after college: They could go to Europe, where they might earn as little as twenty-five thousand dollars a year on a national touring team, or they could stay in the United States and play for free for one of the Amateur Athletic Union teams.*

The Portland Saints, the Ducks' opponent tonight, is an Amateur Athletic Union team. Supported by private donations, including the largesse of the NBA Portland Trail Blazers, the Saints practice twice a week, after the players and coaches come home from their day jobs, and grab whatever games they can.

Tonight's game will not count in the standings. But Jody is making it clear to her team just how much this game means to her.

---

* The opportunities for exceptional female players dramatically increased when the Palo Alto, California–based American Basketball League started its first season in the fall of 1996. Five hundred and fifty of the best women's players showed up in Atlanta in the spring of that year to vie for seventy slots on eight teams. A rival league, the Women's NBA, signed a deal with NBC to televise its games and began a shorter season the following summer. But the financial rewards for this new strata of professional women basketball players in no way mirrored what was available for the men. Salaries in the women's leagues started at about forty thousand dollars, with the very biggest stars commanding perhaps one hundred thousand dollars.

"We need to go out there and get last week out of our system," Jody tells the players in the locker room a few minutes before game time. "We need to get this preseason back on track, and we need to do it tonight."

The girls don't need much motivation. They don't want to go through another week of practices like this past week. They can't stand the thought of seeing Jody's stony face at 7 A.M. every morning. There's only one thing they can do to escape it: win. They go out and do it.

RAGGED EDGE

THE WEEK AFTER THE PORTLAND SAINTS EXHIBITION GAME
is fall term finals week at the university, and the girls are
having a hard time concentrating on basketball. Jess is studying for tests in biology, psychology and psychopathology
while gearing up to take the Graduate Record Examination.
Red has four finals in four days: physics, chemistry, organic
chemistry and calculus.

Universities talk a lot about "scholar-athletes," but the
truth is that many players, especially the men, are athletes first
and scholars second, if at all. They are often funneled into
courses with nicknames like Rocks for Jocks or advised to
pursue majors in recreational management. Special guidance
counselors plan their course schedule with the major objective
of maintaining NCAA-mandated grade point averages so the
players don't lose eligibility. Gifted—or even just hopeful—
male players are hard-pressed to take the academic side of
their lives seriously. Will the NBA or NFL care what their
major is? Why should they study when they imagine a future
secured by a seven-figure contract? Of course, only a small

percentage of college players move on to these kinds of careers, but for men the hope is always there, and it often determines how they live their university years.

For the women, it's different. It is not necessarily that they are brighter—although few male players come to college with the academic credentials of Red, a National Honor Society member, or Eddie, a 4.0 student, or B, who graduated first in her class—it is that they understand that if they don't study hard, if they aren't serious about finding a career-enhancing major, their postgraduation prospects are dim. Karen and Jess are planning to go to graduate school; Red is aiming for medical school. B has her sights set on a high-level career in journalism. Just about everyone on the team has a serious career goal. That's why finals week is a bad week for practice.

When she was a player, Jody understood how important it was to get a decent education, and she did, majoring in biology with plans to become an optometrist. But as a coach, she finds that she cares about how her players do in school as long as it doesn't interfere with how they do on the court. This week, it is interfering. Practice is sluggish, and after the essay writing and the slash-mark strategy, the suicide sprints, the yelling and the locker-room lectures, she is fresh out of motivational ideas.

She is not feeling particularly motivated herself these days. Dealing with the girls is hard enough, but dealing with the unending limbo of her on-again, off-again case is even harder. The stress is cumulative. It is taking its toll both on her body—she is still nursing the same September cold—and her mind. Red's words stick with her: *It wouldn't hurt if you smiled.* She never smiles. She is always on the ragged edge, always boiling over about something. On top of this, there are what Jody has come to view as repeated affronts against the women's basketball program, a series of slights that make her feel as if she's directing a sport no one cares about.

First it was the painters who showed up to work in Mac Court during the team's practice time. Then it was the fire alarm testing. This week it is something more serious. The women's basketball media guide—a magazine-sized publication that features biographies and pictures of the players and the coaches, summaries of past seasons and enough stats and records to satisfy even the most avid fan—is not out yet. The whole idea of the media guide is that it comes out at the beginning of the season to generate interest about the team and help local reporters write about the games, especially early in the season, when they are less familiar with the players. It has been almost a month since the team was officially introduced to the media and three weeks since the season started. There is still no media guide.

The excuse Jody gets from the sports information people, when she calls angrily during finals week, is that everyone is busy working on material for the Rose Bowl. Jody understands the kind of effort that takes. What she doesn't understand—and what pisses her off royally—is that the sports information staff has somehow found the time to produce the *men's* basketball media guide on time.

The day after venting her spleen with the sports information office, Jody comes to Mac Court to find the hallway lined with eight-foot-high framed posters of the men's basketball team. *It wouldn't hurt if you smiled.* Right, thinks Jody. About what? She calls Alan, whom she hasn't heard from in weeks, and unloads. He promises to get right on it.

This week, final exams or not, she is in no mood to tolerate poor practices. She needs something to be working right in her life, and about the only thing she has control of is what the team does on the court. She needs them to do what she can't seem to do: forget everything else when they come to practice. Concentrate and play hard. Some people think there can be problems when a team practices too hard, when players push themselves beyond their physical limits. But Jody knows it's when they don't practice hard enough, when they get sloppy, that accidents can happen.

The day after the men's basketball poster debacle, at practice in the morning, Eddie runs after a ball going out of bounds and whips it back toward the key. Sandie is standing there not paying much attention. The ball hits her square in the face. She topples to the floor, grabbing her nose, blood trickling through her fingers, down her arm, staining the front of her jersey. She thinks her nose is broken. She lies sobbing on the floor under the basket.

The assistant trainer runs over with towel and ice, but Jody keeps her distance. She barely looks at Sandie. People get hurt in practice all the time. Jody has a sixth sense about whether it's serious or not. This one isn't. She doesn't say anything, but she thinks this minor injury has opened a little crack in Sandie, and her frustration about her poor playing, her anger with herself, maybe even a little self-pity, is seeping out. She's lying there too long; she's wallowing in it, thinks Jody.

"Get her off the court or get a stretcher!" Jody yells, exasperated, from the sidelines after a minute or two. There is a cruel edge to her voice. "Let's go." Sandie gets up. It turns out her nose is sore but unbroken, not even bruised.

On the court the next morning, Karen is struggling. She has been feeling oddly lethargic all through the drills. There is no pain in her hips, but she feels as if her Nikes are glued to the floorboards.

"My feet are so slow," she says to Jess as they wait in line during a drill. She shakes her head and tries to pull out of it, pushing herself to run the floor. Nothing feels right this morning. "I'm feeling so slow today," she tells Jess a few minutes later. She tries again. Back in line she turns to B. "I can't seem to get moving," she says. Karen smiles, as she always does, and says it lightly, but she is worried. She has worked so hard to overcome her hip problem. Now she is playing almost pain-free, but she is not having good practices, and she is not having good games. I just need to work harder, she tells herself. I just need to be tough.

Jody watches her from the sidelines and doesn't like what she sees. She admires Karen for working her way back into the lineup, but she feels Karen is denying the extent of her problems, denying the fact that her hip is limiting her play. She still thinks she's going to come back and play like she played last year. Jody just doesn't see it. Karen is not producing on offense because her timing is off. She's not producing on defense because she's afraid of getting hurt. Jody doesn't know what to do.

A week ago, she didn't know what to do about Karen because she needed her in the lineup so badly. Now she doesn't know what to do because she wants her out. Sitting in the bleachers, waiting to play, waiting to take Karen's position, is another Australian godsend, newly arrived, not yet even suited up, a tough-looking, henna-haired kid named Sally Crowe.

Sally is a friend of Roy's. They played together at the Australian Institute of Sports and played with and against each other for years in the national club system. Back in late August, when Roy returned to Eugene from her cross-continental wanderings and started playing casual pickup games with the team—"ratball," they call it—she immediately saw the team's weakness. Back then, Karen was out completely, rehabbing her hip without much hope of being able to play. The team needed a shooting guard.

Roy immediately thought of Sally, a year younger but with just as much experience. Sal had started playing at six, the daughter of a netball- and badminton-playing mother and a father who was once a top player in the Australian Football League. She was seriously competitive at seven, and from nine to sixteen grew up and came of age on the court. She hung out at gyms the way other kids hang out at malls. At sixteen she was playing for the institute. She toured the United States three times with Australian teams, once beating Stanford.

Roy told Jody about Sal back then, and Jody figured, yeah, sure, we're gonna get another windfall from Down Under. But she gave the girl a call. It turned out that Sally wasn't at all interested. Unlike Roy, she was in college in Australia. She had a serious boyfriend. Roy let a few weeks go by and called again. Then Roy's mother called Sally's mother. Then Roy sent Sal information about classes. Then Jody offered her a full-ride scholarship. It was odd offering the scholarship to a player sight unseen, but that's how much Jody trusted Roy's judgment. And that's how desperate Jody was.

Sally began to reconsider. In Australia, she was a young player, playing in a club system with women in their late twenties and early thirties. It was a cliquish group with the mature players keeping aloof of their juniors, treating twenty-one-year-olds like Sally as if they were barely good enough to warm the bench. Sally wasn't getting the playing time she wanted; she wasn't making the progress she hoped for. It was because, with all the veterans on the team—including the coach's wife, an uncomfortable situation all around—not much was expected of her. But at Oregon, she would be an older, experienced player, an elder stateswoman, with the prospect of getting a lot of time on the floor. Roy could vouch for that.

Sally thought hard about it for close to two months before she called Jody and told her she'd come. What Sal figured was she'd get another season under her belt before her own season began in late spring. She thought of Jody's scholarship offer purely in basketball terms: She'd come for the season, take the college classes she needed to be eligible to play and then go back home to her own season, her boyfriend and her own life.

Sal would not be anyone's ideal of the collegiate student-athlete. Her coming was more like bringing in a hired gun. Jody wished she didn't have to go to foreign players to fill out the roster, but the fact was that a number of schools were doing it, and the practice was sanctioned by the NCAA. The top schools that could attract the top U.S. high school players didn't do it, not Stanford or Vanderbilt, Tennessee or North Carolina, but Oregon State had two Swedes and two Croats on the team; Berkeley had two Poles. But even these players didn't come for a season and leave. Jody figured she might take some heat for that. But if Sal was good, it wouldn't matter.

Down near the basket, Karen is guarding Courtney Kanegae, a five-foot-two freshman walk-on. Courtney has the ball. Karen is trying hard to get into the rhythm of this fast-paced drill. Courtney is little and quick, but Karen is quick too. Or used to be. Okay, she thinks to herself, let's do it. Let's move.

She lunges at Courtney, looking to steal the ball. At the same time, Courtney moves toward Karen. Karen's right hand connects with Courtney's shoulder. The fingers jam back. Karen hears a pop. For a moment, the sound makes her so nauseous that she doesn't feel the pain. Then she feels the pain. She freezes in place, feet planted on the floor, white-faced, disoriented. She grabs her hand. It is her shooting hand.

Jody looks over from the sidelines, and instantly she knows. She can tell how Karen is holding her hand. She can tell by how pale she is. When a kid sprains her hand or jams her finger, which happens often, she tries to shake it out. Jody has seen this many times. The girl is hurt but she's talking, moving, massaging the hand, grousing about it. But Karen is just standing there, ashen. Something's broken. Jody knows something's broken.

And she's . . . relieved. Well, that solves that problem, she thinks to herself. It is not a generous thought. It is not a thought soggy with the milk of human kindness. It is the response of a coach assessing the realities of her team, a team she wants and needs to win. Since Sally arrived a few days ago, but really since more than a month ago, when the Australian first committed to coming for the season, Jody has been thinking about how she will manage the inevitable. Her assumption all along has been that Karen will not be capable of playing very well and that Sal will be good. She has imagined giving Sally more and more playing time until she virtually replaces Karen on the court. She has imagined what that would do to Karen and has considered how the other players would take it. She's run it all through her head many times, but she has not been able to figure out how she was going to manage to push Karen from her spot without creating a morale problem. Now, with Karen white with pain under the basket, it seems the problem has been solved for her.

Jody stays on the sidelines. Steph, one of the assistant coaches, rushes to Karen's side, hustling her down to the training room, where they ice the hand. Karen can't feel where the pain is coming from. They place the ice on her middle and ring fingers, waiting for numbness. It doesn't come. In fact, the pain intensifies. Even for Karen, who has learned to tolerate pain, it becomes intolerable.

"Let's go, Karen. We're getting X rays right now," says the assistant trainer. She drives her over to Sacred Heart Hospital.

An hour later, the doctor clips the X ray onto a light board and points to the splintered white twig that is Karen's fourth metacarpal bone, the thin rod that begins at the knuckle under her ring finger and extends to her wrist. It is broken lengthwise.

"You have a broken bone," the doctor says.

Karen looks down. She knew it, but she was hoping for a miracle. Maybe it's just a bad sprain, she kept saying to herself on the way to the hospital. Maybe I just twisted it real bad. She has almost convinced herself that the pop she heard was just a dislocation. They'll just pop it back and I'll be fine. But all the time, under the surface, she knew the truth. And now the doctor is saying it out loud.

She is just letting the doctor's words sink in when she hears him say something else.

"It's a bad break. We are going to have to operate," he says in that deadpan voice doctors use when they have to say things like this.

Karen's slender shoulders slump. Operate? She hadn't even considered that possibility. Operate? This is even more serious than she imagined. She has only a single thought: I can't believe this is happening to me. She looks up and realizes the doctor is speaking again.

"You won't be playing anymore this season," he says. She hears the words, but she doesn't understand them, not at first anyway. She is still processing his last statement, the one about needing an operation. The room is silent except for the hum of the fluorescent lights.

"Are you all right?" the trainer asks Karen. Karen doesn't answer. The three of them sit there in silence. Karen waits for the doctor to leave. Then she breaks down and cries.

The next morning at 7 A.M. she is at practice, her hand in a temporary cast. The cast is resting in a navy blue cotton sling. Karen's eyes are glassy with crying. She is at practice because the rule is you come to practice. If you're a bench-warmer or a redshirt, if you're hurt or rehabbing, you come to practice. This rule probably doesn't extend to players with broken and as-yet-unset bones, but Karen needs to feel she is still part of the team. She follows the rule.

She sits in the bleachers. The girls come up to her, one by one, but they don't know what to say beyond "You feeling okay?" and "I'm so sorry." Even Jess, her best friend, is tongue-tied. In the twenty-four hours since the injury, Jess has been in almost worse shape than Karen.

Jess's anguish, which she contains the way she contains all emotions, her face stony, her eyes cool and distant, has many layers. There's the pure empathic pain she feels for the woman who has been her roommate, teammate and best friend for the past three years. There's the sorrow twinged with a little self-pity about the senior year they talked about so much that they are not going to share. There's the deep confusion about what she, Jess, is going to do, how she is going to be able to keep on being who she is without hurting Karen. If Jess plays and Karen doesn't, will Jess have to hide her excitement about the game? Not talk about the season at all? Maybe she will stay out late after games so she doesn't have to come back to the apartment and face Karen. How can they continue a friendship based on basketball when there is no

basketball for Karen anymore? Jess is not an overly intro-
spective person. She has thought more about Karen and more
about herself in the past twenty-four hours than she has in the
past year.

But Jess's feelings of friendship and her empathy are
balanced by a fierce competitiveness. This is her year. She
has got to do what is best for herself. With Karen out, she's
the only senior on the team. She wants to play. She wants to
make it back to the NCAA tournament. Karen's injury doesn't
change that. Nothing will change that.

Karen sits in the bleachers watching the team go through
the familiar drills. She can't stand it. She can't stand watching
them—big, healthy, already a little breathless, yelling back
and forth to each other "Let's go, ladies" and "Come on,
Ducks." After five minutes, she gets up and leaves the court,
spending the rest of the practice downstairs in the training
room. The following day, the doctors pin together her bone
with three tiny steel rods that will stay in her hand forever.

Saturday afternoon is the next game. The opponent is the
University of Portland, a small private school, not a Pac-10-
caliber school, but not a pushover either. This is one of those
"confidence-building" games Jody has scheduled, a game
Oregon should win.

As the girls warm up on the court, Aretha Franklin belts
out "Respect" over the loudspeakers. The song echoes
through Mac Court, which, just a few minutes before game
time, is almost empty. The girls aren't listening to the music,
but they do look up in the stands and notice the sparse crowd.
Red's father is up there in his usual seat. Jess's parents and
brother are here. Her family has not missed a game since she
was a freshman.

In the reserved seats directly behind the players' bench
are a hundred or so "Daisy Ducks," mostly retirement-aged
women in emerald green sweats and yolk-colored scarves and
retirement-aged men in bottle green polyester trousers, waists
dipping low to cradle their bellies. These are the loyal wom-

en's athletic boosters who buy reserved-seat season tickets and come to every game. The women bring paper plates piled with homemade chocolate chip cookies, with brownies and snickerdoodles, lemon squares and macaroons, that they press on the girls after games. The men walk slowly to their seats, stopping to chat with Jody in front of the bench, to clasp her hand, pat her paternally on the arm.

The game appeals to them; they like to watch the women play. But the real attraction, the reason they come here rather than to the men's games, is the intimacy. Jody knows many of their names. The players recognize the regulars, smile and wave at them, take a moment to joke with them. They can't get this feeling of connectedness at a men's game, with its big, boisterous crowds, the TV cameras, the two-hundred-thousand-dollar-a-year coach. Here they feel like part of an extended family. They are grandparents to the team. After Thursday night home games, the most devoted supporters host a catered party in a nearby campus building. Jody shows up to say a few words. The girls filter in and allow themselves to be congratulated or consoled depending on the night.

In the bleachers just above the reserved seating sits the lesbian contingent, alone and in groups, with and without children, staunch fans who used to play or wished they played or just like to watch women play. Last year someone in the athletic department got wind of a rumor that some lesbian fans were planning to bring a big hand-painted banner to Mac Court that read "Dykes for Ducks." There was much consternation about this, but the banner never materialized. Lesbian supporters elsewhere, however, have been known to go public. Down in Berkeley, a group once sat in the stands with placards that read 3 CHEERS FOR THE 3-POINT QUEER, an homage to the team's solid outside shooter who was an out lesbian.

The relationship between lesbian supporters and teams, whether the teams have lesbian players or not, is a complex one. On the one hand, coaches, athletic directors and the players themselves welcome the solid and enthusiastic support they get from that group of fans who happen to be lesbians. On the other hand, there is a feeling, not often publicly expressed, that visible lesbian support will hurt women's basketball.

It is not so much that the coaches or the players are overtly homophobic, although there may be some of that going on; it is rather that most of them accept the societal precept that homosexuality is a stigma, that to call a player a lesbian is to insult her. Women athletes, gay and straight, have grown up in a culture steeped in traditional gender roles, a culture that allows, encourages and expects men to be strong, aggressive and competitive—and looks with suspicion on women who exhibit these same traits (and men who do not). Women are nurturing not combative, soft not hard, passive not aggressive. If real men don't eat quiche, then real women don't grab rebounds.

One of the first questions some parents ask Jody when she makes home recruiting visits to their heterosexual, high school–aged daughters is: "Are there any gay players on your team?" Most parents don't articulate it so forthrightly, but they hint; they scrutinize photographs; they ask pointedly about Jody's marital status. Some are afraid their daughters will be accosted in the locker room by lesbian teammates, that most elemental and mistaken of heterosexual fears. Most are concerned that their daughters will be stigmatized by any association with lesbianism. A "Dykes for Ducks" banner, if indeed one was ever planned, would have been a catastrophe. The enthusiasm and support of the lesbian fans is vital, but their contribution cannot be publicly acknowledged.

The other group of stalwart fans besides the Daisy Ducks and the lesbian contingent are the little girls. They are seven, eight, nine and ten, skinny and skittish, dressed in scuffed-knee jeans and Oregon T-shirts. They play on city teams already and come to watch the women they hope to someday become. They are of that protected, preadolescent age when girls can have big dreams, that time before they learn the hard lessons about what girls should and shouldn't hope for, what real women can and can't do.

The little girls know the players' names, and they have favorites, but mostly they can't take their eyes off Jody. Sometimes a parent will walk a daughter to the players' bench while the team is warming up.

"Coach Runge, this is my daughter Jenny," or Anna or Alexis, the parent will say. "She just wanted to meet you." Jody will bend from the waist, extend her long arm and shake the girl's hand. The girl will stand motionless and wide-eyed, then break ranks and run back to her friends, giggling. She will talk about the experience for weeks afterward.

The players finish their warm-up in front of a few hundred fans and head for the locker room. Karen is down there, standing off to one side dressed in a long black wool jumper with a hint of gold jewelry, an outfit one might wear to a funeral. Her hair hangs loose to her shoulders, dark, straight and shiny. She holds her right hand high above her heart, the big cast thick and creamy white. Next to it, her forearm is a slender reed. She listens to Jody go through the opponent's starting roster, talking about plays and strategies for tonight's game. She looks intently at the board as Jody draws the plays with a colored marker.

"You can go out and do either of two things right off," Jody is saying. "You can go out there and put their tail between their legs or you can let 'em think they can win it."

Karen has heard it all before, but tonight it sounds different. She looks over at the girls in their white uniforms sprawled on the long couch and the folding chairs. She cradles her hand. Even with the codeine and Tylenol, it still hurts too much to let her arm hang free. This is what it's going to be like for me now, she thinks: always on the outside. She keeps herself under control, but just barely. "This is hard," she whispers as she walks upstairs with the team. They are making too much noise to hear her.

B is pumped tonight. With Karen out, she will be in the Oregon starting lineup for the first time in her career. She struts out on the floor, singing to herself. She is not swelled-headed about it, just excited, ebullient the way B is ebullient about life in general, determined to go in there and show Jody she can do the job. Almost immediately, B grabs a rebound. She sinks a basket and draws a foul. She hauls down another rebound. Jody looks on approvingly. B is six-foot-one, but she's playing even bigger tonight, carving out space for herself with her long arms, elbows up and out, torso twisting as she pulls the ball to her chest. She's not fast, but she's keeping up.

Then, all of a sudden, like a spigot turned counterclockwise, B shuts down. One minute she's taking control, the next she's just taking up space. Jody stops her usual pacing for a moment and stares at B lagging behind the others as the team gets into its defense. She's not making anything happen out there. Jody shakes her head and looks to the bench.

The Ducks are ahead by six. Red and Roy are playing well; Eddie looks solid. Jody decides to take a gamble.

"Sal," she calls to Sally Crowe, who has not yet even practiced with the team, who was only just this morning certified by the NCAA as eligible to play. "Sal, in for B."

Sally whips off her warm-up jersey and sprints to the scoring table, where she kneels, waiting to be called in. She is a tough, scrappy-looking woman despite the delicate English coloring: pale skin that mottles easily, freckled arms, pale legs that almost match the white of her uniform shorts. She wears her henna-ed hair chopped short, someplace between punk and tomboy. She is not tall, only five-foot-nine, but she moves with such confidence that she seems bigger.

She goes in full tilt. She's watched the team in practice for a few days, seen some game films and talked to Jody, but she's never actually run any of the plays. Less than a minute on the court and she drives to the basket, drawing a foul as she skids to the floor. It's a bad fall, facedown. Sally stays there, splayed under the basket. Jody stops midpace and clenches her fists. The bench is up. The crowd is silent. Everyone waits.

Sally lifts herself up to one knee, then stands tall, shaking out her arm. The crowd applauds. Sal looks up for a moment, surprised. By now there are 1,300 people in the stands. It's not like this in Australia, where women's sports enjoy little popularity, where a few dozen people watch games in silence. Red walks over and wraps a long arm around Sally's shoulders, and the two redheads, the two tough girls, walk back to the key. Sally makes both her free throws.

From then on, it's Sally who makes things happen on the court. She makes four steals, grabbing at the ball aggressively, fighting for it on the ground, at one point somersaulting into the stands. She pulls down four rebounds. She mixes it up inside, attracting three more fouls and sinking every free throw.

Jody is having a hard time believing her good fortune. Here's a girl she never even scouted, a girl no one but Roy had ever seen play. She arrives in the country a week ago, never runs so much as a drill with the team and goes out there and plays like this. It is not lost on Jody that Sally is wearing number 23. That's Missy Crowshaw's old number—Missy, last year's fiery point guard, the team's spark plug.

The bigger kids last year may have provided more of the points, but Missy was the engine. Missy was the heart. What Missy had, Eddie doesn't have. Neither does Jess. Karen didn't have it either. But Sally's got it. Jody keeps Sally in for twenty-three minutes, watching her pick up the offensive plays and bluff her way through the defense. That's experience, thinks Jody. No, she amends that: That's a girl with fire.

The game is much closer than it should be. Roy and Red get into foul trouble in the first half and have to slack off. The shots aren't dropping. A halftime lead of thirteen evaporates to three with less than a minute left in the game. At the thirteen-second mark, Sally is fouled and goes to the free throw line. She makes both shots, and Oregon hangs on to win. It's not the kind of win Jody wants. It's not the kind of playing that's going to get the Ducks anywhere in the Pac-10, but it's a victory, and she'll take it.

After the game, Sally gets asked into the media room. Bob Rodman from the *Register-Guard* is the only one down there. He asks her how she managed to play so well without practicing.

"When you work hard, you can fit in," Sally tells him. "It comes from the heart."

Jody is outside the door, listening. She smiles.

When she gets to her office Monday after the usual early morning practice, Jody finds a fax waiting. "Dear Dan and Dave," it begins, "I have patiently abided by our agreement to not speak with the press and not proceed on my client's behalf to address serious Title IX issues. . . ." Jody takes the fax, walks into her office and closes the door. It's a three-page, single-spaced letter from her lawyer, Alan, to the president of the university and the acting athletic director. Jody is glad that her conversation with her lawyer last week had some effect. She sits behind her big, neat desk and reads.

"I am sure that you recall at the end of our telephone conversation"—Jody figures he's referring to the conference call three weeks ago—"that I urged you to make this matter a priority in that it was quickly becoming the number one priority of my law office. It has now moved to the front burner."

This is what Jody has wanted to hear for months. She only hopes it's true. She reads on as Alan berates Dan and Dave for their "complete and blatant disregard" for their word. Their word, according to Alan, was a verbal promise to get back to him with a progress report on the big-money donor. "Perhaps a simple phone call from either of you or even an acknowledgment of the December 1 deadline would have generated some hope that either of you had any intention of abiding by your word and addressing this issue."

Alan goes on to take special note of the late media guide and the sudden appearance of the larger-than-life posters of the men's basketball team. This is a "slap in the face to the women's basketball program," he writes. It follows a "pattern of discrimination against women at the University of Oregon and will not be tolerated."

Alan demands immediate placement of larger-than-life photographs of the senior women on the team. He demands the immediate production of the women's media guide. He wants reasonable practice times for the women, upgrades to their locker room and, by noon the following day, a new four-year, seventy-thousand-dollar contract for Jody. "I do not intend to sit idly by while the University of Oregon, through its administration and athletic director, blatantly ignores and prejudices the rights of females at the University." Alan hints that he may be coming out to Eugene quite soon to "address all my client's rights and concerns"; that is, to file the lawsuit.

Behind that fax, Jody finds another. It is Pete Swan's answer to Alan, dated the same day. Alan has addressed the president as "Dave"; Pete addresses Alan as "Mr. Manheim."

"Mr. Manheim," he has written, "this is in response to your regrettable and intemperate FAX. . . ." Oh no, Jody thinks. Not more chest bumping. Not more of these lawyer games. But it's more than chest bumping. Pete is genuinely peeved. The president is moving toward contact with the potential donor, he writes to Alan, and never promised that he'd get back to you on a particular day. "The President and Athletic Director find it ironic and disappointing that after several weeks' delay on your part in agreeing to support the President's endowment initiative as a constructive reaction to Jody's concerns, you now appear to demand short (and unagreed to) deadlines from a major university's leader and an almost equally busy philanthropist."

Pete tells Alan that the president has, in fact, arranged a luncheon meeting with the potential donor and that Jody will be involved in follow-up meetings. "It is safe to say that my clients feel these sporadic outbursts of yours do nothing for and materially distract everyone from what we believe are

Jody's and the University's mutual interest in dealing with
gender equity issues."

Jody goes over the two faxes again, this time slowly,
trying to read between the lines. Is Alan about to drop everything and fly out to file a lawsuit? Is this twenty-four-hour
deadline for a new contract for real? Is this *it*? She has no
idea. It all sounds too familiar. Maybe the president is going
to step in and save the day, announce that he's reeled in the
big fish. Or maybe this is all just talk on both sides. Jody is
almost glad she has no time to ponder this more deeply. She's
got two days to get the team ready for the first road trip.

On Wednesday, the team flies to Idaho. The next night,
in Pocatello, Sally scores seventeen points and makes eight
steals against Idaho State. But it is really Jess's game, the
game she needs to play well in to show herself and the others
that she's fine without Karen, that she can hold up her end as
the sole senior on the team, as the team's captain. It is her
first road trip in three years without Karen, and she feels
strange and disconnected. No one to sit next to on the plane.
No one to talk to at dinner. With Karen around, Jess did not
have to make any other friends on the team, and she didn't.

Although fierce on the court, Jess is quiet and shy away
from basketball. The youngest of five children, she grew up
in Washington State in a two-story farmhouse surrounded by
asparagus, mint and hayfields three miles out of town on
gravel roads. It is the same house her father was raised in.
Jess's whole family is basketball-crazy, from her youthful-
looking mother, who played in high school, to her father, who
filled his children's minds with sports from infancy. Her two
older brothers, who now farm land next to their parents',
played basketball in high school. The older sisters played too,
although one broke ranks to play volleyball in her junior college days.

Until eighth grade, Jess went to a small, private Christian
school, the same one all her older siblings attended. She
switched to public school for only one reason: basketball.

Continuing in the Christian school would have meant playing in the B league; the local high school had a AA team. Ever since third grade, when she was water girl for her older sister's team, Jess's life has revolved around basketball. By junior high, she knew she wanted to play college ball. In high school, she was team captain, two-time most valuable player, her school's career scoring leader and the all-time AA state tournament scoring pacesetter.

She had long dreamed of playing in the Pac-10 at a university close enough to home so that her parents, who had never missed a game she and her siblings played, could continue the tradition for another four years. Oregon gave her the chance, and she had done well, averaging eleven points a game by her junior year, scoring in the double digits in fifteen games that year and placing fifth in the Pac-10 for three-point accuracy. Jess was deadly from outside. She had this way of sizing up the basket fast, of staring at it hard, not squinting but wide-eyed, the whites of her eyes like an ocean, the irises floating free. Then she'd lob the ball in a graceful arc from her fingertips in a textbook-pretty shot.

When she made it, which she often did—eight three-pointers against USC last year—she never smiled, never hotdogged, never looked up to the stands where her family was invariably sitting. Instead, she and Karen slapped hands, and Jess was off down the court, ready to plant herself in front of some player whose life she would make temporarily miserable. But now there is no Karen, and there won't be all season. Jess can't believe how she has taken that friendship for granted, how alone she feels out on the road. But that is all the more reason to rise to the occasion, to—as Jody says when a player is feeling tired or off-kilter—suck it up.

At Idaho State, Jess scores twenty-eight points, including five three-pointers, in twenty-nine minutes. The next night, in Provo, Utah, two and a half minutes into the game against Brigham Young University, Jess lunges for a ball going out of bounds, comes down on an opponent's foot and wrenches her ankle. She falls to the ground, grimacing, and stays down.

She has torn two ligaments and will be out, sidelined, for at least four weeks.

The Ducks win both nights.

Jody returns from the road trip to find a copy of another fax Pete has sent to Alan. It has the calm, measured tone of a letter written by a man who has waited for his anger to cool. In four long paragraphs, the university's counsel discusses and dismisses the concerns Alan raised in last week's fax, the ones that didn't refer to Jody's salary. There are two almost Nixonian paragraphs of deniability. "The deferral of the women's basketball media guide was unknown to higher-level administrators," Pete writes at the end of one paragraph. On the next page, referring to the appearance of the eight-foot-high framed photographs of the male players, Pete writes: "Both the Athletic Department senior administrators and our promotions people were unaware of the project until the pictures appeared."

Jody snorts. More excuses. That's how she sees it. Maybe the late media guide and the men's posters and the rotten practice times and the unventilated locker room with no showers are not part of some grand scheme to disadvantage women's basketball. Maybe they are just separate, ill-conceived decisions that cumulatively disadvantage women's basketball. Jody doesn't care which. She just wants it fixed.

At the end of the letter, Pete tells Alan that the president's initial meeting with the prospective donor "went quite well" and that Jody will be included in the next meeting, which they are trying to arrange for early January. Jody is not heartened by the news. To her, it's just more stalling, more of a chance for the team to do poorly, for her stock to go down.

There is a good chance the team will do poorly. The Ducks have won five of their six games, including the exhibition, and officially have a 4–1 record. That looks good on the stat page, but Jody knows just how flimsy it is. The wins are all against teams Oregon was supposed to beat, and most of those games were much closer than they should have been. Drake was the only team that offered a real challenge, and Oregon lost that game. Now, with Jess out, the team is playing with three sophomores and two newcomers and faces its two toughest nonconference games and the entire Pac-10 season. Jody is not sanguine about the prospects.

Her position off the court is weak too. She knows that once the Pac-10 season begins in two weeks she will have no time to devote to her case. She knows once the Pac-10 season begins, she can't have Alan flying out to file the suit. She'll be on the road. She'll be in practice. She'll be in conferences with the players, on the phone with the media, in meetings with her assistants, at functions with the boosters. She will have to focus on basketball, become single-minded about the season if she hopes to accomplish anything.

She assumes the university administration has this figured out. The way she sees it, the university has done its best to stall any action, and Alan, through his inattention, has let that happen. Now she is in the position she most dreaded months back, when the discussions with her lawyer began: She is a month into the season, a few games away from Pac-10 play, and absolutely nothing is resolved. She has no time to think about this latest fax from Pete. In a few days, the team will face Vanderbilt, the toughest opponent before conference play begins. The week after is Santa Clara, another challenge.

Before the Ducks face Vanderbilt, they are scheduled to play a home game against the University of Texas at Arlington. It's one of those we-should-win games that go slightly sour. In the first half, Oregon outscores Arlington almost two to one and goes to the locker room fifteen points up. In the second half, the Oregon defense takes a prolonged siesta, allowing the opponents to score forty-two points. It turns out to be something of a nail-biter, this game against a visiting team that has won only one of its last eight games. Oregon takes it by seven, but it's a sloppy win. It does nothing to prepare the team for Vanderbilt.

Maybe nothing could. Vanderbilt is an excellent team, strong, quick and deep, a team with a long winning tradition. It is not a pretty game. B, Red and Roy all make early baskets, but in the first five minutes of the half, Vanderbilt hits four three-pointers, and Oregon never leads again, never comes close. Toward the end of the half, in the midst of a demoralizing twelve-to-nothing Vanderbilt run, Red tries to take control. She has the ball a few feet from the basket. When she has the ball in this close, she always takes a shot, no matter how many defenders are around, no matter how heavy the traffic. She has polished a whole set of moves for just this circumstance. She goes through them: lunges left, fakes, moves right, tosses a head fake, dips her shoulder and charges. She moves with strength, with certainty. She has evaded two defenders. She puts up the shot. From out of nowhere, the long arm of a six-foot-seven Vanderbilt player reaches out effortlessly to deflect the ball from its arc to the basket. Red can't believe it. She also can't recover from it. This night, it breaks her spirit.

Oregon loses big, by almost thirty points. But it's not just the magnitude of the loss that worries Jody. She expected to lose this one—although not this badly. She never said anything like this to the players, but she thought it; she prepared herself mentally for it. No, it's not the loss that has her screaming in the locker room. It's that no one on the team "stepped up," which is coach talk for assuming leadership, asserting oneself, going beyond one's role to make things happen. This is exactly what she fears most from this team, this lack of confidence, this timidity in the face of adversity.

She knew this was going to be a problem months ago, long before a single game was played, long before the first practice of the season. When she sat in her office that summer day staring at the names she had written on the board, the likely starters, she knew this season would be uphill all the

way. These were young players, too young. They were, with
the exception of Red, unsure of themselves. They lacked the
killer instinct. She had hoped then, and still hopes now, that
she can turn this around. She is banking on the combination
of tough practices and a tough coach: a woman with power
and authority and grit, a woman with an unyielding game face
and a relentless set of expectations. She is willing to be—she
wants to be—that person, the one who pushes them, the one
they love to hate. But this big loss to Vanderbilt shows her
just how vulnerable the team is. If the girls are not up at the
half, they don't win. They don't have what it takes to fight
back when they're down.

The problem is not just mental; it's physical too. The
starters are so exhausted that they have nothing left to give in
the last five minutes of the game. But Jody has to play them
almost every minute. With Jess out of the lineup, B is starting.
That leaves only Sandie to go to on the bench. The three
freshmen, Courtney, Timmy and Neiman, are a long way
away from being able to contribute. Jody looks at the stats on
her clipboard. Vanderbilt played all nine of its players about
equally, getting lots of rest time for its starters and an astounding forty-six points from the bench. Three of Oregon's starters
played virtually without rest. The Oregon bench contributed
nine points. These are problems that won't go away.

The Vanderbilt game is Wednesday, four days before
Christmas. The Santa Clara game is not scheduled until Friday
of the following week. Jody wishes she could keep everyone
in town practicing hard, but she knows she has to let them go
spend time with their families. She realizes, grudgingly, that
it's holiday season, that the girls have lives outside of basketball, even if their coach doesn't. Maybe it's for the best
anyway. They all need to put some distance between themselves and the Vanderbilt humiliation.

When practice starts up again after the weekend, Jody
acts as if Vanderbilt never happened. The focus is Santa Clara.

"We've got to turn up the intensity," she tells the team

at morning practice two days before the game. "We've got to start playing like we want to be playing because there are no more freebies, no more easy ones. You can't coast and expect to win in the Pac-10, ladies."

Santa Clara is a tough, mature team that made it to the NCAA tournament last year, the team Oregon beat in a hard-fought first-round game. Now they're coming back to Mac Court for the first time since that defeat, and Jody is playing up the revenge angle. "They're coming to get us," she tells the girls at the next practice. "They want to storm in here and make up for last year. They want to embarrass us on our home court because we knocked them out of the tournament."

It's not clear that all this coach talk is having any effect. The girls are in high spirits after a week away from classes and some vacation time with their families. Jody wants them to put on their game face, to get serious, get tough. They want to scrimmage and go home.

On Friday, game day, Jody continues to worry about the team's lack of intensity.

"You've been pretty loosey-goosey in practice," she tells them in the locker room a few minutes before game time. "I'm gonna trust that you've got it together."

Jody has been a little loosey-goosey herself these past few days. Her parents have been staying with her since Christmas Day, and they're beginning to drive her crazy. She may mourn her lack of a social life, but she has gotten used to living alone and calling all the shots. For the past week, she has had no time alone, no time to de-stress, to be quiet and think.

She's taking a moment now before the game, standing in front of the board at the head of the locker room, writing down the Santa Clara starters, making notes about strategy and collecting her thoughts. The girls are upstairs warming up. Dennis Runge, Jody's father, sprawls on one of the fold-up chairs facing the board. He's so big that the chair under him looks like nursery furniture.

He watches Jody intently. Her back is to him, but she

No one expected much from the University of Oregon Ducks that season. The team had lost its three top players and was headed for mediocrity. Second-year coach Jody Runge (right) and assistant coach Stephanie Osburn knew the team was shallow, inexperienced, and tentative on the court. (CURT JENSEN)

The only two seniors on the team were Karen Healea (left) and Jessica Schutt, best friends and roommates since they came to the university. Others might be concerned about how the team would fare, but all Karen and Jess could talk about was the terrific senior year they would be sharing. (JOHN GIUSTINA)

At 6′5′′, Sandie Edwards was the natural choice to play center, but both she and Jody knew she wasn't strong or confident enough for a starting position in the Pac-10. Still, Jody had few options. (JOHN GIUSTINA)

The team's prospects changed suddenly when Jody managed to tempt Renae Fegent (Roy), a twenty-one-year-old, 6′3′′ Australian, to join the team. Renae, burned out from five years of playing in the Australian national league, had come to the U.S. for an extended vacation. Basketball was not on her agenda until Jody put it there. (CURT JENSEN)

Cindie Edamura (Eddie) would have to start at point guard, although the position had defeated her the year before. She was smart and quick, but she lacked the cockiness and self-confidence the position demanded. Jody respected her work ethic and took special care to praise her. (JOHN GIUSTINA)

Jody dressed meticulously for each game, sometimes wearing three-inch pumps that left her wincing in pain. But she was 6´6´´ with the shoes on—a mighty presence on the sidelines. (CURT JENSEN)

Of all the players, Arianne Boyer (Red) was the one for whom Jody had the highest hopes. Red could be an all-American if she wanted to, Jody thought. The two strong, stubborn women tangled all year. Jody thought Red didn't work hard enough. Red was only a sophomore and thought Jody expected too much of her. (CURT JENSEN)

Frustrations mounted during the season for Jody. Her equity case was stalled. Her lawyer wasn't returning her phone calls. The team, already among the shallowest in the league, was plagued by injuries. On top of that, Jody was constantly appalled by the officiating. Officials for women's games were paid considerably less than those who worked the men's games. She thought you got what you paid for. (CURT JENSEN)

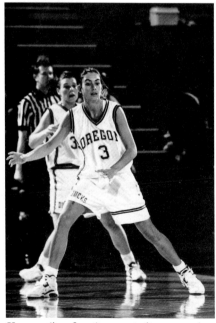

Karen (in front) spent long weeks rehabing a hip problem before she could rejoin the team. But she soon suffered another serious injury. Her much-anticipated senior year was not to be. (JOHN GIUSTINA)

Eddie was determined to exorcise past demons and make good that seaon. In practise, she worked the hardest; on the court she was intense and focused. (JOHN GIUSTINA)

Whenever Red got the ball near the basket, she fought for the shot. It didn't matter how many opponents were on her. (CURT JENSEN)

Sally Crowe (with the ball) was another godsend from Australia. Jody couldn't believe her luck. Still, the Ducks—like most of the other Pac-10 teams—could never get the best of Stanford. Tara VanDerveer's team was just too talented, too deep, and too well coached to beat. (CURT JENSEN)

Across the country, women's basketball was attracting larger and larger crowds. In Jody's second season as coach, the Ducks were consistently drawing crowds four times the size as the year before. The fans, many of them girls and women, felt a special affinity for the team and its players. (CURT JENSEN)

Jess was having a bad year, and no one knew what to do about it. (JOHN GIUSTINA)

Betty Ann Boeving (B), on the other hand, was having a great year. When she was in what she called the B-zone, she couldn't miss. Off the court, her enthusiasm was boundless. (CURT JENSEN)

Jody loved it when a game was televised, both for the exposure the team got and the frequent TV time-outs that kept everyone rested. But not many of the women's games were carried on the local sports network that season. This was one of the inequities Jody wanted to remedy when she considered suing the university for Title IX violations. (CURT JENSEN)

Sal turned out to be the team's fiercest competitor. She should have stepped up to take a leadership role, but she didn't want to take anything away from Jess. (CURT JENSEN)

Red was the power player with all the right moves. As the season progressed, she and Jody reached an uneasy detente. (CURT JENSEN)

What everyone thought would be a "building year"—coach talk for a losing year—turned out quite differently. But the bench, with the exception of B (far left), struggled all season. Freshman Kirsten McKnight (Timmy) and Cicely Brewster, the promising 6′2′′ transfer student from southern California, saw little action. (JOHN GIUSTINA)

By the end of Jody's second season, women's basketball at the University of Oregon was poised for a breakthrough. The team had earned, and its coach had fought hard for, respect. Making it back to the NCAA tournament and "packing the Pit"—filling Mac Court to the rafters—were proof of that. (JOHN GIUSTINA)

feels his eyes. The only sound is the soft squeak of the marker on the board. Moments pass.

"You have two number thirty-twos up there," Dennis says, breaking the silence. Jody has mistakenly written the same number for two Santa Clara players. She stands back and looks, then erases her mistake and goes on. Dennis nods slowly. Jody doesn't take her eyes off the board.

The girls come thundering back from their warm-up. B will be starting again tonight because of Jess's ankle injury, and she's beside herself with joy, like a big puppy in a park. Of course she wishes Jess weren't injured—B is the ultimate team player—but she also realizes that the injury is her good fortune. Jody is always talking about "stepping up," about the younger players moving in to contribute when they're needed. That's what B wants to do tonight. She wants to step up.

"All right, quiet down out there," Jody says, turning from the board to face her players. She sets her jaw. She's going to give them one more go-out-and-get-'em talk and see if it takes. "This Santa Clara team . . . they've come in here complaining about everything." Jody pretends to whine. "The practice time is too late; the training room is closed; it's *raining.*" She sighs dramatically. "I'm tired of their shit. Let's get them *out of here.*"

She lets that sink in for a few seconds, and then plays her trump card. "Here's how it is, ladies: You beat 'em, you get two days off. You lose, you practice hard for the next four days. It's as simple as that. Now go out there and play like a Pac-10 team."

Six minutes into the game, and Jody is already pacing back and forth in front of the bench so furiously that it seems she'll wear a trough into the polished floorboards. But all the intensity is coming from her. On the court, the starters have yet to score a field goal. There are two points up on the scoreboard for Oregon, but they came from a pair of free throws by Sally. Santa Clara has made five baskets, two of them

three-pointers. Roy misses two easy layups. Her shoulders are
hunched, her head down as she lopes across the court. Jody
keeps her in. Let her get it out of her system, Jody thinks.
Roy has been top scorer in most of the Ducks' games. She
just needs to work it out.

With Roy cold and Jess sitting on the bench with a boot
on her ankle, Red knows she'll have to play hard. But it makes
it tough on her when Roy isn't in the groove. The two of
them, the center and the big forward, play off each other.
Eddie dribbles the ball upcourt, fast and slick, zigzagging,
stopping, changing direction, and fires the ball to B, alone in
the corner. Santa Clara isn't afraid of B, so there's no one out
there guarding her. In fact, Santa Clara isn't intimidated by
the Ducks at all, and so far the Ducks have given them no
reason to be. When the visiting players came out and saw
Karen sitting on the bench with her broken hand and Jess
sitting on the bench with her bad ankle, they smiled at each
other. Piece of cake, they thought. We're playing a bunch of
sophomores.

B looks to pass, but sees she's open, and it's her shot.
She's outside the three-point line. She shoots with that high
arc her father taught her in the driveway at home when he
put trash cans in front of her, at age seven, and showed her
how to loop the ball over the heads of the defenders. Her
father was the high school player of the year in Nevada, went
on to play basketball for the University of San Francisco and
later, to turn his family into a bunch of sports nuts. The Boevings, from six-foot-eight Hans to five-eleven Barbara to the
two big kids they bred, B and her older brother Bob, weren't
spectators; they were a family of players—basketball, volleyball, soccer, tennis, Ping-Pong, whatever was available. In
Danville, California, the bedroom community east of Oakland
where they lived, they could play outdoors all year round.

B got serious about basketball early, a first grader watching her big brother play and her father coach. During her
sophomore year in high school, when B had already become
the star of her team, her father sat her down for a serious talk.

"Is this something you really want to go after?" he asked her. "Yes," she said, without hesitation. For the next three summers, the Boevings financed their daughter's attendance at summer basketball camps. The summer between her junior and senior years, between camps and tournaments, B was home a total of fourteen days.

That summer, playing in a championship game in Santa Barbara, B dislocated her finger. She stood there on the court, momentarily stunned. Then she grabbed the finger, pulled it, popped it back in and kept playing. In the stands, scouting, was Oregon assistant coach Stephanie Osburn. She was impressed.

B went on to be even more impressive, averaging twenty-two points a game as a senior while breaking fifteen school records. She topped it off by being named a high school all-American by *USA Today*, Sports Girl of the Year by *Teen* magazine and female scholar-athlete of the year by the California Interscholastic Federation.

B watches her shot arc to the basket. It's in. She grins uncontrollably. No game face for her. A minute later, she makes an eighteen-footer, then sinks two free throws, then a layup. B is not thinking anymore. When you're in a zone, the body takes over and the mind quiets. You need nothing but adrenaline and the ball.

It is beginning to dawn on the bench that B can't miss tonight.

"Pass it to B!" Courtney, the freshman, yells from the bench. "She's in a B-zone. Give her the ball."

At halftime, B has scored thirteen points and is 100 percent from the floor. Red has contributed a solid ten. Roy is scoreless. The Ducks are up by three, but they know it's anybody's game.

B bounds down the stairs to the basement locker room. She can't sit down.

"We can win this one, you guys. We can win this." She's stomping around, yelling and sweating.

Roy sits quietly on the couch, staring at her Nikes. "I

don't know what's wrong with my shot," she says softly, more to herself than to anyone else. B is drowning her out, but Sandie, sitting next to Roy, hears. Sandie has had a bad half too.

"Two fouls and no points, that's what I've got," Sandie says to Roy. Sandie is on the verge of tears. Her face is white. Her hands are shaking. Jody keeps putting her in, and Sandie keeps screwing up.

Jody is concerned about Roy and Sandie, but she's more concerned about the officiating tonight. It's been awful. Coaches always criticize calls, seeing fouls where officials are blind. It's part of the game to yell at the refs, to badger them just short of being called for a technical foul. But this time, this one official, a blond guy with a tight perm who looks like Gene Wilder's younger brother, has been calling a terrible game.

Jody is disgusted. She fought the battle for equity in officiating last year, and hoped to see good things come of it this season. Now the women's games are officiated by three refs, just like the men's games, not two as they used to be. But because the pay is so much lower—$250 a game for the women's officials compared to $445 for the men's—the experience and skill of the women's officials leaves much to be desired.

Despite the bad calls, the Ducks pull away from Santa Clara in the second half. B can't miss: three pointers, layups, jump shots, free throws—she gets them all. The basket feels ten feet wide.

"D'ya see that?" Courtney yells from the bench. "She closed her eyes and hit that one. She *closed her eyes.*"

But even with B putting on a show—she eventually scores twenty-nine points, a career high—this is not an easy game for the Ducks to win. Santa Clara is not rolling over. This is good, thinks Jody as she paces. This is Pac-10 intensity out there.

With fifteen seconds on the clock, the score is Oregon 61, Santa Clara 59, with Eddie on the free throw line to shoot one. If she makes it, Santa Clara will have to come back with a three-point play to tie the game. Eddie is a good free throw shooter. She stands at the line struggling to control her nerves. The arena quiets. There are 1,400 people in the stands. Eddie puts it up. Her form, as always, is lovely. But the ball hits the glass and bounces back.

B jumps up, and in the middle of three Santa Clara players, grabs the rebound. B doesn't often go up for rebounds. She's too slow and she just can't get her feet that high off the floor. This is her only rebound of the game. She is immediately fouled. At the line, in the B-zone, she sinks both of them.

"She's unconscious!" yells Courtney. "That girl's unconscious." Oregon wins by four.

B is grinning like a baby: Her whole face, her whole body is grinning. She bounds off the court with Red hanging on her shoulders.

"Someone hose that girl off," says Courtney as they run into the locker room. Courtney has not played yet this season and doesn't have much hope of doing so. But tonight she has shown herself to be the kind of team player, the kind of cheerleader that Jody wants on the squad.

Jody stands smiling but composed in front of the locker room. This win over Santa Clara has given her some hope that the team can actually compete at the level it needs to. All along she's been telling everyone—the media, her superiors in the athletic department, her friends—that this is going to be a "building season," a year during which inexperienced players lose, but learn to play the game. But now, for the first time, she begins to think she might be wrong. Maybe this team can go someplace.

"That was a great game," she tells them. "You know why that was a great game?"

"Because we won!" someone yells.

"No," Jody says patiently. "Because you took care of each other out there. Because you played Pac-10 ball."

P-A-C-T-E-N

THE PAC-10 SEASON BEGINS WITH A ROAD TRIP, AND THE road trip begins with a five-hour delay at the San Francisco airport while four and a half inches of rain pelt the length of coastal California. Two days before, the weather had been perfect for the eighty-first annual Rose Bowl game, the athletic extravaganza that had eclipsed all else not just for University of Oregon sports fans, two generations of whom had never seen their team elevated to such heights, but for administrators and staff as well.

The university's news bureau, alumni association, marketing and merchandising office and sports information staff had dropped virtually everything else to concentrate on Rose Bowl plans and promotion. It was not just a game; it was a wide-open public relations opportunity, thought of by those who think of such things as a chance to grab media exposure for the president of the university, an opportunity to promote the university on national television and a boon to everything from potential donations to the recruitment of premium-tuition-paying out-of-state students.

The president, along with a 130-person delegation of handpicked "friends" or potential friends of the university, three vice presidents, the athletic director, two dozen other university personnel, seventy-one football coaches, trainers and support staff, ninety-six football players, a 180-member marching band and forty thousand fans flew down for the occasion. This was going to be, among other things, an opportunity for Dave to talk serious business with the potential big-money donor for women's basketball.

Stranded at the airport two days later, Jody doesn't know yet how this has turned out, or even if Dave found the time to talk with the prospect amid his other commitments. She does know, as does everyone else, how Rich Brooks's team fared. The Ducks lost to Penn State 38–20. Jody watched the game on TV and was sorry to see Oregon fall apart in the fourth quarter. But she was happy the whole thing was over. Maybe now the sports information people would start paying attention to women's basketball. Maybe she'd see more people at the games.

The California sunshine of a few days past has been replaced not just by rain—Oregonians are used to rain—but by a California-scale disaster, with chunks of roads giving way and cars stranded in intersections with water swirling to their windshields, with disaster teams and helicopters and more news coverage than a war in Central America. Jody and the team finally catch a flight out of San Francisco for Los Angeles and arrive at the hotel, a Holiday Inn overlooking the San Diego freeway, past midnight.

The girls sleep the next morning until eleven, beginning what will be a three-day routine that alternates between long periods of tedium and short bursts of extreme exertion. On the road, the girls sleep ten hours a night, eat many and formidable meals and take long afternoon naps. They drag themselves from hotel room to restaurant back to hotel room with a deep and abiding sluggishness. They seem to be hoarding energy, saving everything for the games.

On road trips, these college women are twelve years old

again, and like kids, free of all responsibility except the responsibility to play. Kelly, the most junior of the assistant coaches, makes all the travel and hotel arrangements for them, planning the itinerary, holding the tickets, assigning the rooms, corralling them from place to place. She makes the restaurant reservations, holds the money and pays their tabs. Buses wait to take them where they need to go. The equipment manager collects their sweaty uniforms, hauls them down to the hotel laundry room and washes them. Their coach plans their days, from wake-up calls to lights-out. Everything is taken care of for them. They travel in a cocoon more tightly woven than any family.

On the chartered bus from the hotel to the UCLA campus, where the first of the two Pac-10 games will be held, the girls are quiet, each sitting alone, sprawled across two seats. It is raining too hard to see anything out the windows. B closes her eyes and leans back. She is visualizing the court, the tip-off; she is watching herself play, thinking herself into a good game. Jess, who came along for the ride but whose ankle is not ready to be played on, stares straight ahead, expressionless. It has been hard for her to sit on the bench these past three weeks since the injury, hard to watch the team win without her. Of course she wants the team to win, and of course she's happy that B has stepped up and played well. But she can't help feeling a twinge of ego. She'd like to think the team needs her, that her presence is missed. But of the five games played since her injury, the Ducks have won four. At the Santa Clara game last week, B, playing Jess's position, scored a career-high twenty-nine points. Jess is beginning to think she'll have to fight to get her place back on the team.

She's a senior, and that pisses her off. Jody is fully aware of the dynamic. She thinks a little competition is just what Jess needs. She hopes after Jess is finished being angry she will be motivated. But first the tendons have to mend, and that's not going to happen during this road trip. So Jess isn't sitting in the bus thinking about the game. She's thinking about Karen. She's thinking about Karen not being here. She looks around the bus. Eddie and Sandie are talking to each other in low voices. Roy is facing backward joking with Sally. The freshmen are whispering among themselves. Jessica, she thinks to herself, you're going to have to make some new friends, and fast.

The game tonight against UCLA is in Pauley Pavilion, a sports arena so vast and spacious, so clean and sleek and sophisticated that it makes Mac Court, with its steep wooden bleachers and gaudy green-and-yellow paint job, look like a backwoods cousin who shows up at a party in a flowery dress and cheap jewelry. The girls love Mac Court, but here in Los Angeles, it's a different world. Both teams are warming up on the court, the tall, mostly black women of UCLA and the shorter, mostly white women of the University of Oregon. One of the UCLA assistant coaches saunters up to the Ducks' bench. All these folks know one another. They come up through the ranks together. They regularly cross paths on the recruiting trail.

"So, what did ya do today?" the coach asks Stephanie.

Steph smiles. "Ate and slept," she says. "What did you do?"

"Watched films of OSU all afternoon," the other coach says. UCLA will be playing Oregon State in two days.

Next to Steph, assistant coach Joe Jackson looks on. "Watched OSU films," he mutters under his breath. "You're playing *us* tonight, not Oregon State." He grips his clipboard tight to keep from saying something.

Jody is in the locker room by herself scrawling notes on the chalkboard. When she emerges to see how the warm-up is going, she has her game face on: haughty, unflappable, self-assured. Dressed in her best outfit, the cream white swan suit with matching three-inch pumps, she strides past the UCLA bench with only a small nod in their direction. These moves are orchestrated, ritualized. She stands on the sidelines for a moment watching the warm-up, then about-faces and marches back to the locker room. On the court, the girls don't seem to notice her. But as soon as she heads toward the locker room, they stop their drills and follow her.

The girls file in, sit on hard benches, fidget, stretch, tie and retie their Nikes as they listen to Jody and peer at the diagrams she scribbles on the board. When she's finished with the game plan, a ten-minute nonstop monologue, she pauses for a breath and surveys the team. They're so young, she thinks to herself for the umpteenth time, so green. UCLA is not one of the tougher teams in the conference. Led by a second-year coach, ranked fifth in the Pac-10 last year to Oregon's third, hampered by the loss of four seniors including their best player, the Bruins are definitely beatable. But Jody doesn't know if her team of sophomores and newcomers can handle Pac-10 play. Tonight, she'll see. She takes another breath.

"This is the most important game we will play in the Pac-10," she says slowly, taking the time to make eye contact with everyone in the room. "It is absolutely imperative that we win this game." She doesn't know if she's motivating them or scaring them, but either way, she's got their attention. She can see them get serious. That's what she wants to see: their game face.

"This is it, ladies," she tells them. "This is why we played all those preconference games. It was for this moment." She lets that sink in. "We must go out and play like we're not saving it for anything else. I want everybody's best individual effort. And"—her voice is rising now—"I want nothing less than a win."

The girls get up to leave, encouraging one another with the usual high fives and "Go, Ducks," but Joe, the assistant coach, interrupts. The team is accustomed to Jody's voice with its high-pitched Midwestern twang. Joe's is deep and resonant. It carries far.

"Listen," he says. "Their coaches spent the whole day looking at *OSU* game tapes." He emphasizes the OSU—Oregon's biggest rival—taunting them with it. "It looks to me

like this team is looking right past you. Like you're getting
no respect at all. They see Jess in street clothes; they don't
see Karen, and they think the rest of you are crap." He's
having fun with this, but he's also quite serious. "I don't
know about you," he says, his voice rising, his cadence like
a politician on the stump, "but that pisses me off. I want to
go out there and beat their butts."

They walk out into the arena, all nerves. Barely three
hundred of Pauley Pavilion's thirteen thousand seats are filled.
The band is earsplitting. UCLA wins the tip-off and immediately sinks a three-pointer. It's a bad way to start, but it
forces the girls to focus fast. B scores, then scores again. Red
puts in a layup. Sally sinks a three-pointer. Jody, who has
been pacing since the first play, stalking the sidelines like a
big cat in a small cage, ratchets it down a notch. She doesn't
relax, but she walks slower. She watches as the Ducks open
a margin of five, then seven, nine, eleven points. This is what
she likes to see: good, hard playing, everyone working the
floor, tough defense. But just as she begins to relax a little
more, the rhythm of the game changes. The girls slack off.
B takes a bad shot. The defense shuts down. Sally makes a
stupid foul. Roy makes a stupid foul. The Ducks end the half
up by seven, but Jody is seething. She can't wait to get into
the locker room to unload.

When she does, a minute later, it's not pretty. Her face
is flushed, her fists are clenched, and she's screaming—not
yelling, not shouting, but screaming.

"I don't know how many more bonehead moves you
could make with a few seconds left to play!" She stamps her
foot. "We should be up by twenty!"

Roy hunches over and stares at the floor. Red looks Jody
in the eye. She's acting like we're losing instead of winning,
Red thinks to herself. Red has played a good half, sinking five
of six field goals, grabbing four rebounds and chalking up
three assists. She wishes that just once Jody would acknowledge her, say something positive. Red likes to think that she
doesn't need Jody's approval, that she's not the type to go

out of her way to please anyone, but she does need something, even if it's only periodic feeding and watering of the ego. Jody doesn't do that, not for her, not for anyone. But Red hasn't figured that out yet. She's still trying to imagine what it will take to earn a good word from Jody.

Red knows, they all know, that there's no percentage in getting Jody angry. You screw up a game, you end up paying for it with a week's worth of grueling practice. That's the deal. They wait for Jody to scream herself out. Then they go out in the second half and pour it on, increasing their lead despite officiating that has Joe and Steph alternately slamming down their clipboards, jumping off the bench and jabbing their fingers at the referees. Jody knows the calls go against you when you play on the road. She stays calm and watches Oregon widen its lead. With three minutes left to go, the Ducks are up by twenty-three points.

"Don't you want to put in some subs?" Joe asks Jody as she walks by the bench. He's concerned one of the starters will get hurt. There's no need for the first team to be playing now. There's no chance for UCLA to come back.

Jody has been thinking about subs for the past few minutes. The subs are the Achilles heel of the team. Beyond Sandie, there is no one she feels she can go to on the bench. She thinks about Courtney, the backup point guard, who has not yet played a single moment in any game. Courtney's parents are in the stands, in from Pasadena. Tomorrow the entire team is invited to their house for dinner. Jody considers putting in Courtney, a kind of gift, so her parents can see her play. But she nixes the idea. Courtney's not ready for the Pac-10. She might embarrass herself out there.

"No subs," she hisses at Joe. UCLA's attitude has pissed her off, especially the fact that the coaching staff didn't view Oregon as a worthy opponent. The officiating has finally managed to piss her off. And she hates the band.

"I want to beat the shit out of them," she says to Joe.

They do.

The Ducks win by twenty-five points, a big victory anytime, but here, on the road, the first game of the conference season, it is a huge win. B scores twenty points. Red ends the game with twenty-one points and eleven rebounds, tops in both categories. When Red does well, she is not bashful about showing how proud she is of herself. Her teammates have learned to take this in stride. Red isn't boasting; she isn't hotdogging. She's just "being Red."

Tonight, she figures her contribution on the court is worth special mention. She can't believe how Jody, talking to a reporter just after the game, explains the win. It's as if the coach is going out of her way to underplay what Red has done.

"It just happens that on a given night somebody will show up and play well," Jody says to the reporter. "Tonight it was Red."

After the game, the girls put on their sweats over their uniforms—there are no locker-room shower facilities provided—and go out to mingle with the small group of Oregon supporters in the crowd. Four sets of parents have traveled to come to this game.

Sandie, Red, Steph and Joe stand in front of the UCLA sports information desk on the sidelines, trying to find out if the Oregon men's basketball team, playing UCLA in Eugene tonight, won its game. The UCLA sports guy has Mac Court on the line. He listens intently, then shakes his head.

"The Ducks won by ten points," he announces.

"All right!" yells Red. She and Sandie exchange high fives and shout the news crosscourt to the other girls, who cheer loudly. When they walk out of the arena a few minutes later, Sandie turns to Red.

"So, do you think the men are cheering us right now?" Red gives her a look. "Yeah, right."

The next evening, after a long day of napping, eating and napping as horizontal rain pummels the windows of the Holiday Inn, the team is bused to Courtney's parents' house in Pasadena. After the sterility of the hotel and the numbing landscape of freeways and urban boulevards, the City of Roses comes as a relief. Courtney's parents live in a lovely old California bungalow on a cloistered, tree-lined street. In front is a lush, densely landscaped yard; in back is the obligatory pool. Inside is a buffet that immediately animates the girls. If there's anything they like better than playing basketball, it is eating.

At a time when so many young women suffer eating disorders, when six-year-old girls put themselves on diets, when millions of otherwise sane and successful women measure their "goodness" by what they ate or resisted the temptation to eat that day, there is something wonderful, something transcendent about the unapologetically big appetites of the players. They descend on the upscale hors d'oeuvre table, piling their plates with shrimp, smoked salmon, cheeses and bread, eating quickly and coming back for more. They are proud of their appetites, even boastful.

"This is my third plate," Roy brags to Sally. Sally looks impressed, then walks back over to the buffet herself.

Courtney's parents are hosting this meal for almost two dozen people—the team, coaches, trainer, three sets of parents, even the chartered bus driver—as a rite of passage, both for them as new team parents and for Courtney as a freshman. This evening, carried along by her parents' high spirits and generosity, will help integrate Courtney into the team.

Parents can play a big part on the team. They have already played a big part in their daughters' sports lives, supporting their athletic aspirations since elementary school. For a decade of winters and springs, they lived basketball game by game. During the summers, they footed the bills for high-cost basketball camps, planning their own lives and vacations around their daughters' activities. Later, they fielded the phone calls from recruiters, sat for home visits and helped their daughters sort out offers. By now they have worked up a considerable stake, both emotional and financial, in their daughters' success on the team.

For the mothers, their Pac-10 daughters represent the opportunities they never had or perhaps never even dreamed of
having. They marvel at these strong, hard-muscled young
women they raised and are comforted by the team that surrounds them, the friendly, boisterous, healthy girls who are
now their daughters' closest companions. Much can happen
to a young woman in college, not all of it good, and sports
might be a shield against the worst, the mothers think. At any
rate, it will keep their daughters believing in their own power,
and that is worth any sacrifices the mothers have had to make.
It is, in fact, worth more than any scholarship their daughters
will earn.

The fathers come to the experience from a different
place. For some, there is the pure joy of watching talent they
nurtured through countless Saturday afternoons in the driveway playing Horse. To others, women's sports is a fall-
back position: they prayed for sons but got daughters
instead and decided to make the best of it. Some fathers had
college careers as athletes and want—need—to experience
again the highs and lows of the season, this time vicariously
through their daughters. Some are just sports nuts who love to
watch—their kid, any kid; basketball, football, any sport. Sandie's and Karen's fathers are "stage parents," the kind who
push and prod, who yell from the sidelines, who can't help
continuing to insert themselves into their now-adult daughters'
sports lives. They can't stop coaching; they can't stop criti-
cizing. They are Mama Rose to their daughters' Gypsy Rose
Lee.

But most of the parents are not like that. For them, this
final athletic endeavor of their daughters has provided them
with a new and separate identity: They are the Parents of
Pac-10 Players. They go to every game they can. They so-
cialize with one another. When the team plays on the road
near their homes, they host a dinner like this one Courtney's
parents have arranged. It strengthens their connection to their
daughters' lives. It gives them a chance to check out their

daughters' teammates, the coaches, the way the women inter-
act. They want to be reassured that they have made the right
choice in sending their daughters to Oregon.

They also want to be part of this community of parents
who sit sipping white wine around various dinner tables up
and down the West Coast, reliving past victories and reveling
in the high spirits of their daughters. This community of parents is a curiously female phenomenon. None of the men's
teams act as such a magnet, although certainly individual parents attend games to cheer on their sons.

At Courtney's parents' house tonight, the emerging dynamics of the team are obvious. Jody isn't here—she's the
only one of the traveling group missing—because she's scouting a high school game south of Los Angeles. Maybe she had
to go to the game. But maybe she was looking for an excuse
not to be part of this informal evening. She knows her presence would cramp the girls' style. But more than that, she is
not interested in having the team see her in this garrulous
social free-for-all over which she has no control. She has to
be Coach.

Then there's Red, the perpetual outsider. The rest of the
team is sitting at card tables set up in the living room. Red
sits at the head of the big table in the dining room, methodically forking down her third plate of bloody roast beef and
holding court over a group of parents. Besides Courtney's
parents, Jess's, B's and Timmy's are here tonight. Red is the
only one under forty-five at the table, and she loves it. The
parents allow her to be the center of attention; they encourage
it. She regales them with stories of past road trips. She tells
jokes between mouthfuls of food. She is more at ease with
this group than with her peers. She has spent so much of her
young adulthood not fitting in—big, strong, smart, a loner—
that she has not learned how to be social with people her own
age. She has never been part of the social dynamic of the
team. Last year, when there were team parties or functions,
she was a no-show. This year she is making some first, tentative efforts.

Meanwhile, B and her big brother Bob (throughout high school known as the Twin Towers) are challenging all comers to Ping-Pong in the poolside rec room. They've eaten quickly and moved on to what they love best: competition. After B and Bob beat every successive twosome, they move to the Foosball table and start all over again. Hours go by and they are still out there, two big, good-natured kids with an undepleted store of energy and goodwill. Other kids go out, play a few games, tire, come back in to watch a movie on video in the den, eat another piece of cake. But B and Bob play on.

The freshmen have taken over the living room. They are conducting a long, detailed and silly conversation about the tattoos they will get if Oregon wins the Pac-10 championship this year. Opening the season last night with a big victory on the road has made them giddy. They dare each other.

"Come on, come on, where'll ya get it?" asks Kristen Neiman, who everyone just calls Neiman.

Steph, who's just walked in, volunteers to be tattooed across her forehead. The girls laugh.

"No, no, I mean it. I'm serious here," says Neiman. They are silent for a moment, pondering the question.

"Across my toes," says Courtney, spelling out P-A-C-T-E-N as she points to each toe in turn. "Uh-oh, that leaves four toes," she says, shaking her head.

"I'll get it across my butt," says Neiman. "You know, Pac"—she draws a line in the air, then hesitates—"Ten." Anything seems possible tonight.

On the ride home, Roy, Sally and Eddie lead the back of the bus in the scores from *The Sound of Music*, *West Side Story* and *Grease*. They work up a sweat back there, gesturing wildly, singing loud enough to make themselves forget the tunes, singing so loud they drown out the rain that hammers the roof of the bus. They are completely without inhibition, a bus full of preteens on a field trip.

Red, who has chosen a seat toward the front of the bus near the parents and coaches, turns around and joins in. She sings just as loud as the others, but there is an awkwardness about her. This joining in does not come naturally. Even Jess, always so quiet, so focused, so self-contained, starts singing. Only Cicely, the team's one black player, is not part of it.

Cicely has not been popular with her teammates. In practice, she still has problems with the plays, and because she's not where she needs to be, she ends up hurting people. Sandie gives her a wide berth. The starters have learned to steer clear of her. Off the court, she has not made a friend of a single teammate. She can't seem to relax around them. Their jokes, their songs, their easiness with each other—like tonight—mystify her. She shares a small, slightly shabby house near campus with Roy and Sally, but she doesn't share their good times. She keeps to her room, keeps to herself. Even when she does join the team for a party or an event, she is always off to the side, a spectator.

Partly it's because she's black and they're not. She is, in fact, only the fourteenth black woman to play basketball for Oregon since it became an intercollegiate sport more than two decades ago. But race doesn't quite explain it, because Cicely isn't necessarily any more comfortable with the other black athletes at school.

It seems to be more a matter of personality than skin tone. Cicely is not the fun-loving type. There is a stiffness, a formality about her that isn't present in the other girls. She is laced straighter than they are. She doesn't drink—not that anyone on the team is a great imbiber, but they are relaxed about it. She doesn't curse or even just talk a little trash in the locker room. She rarely dates. She is a shy, quiet, religious girl from a small, close-knit family. She just doesn't fool around, and that separates her from everyone. In the bus tonight, in the middle of the raucous songfest, Cicely sits very straight in her seat, facing forward in the dark.

The next evening, the silliness is gone. The team is crammed into a small, windowless conference room at the University of Southern California student recreation center. There are no lockers, no showers, no benches, only a central conference table with hard-backed chairs lining the perimeter of the room. This will be their locker room tonight. Across the hall, the USC team is gathered in a slightly larger classroom. The teams will meet each other not in an arena, but in a high school–sized practice gym where a few rows of bleachers will be pulled down from the wall minutes before game time.

This is USC, the sports powerhouse, last year's Pac-10 champs, the team that won back-to-back NCAA championships in the mid-1980s when Cheryl Miller played. Miller was the first superstar of women's basketball, a four-time all-American who went on to lead the U.S. women's basketball team to a gold medal at the 1984 Olympics and land a sportscasting job at ABC. Now she is back coaching the USC team. With all that, the team dresses in a classroom and plays in a practice gym in front of three hundred fans.

In the Ducks' "locker room," Jody is trying to write the plays on the board in the front of the room, but the marker she was given is almost out of ink. Steph goes out to the front desk to get another but comes back empty-handed.

"They say they don't have any more markers," she tells Jody.

Jody looks disgusted. She presses harder on the felt tip.

Jody doesn't have much respect for this USC team. It has nothing to do with the record, which is impressive: number one in the conference last year, number seven in the nation, NCAA regional finalist. Cheryl Miller was a great player, Jody will give her that, but she isn't much of a coach. Jody thinks the USC players are undisciplined. Miller lets them talk trash on the court. She lets them show off, dress sloppily, affect an attitude.

The Oregon women go through their structured warmup, an orchestrated set of drills, crisp and choreographed. They are silent and focused, working up a sweat. Under the opposite basket, the USC women laugh and joke, call to each other, slap hands. Two players dance to the rap music coming over the PA system. Occasionally someone puts up a shot.

It's as if they feel they don't need to warm up for an opponent the likes of Oregon. Their ease, their insouciance, their confidence are unhinging.

"I want this team to kiss our ass," says Sandie, back in the makeshift locker room after the warm-up. She is trying to sound tough, but she is pale and shaky.

"I hate this team," says Red.

"Yeah, I hate this team too," says Sally. Everyone laughs, breaking the tension. Sally doesn't even know this team. She doesn't know any of these teams and has no history playing in the conference. But she is a team player, and she knows what to say.

Jody starts in. She looks elegant in her taupe pantsuit, her long nails manicured, her hair freshly washed, her makeup perfect. She spends time getting ready for each game, and it shows. On the road like this, the first thing she does when she checks into a hotel is call down to housekeeping for an iron and ironing board. She's learned that you don't wait until an hour before you have to dress to get the iron. You stake your claim early. Tonight she looks like she's stepped out of the pages of *Town and Country.*

"We gotta deny the high post . . . trail on the press . . . short the gap . . . pin the backside." When she speaks the code of basketball, she could be any guy in sweatpants and smelly sneakers. The difference between the way she looks and the way she talks is at once disconcerting and liberating.

"If you win this basketball game, ladies," she tells them when she's shifted from strategy to motivation, "you can win the Pac-10 championship." The women look up, a little startled. "I'm serious," says Jody. "This is a tough game on the road. You do this, and you can do anything."

The girls come together in a huddle. "Listen, they were *dancing* to their warm-up music out there," one of them says. "They weren't even warming up."

"I really wanna get them," says Sandie.

B, who is usually smiling and good-natured, looks steely-eyed. "Let's win this one," she says.

Jody stands outside the circle, watching and listening. She smiles a small smile. If they can win this one, they will have earned her respect.

On the court, the Ducks come out strong. They stick to the strategy Jody has outlined and play hard. Physically, they're doing fine, keeping even. Sally is having a great shooting night. Sandie makes both of her field goal attempts. Red is pulling down the rebounds. But psychologically, this USC team is beginning to bother them.

The team has attitude with a capital A. The players wear their shorts oversized and slung so low they can barely keep their jerseys tucked in. It's a hip urban grunge style somewhere between skateboard chic and modern-day pachuco. One of their guards does this fancy show-off dribble behind her back. They all talk trash on the court.

"You touch me once more, I'll deck you," the USC point guard yells at Eddie after they bump each other in the backcourt. Eddie is neither cocky nor aggressive—two vaunted traits of point guards—but she's very smart, and she knows what she has to do to stay out of trouble. Eddie gives the USC player a look and bumps her again as she dribbles upcourt.

When the guard catches up to her, she yells, "I owe you one!" in Eddie's face.

"Whatever," Eddie yells back. But it's false bravado. She's feeling intimidated. She is doubting herself. During a time-out, Eddie bites her nails. Her hands are shaking.

Then there's the band. They are camped out across from the UO bench, and whenever Jody calls a time-out, they begin playing as loud as they can. Jody is shouting instructions an inch away from her players, but they can't hear her. They have to read her lips. When Oregon goes to shoot a basket, the tuba player gives a blast; when an Oregon player stands at the free throw line, the band creates an earsplitting cacophony. Band members sing spontaneous and insulting ditties, needling the girls as they run up the court or in-bound the ball. It's hard to know where fun ends and rudeness begins, where an excess of school spirit becomes bad sportsmanship. The USC band is known throughout the conference for pushing the line.

The Ducks play through it, through the band and the trash talk and the calls that don't go their way. But they've lost the confidence they had when they started the game, the confidence they had last night when they were planning their victory tattoos. Jody can see it out there. She can feel it. At halftime, Oregon trails by only one point, but Jody knows she has to do something or the team will lose this game.

In the conference-cum-locker room, she is cooler and quieter than the players have ever seen her.

"I have every confidence in you," she tells them. This is far from the truth, but at this moment, it is the right thing to say. "I don't know why you don't have every confidence in yourself." She is talking softly. She knows they are rattled. Maybe she can calm them down enough to go out there and play the way she thinks they're capable of playing.

"They're not doing anything special out there, are they? Anything we haven't seen before? Anything we aren't prepared for?" she asks quietly.

"No." Several players say it at once.

"Are they in good shape? Are they in better shape than you are?" she asks softly.

"No."

"You're playing like you're scared," she tells them. "You have to play to win. You can't play not to lose."

They hear her, but they can't seem to translate the words into action on the court. In the second half, USC quickly pulls ahead by seven. Jody calls a time-out and pumps them up again. She knows it's possible to win this game, and she wants the win badly. To start the conference season by defeating last year's Pac-10 champion on their home court—that would send a clear message about Oregon and about its coach, a message not just to rival teams but to Jody's bosses.

They go out, regroup and recapture a slim lead with five

minutes left. Joe, the assistant coach, looks up at the game clock. Five minutes, that's a lot of time, he thinks to himself. That's too much time. Jody is pacing the sidelines, her fists clenched.

The play is getting a little ragged, but Oregon stays with it. Red sinks a layup, putting Oregon ahead by four points. Joe exhales a long breath and sneaks another look at the clock: 1:58. Jody unclenches her fists for a moment. Her long nails have cut into the meat of her palms, leaving angry red slits.

Then something odd happens: It suddenly dawns on the Oregon players out on the floor that they might just win this game if they don't blow it.

So they blow it.

They are a young team, and clutch playing is a learned art. With a minute and a half to play, Roy reaches in over the shoulders of a USC player and fouls her. The girl makes both shots, cutting the Oregon lead to two. Then with fifty-three seconds left, Roy fouls again, and USC ties it.

That's five for Roy. She's out of the game. Jody sends in Sandie. With fifteen seconds on the clock, USC's best shooter outmaneuvers Sandie in the key and posts up to hit a short jumper. Sandie has no choice but to foul her. The girl sinks both free throws, and USC is up by two. When it's Oregon's ball, Sal is called for traveling. She doesn't actually take a step; it's this little hip-hop thing she sometimes does at the end of a dribble, a move she doesn't get called for in Australia, a move Jody has been trying to train out of her. But she's been doing it for so long that it's second nature. Oregon loses the ball. Then Oregon is forced to foul again to prevent an easy shot. The USC player is cool at the line. Both free throws go in.

The margin is now four with three seconds on the clock. Sal gets the ball at half-court. There is no time to pass and barely time to think. She rushes forward and hefts the ball in the general direction of the basket. The three-point shot goes in the same moment the buzzer sounds.

Oregon loses its second conference game by a single point.

The players file down a flight of stairs to their assigned room. Jody follows slowly, silent, her head bent. If she were constitutionally capable of slumping, she would. She waits outside the room, head down, composing herself while the players find seats inside. No one talks. No one moves. The girls don't even bend to untie their sneakers. Jody walks in, and all eyes are immediately on her.

She stands there, in front of the room, for a moment.

"We didn't play very smart," she says, her voice barely audible. She is silent for what seems like a long time as she fights to control her emotions. "It's tough to win on the road," she finally says. Her voice is wavering. Then there's another long silence. "There's not much else to say." She walks out of the room, and the door closes behind her with a click.

Eddie is in the corner, stone-faced, staring at the floor. Roy sits cradling her head in both hands. Sally's face is blotchy, her eyes rimmed with red. Even the ever-effervescent B looks despondent. They sit there like that, silent, almost stupefied, for three or four minutes. Then slowly, as if struggling against some great weight, they start to move. They untie their Nikes; they cut the tape from their ankles; they shed their jerseys and put on sweatshirts. One by one, silently, they head out the door, across the lobby and into the waiting chartered bus.

After games on the road, the tradition is to go out for a big dinner. The reservations were made this afternoon. Now no one wants to go. When the bus arrives at the hotel, Jody immediately heads up to her room. The others linger, not knowing what to do. Of the seven women who played in tonight's game, only Red goes out to dinner. She can't resist. It's a steak place.

The following afternoon, the team is back in Eugene. At the airport, Jody runs into Dave Frohnmayer, who is just now returning from the Rose Bowl commitments that have kept him a week and a half in Southern California. Yes, he tells her, he did have a chance to meet with the prospective donor, the woman he has in mind to endow the women's basketball program. There's another meeting scheduled for the end of the month.

"But don't get your hopes up," he says. He knows how long these things can take.

Don't get your hopes up? Jody misreads his caution for negativity and is mystified by his attitude. If *he* has so little hope, why should *she* be hanging on? After all, it is talk of this endowment that has kept Alan from filing the lawsuit. It is talk of this endowment that has kept Jody in check. But now the president himself is saying—or at least Jody is hearing—that the endowment idea is going nowhere.

Was all the talk about the donor just a stalling tactic? Jody wonders, not for the first time. If it was, it worked. The Pac-10 season has started, and there is no way Jody is going to become involved in either negotiations or a lawsuit for the next three months.

There's only one way I'm going to get what I want, she tells herself as she walks through the airport, and that's if I coach a winning team.

CIVIL WAR

IT DOESN'T MATTER WHAT YEAR OR WHICH SPORT, ANY GAME that pits the University of Oregon against Oregon State University is a big game. The state's two largest schools, located just forty miles apart, nourish the usual intrastate rivalry, with the athletic contests invariably billed as "civil wars." But in Oregon, with its relatively small population and sparse educational resources, the rivalry seems less good-natured joshing than grim competition.

Outside the fabricated arena of intercollegiate athletics, the two schools are locked in an ongoing contest for the hearts and minds—and dollars—of Oregonians. OSU, the Moo U of the state, with its majors in poultry production and swine industries and its courses in beverage management and stochastic hydrology, is a favorite of ruralites who want to send their kids to college but don't want them coming home with any dangerous ideas, and with the agriculture, fishing and timber industries that have traditionally made up the economic heart of the state. The University of Oregon is the closest the state gets to Ivy League, with its share of Fulbright scholars and NEH recipients, famous poets and radical sociologists, Nobelists and esteemed members of the National Academy of Sciences. The students are generally hipper than Oregon Staters, with more body piercings per square inch and broader social agendas.

It happens that the University of Oregon's first Pac-10 home game this season is against country cousin Oregon State. The girls have four days to recover from the California trip before facing their state rival in Mac Court. The Ducks are bringing a 1–1 conference record to this game. It is not what Jody hoped—she thought the team could and should have taken USC—but it is not a bad start. Every game the team wins brings the Ducks closer to a return trip to the NCAA tournament. An invitation is a badge of honor, the sine qua non of the season; back-to-back invitations are the beginning of a dynasty. Every win helps the program more generally, helps future recruiting and—this is never far from Jody's mind—puts her personally in a better negotiating position.

She is haunted by the idea that the people she works for are hoping for the team to have a poor season. She will be so much easier to negotiate with if she fails. Perhaps they won't want to negotiate at all. She will be gone, and she thinks the equity issues she has raised will disappear with her. Her failure, the team's failure, would be an easy way out for the university. From now, mid-January, until the final games of the season in mid-March, every game counts.

The day before the Oregon State game, Jody's team is in the locker room rearranging chairs to face the video monitor. The girls want to watch tape of the UCLA game. They are eager to relive the glory of that victory, to revel in each good shot. But Jody will have none of it. Her idea of firing them up is to show them last year's game tape against OSU, a game they lost badly.

"You want to watch yourself win because you want

praise," she tells them. "But this isn't the time for praise. This is the time for work. We need to identify our weaknesses."

There is an audible sigh. Jody wishes that this group of players had the same intensity of purpose, the same fire she had when she played college ball. "You need to take this as a challenge, not a negative," she says, hitting the play button.

The film is not pretty. Eddie winces as she watches. That game was her low point last year. She played thirty-one minutes, never scored and turned over the ball six times. The turnovers were the worst. Oregon State's five-foot-eleven Swedish star came after five-foot-six Eddie with a vengeance, elbowing her, pushing her, blocking her, then rapping the ball from her hands and striding crosscourt to score. Eddie was an eighteen-year-old girl from a Canadian town no one ever heard of who never quite believed she had made it to the Pac-10, let alone into the starting lineup. She was the smallest player on the team, the only freshman, the short, quiet kid in the land of the big and bold. Even the grade school girls who rounded up the practice balls for the team exuded more self-confidence on the court.

But for all her lack of self-assurance, Eddie was a natural athlete and tough competitor. She had been playing basketball since she joined a city youth league in fourth grade in Kamloops, British Columbia, a seventy-thousand-population mill town northeast of Vancouver. She grew up tussling with the kids on her block, all boys, and playing on the boys' soccer and hockey teams, where she was known as "George." She didn't make friends with a girl until she was twelve years old.

When the time came to think about college, Eddie only considered schools in British Columbia. U.S. colleges, she was told, didn't have high academic standards. But Eddie and her family did. The daughter of two schoolteachers, she had internalized their work ethic and the value they placed on education. She was also a third-generation Japanese Canadian whose grandparents spent the war years in internment camps in the interior, and she had internalized the quiet fierceness, the compulsion to excel that has been the hallmark of so many children and grandchildren of Asian immigrants. Eddie maintained a perfect 4.0 grade average throughout high school while leading her AA team to the provincial championships her senior year, averaging more than seventeen points a game and, off-season, lettering in three other sports.

The high standards she set for herself were the source of her success, but they were also the source of her biggest problem, her lack of self-confidence. She could never do enough, never play hard enough, run fast enough, be in good enough shape. Every win was an occasion for self-criticism rather than self-congratulation—what she could have done, how much better she could have done it. She had a way of dismissing her victories and underplaying her achievements that went far beyond humility but not quite as far as neurosis.

With all her high school sports successes, she didn't believe she was capable of playing ball at a big U.S. school. In her junior year, when a British Columbia college offered her a partial scholarship, she was ready to take it without visiting another school. It was a big deal to be offered the scholarship, and she would have signed right then if her high school coach had not persuaded her to see what else was out there.

Oregon had scouted her and was interested, but didn't recruit hard. Still, she was dazzled by her visit to campus, bowled over that the school had paid her way down, impressed that she was put up in a motel, that she was taken to restaurants. Things like this didn't happen to kids from her high school. No high school girl was recruited like this in Canada. Later, she realized it was just a standard recruiting visit, maybe even a little scaled down. But at the time, she was awestruck. She felt like royalty. She couldn't resist. She came to Oregon but was sure she would spend the next four years warming a spot on the bench.

As it turned out, Jody needed her right away, and Eddie was in the starting lineup for the first thirteen games of the season. Her thirteenth game as a starter was the OSU game, the one she is watching right now on videotape.

What am I doing in the Pac-10? Eddie remembers thinking to herself as she was battered and pushed all over the court during that game. Who am I kidding? I can't do this. I can't handle this. Eddie rarely showed emotion, and she never cried. That night after the game, she cried in the locker room. All of her self-doubts were confirmed when Jody pulled her out of the starting lineup. She never started in another game through the rest of the season.

Jody dubbed that game "Eddie's baby game" in an attempt to assign it to a distant past, to defuse its power by poking fun at it. But seeing it again on videotape today, Eddie is shaken anew. That game was—and still is—her greatest humiliation. Part of her knows she is no longer that scared freshman. She has started in all twelve games this season and has earned the spot with hard work; she has handled the ball well. But part of her still is that frightened kid, the little one, the provincial Canadian in awe of the power of U.S. sport. She tells herself that this year the OSU game will be different—but she only half believes it.

The next afternoon, the day of the game, Eddie lies in her bed in the apartment she shares with Sandie. The idea is to take a "power nap" before the game, but Eddie is not sleeping. She's turning the game over in her mind. This year I have to do it, she is thinking. There's no one else, no one to step in for me, no one to take over. This is my responsibility. She closes her eyes. She tries to work up a kind of defiance, an attitude. She wants to show OSU she's not the same person she was a year ago. She wants to go in there and turn some heads. She tries to relax her body. It's three hours until game time.

In the other bedroom, Sandie is curled under her comforter berating herself for how she's been playing this season. She's disgusted. She knows Jody is too, not to mention her father. She knows she goes out there and plays scared. She doesn't shoot the ball when she should. She makes stupid fouls. She goes back to the bench, hangdog, feeling like a failure. This afternoon, thinking about it, her fear begins to turn to anger. I'm sick of playing timid, she thinks to herself. I'm sick of just going through the motions. If I'm gonna play, I'm gonna have to go for it. In the anger, she finds a kind of strength. Finally, she sleeps.

In the locker room at 6:30, a half hour before game time, Eddie is so keyed up she can't stop jiggling her legs. Around her, her teammates are talking, settling into their seats, tying their sneakers. Eddie sits ruler-straight on one of the folding chairs, staring forward at nothing, legs jiggling. She asks Stacy, the equipment manager, to get her a basketball. Holding it on her lap calms her a little. Sally sits next to her and starts talking strategy. Sal knows how nervous Eddie is. She understands what this game means to Eddie, and she wants to help her get through it. She likes Eddie a lot. She believes in Eddie more than Eddie believes in herself.

Sandie, in her usual place on the long couch, looks pale, but determined. Something has replaced the fear that's always evident on her face, that startled, deer-in-the-headlights look. It's not confidence, but it's a kind of focus, a resolve. This is the closest she has ever come to having a game face.

In front of the room, Jody is taking control. Every game she has to search for the key to ignite the girls, a locker-room speech different from the last one, a speech that presents a new, compelling reason to play hard. At UCLA it was the start-of-the-conference-season-let's-show-'em-what-we're-made-of speech. At USC it was the they-have-an-attitude-let's-cut-them-down-to-size speech. With Santa Clara it was the grudge-match speech. Tonight she has an easy job: Everyone wants to beat OSU.

What compels the players is equal portions of intrastate rivalry and animosity. OSU is the kind of team the players love to hate: very strong, very physical, with a reputation for being mean, for bashing and banging. Even Roy and Sally, who have never played OSU, have worked up an attitude for tonight.

"Our teammates just tell us who not to like, and we don't

like them," Roy tells a reporter before the game. OSU is ranked twenty-first in the nation. The University of Oregon, with an identical 7–3 record, has not made it into the top twenty-five.

Jody waits for the girls' attention. Then she begins her speech, talking louder than usual, her voice tight with tension.

"Their intent is to get belligerent and come out and intimidate you," she says. "They're here to see if they can embarrass the hell out of us. If you let them see you flustered, if you let them see you shook, it will ignite them."

Eddie's legs are jiggling.

"Listen," she tells the girls, "they're packin' for bear out there. But you, you're not cut from the same cloth. You're gonna persevere because of your character, because you know how to stick together. Now this is our night. Let's go out and play like it."

It is one of her better speeches, mostly because it rings true. In the Pac-10, it seems all the successful teams affect some kind of an attitude. Cheryl Miller's USC team talks trash. The OSU team bangs and batters. The University of Washington team comes on cocky. Stanford . . . well, Stanford is in a class by itself. Stanford's well-earned self-confidence isn't showy; it is regal.

The Ducks, however, are without pretension, possibly because they have not yet earned the right to be pretentious but more probably because they are just not the type. Their style of play isn't flamboyant. They dress regulation. They don't strut; they don't curse. They don't walk onto a court, even their own, as if they owned it (much to Jody's chagrin). They are mostly nice small-town and suburban girls from traditional-value families who blush when they talk to reporters and love giving autographs to the bevies of ten-year-old girls that surround them after every home game.

But what mostly distinguishes them from the players on the other teams they face is that the Oregon players, most of them at least, genuinely like each other. They were recruited elsewhere, but they chose Oregon because they saw it as a friendly place with a team that offered an instant family. They were smart enough to see the tensions on other teams, the prima donnas, the selfish post players who never passed, the guards who tried to outdo each other, the hungry second string that almost wished for injuries to the starters, the racial tensions just below the surface. At Oregon, the competition was the other team, not each other. It is that stick-together character that Jody is tapping into tonight. The team will need it.

The girls come out on the court, greeted by a crowd of five thousand, the largest and loudest yet this year. They listen as the OSU starters are introduced. Four of the five are foreigners, two from Sweden, two from Croatia; Aki Hill, the OSU coach who has supported Jody in her equity battle, faces the same problems in recruiting as does her Oregon counterpart. The very best players in the state are recruited away to schools with winning traditions. The very best regional players who want to play in the Pac-10 go to Stanford or the University of Washington. So Aki recruits in Europe; Jody gets godsends from Australia. They have to in order to survive, in order to win.

The Oregon State players are tough. They are showing that on the floor tonight. For six minutes in the first half, Oregon is held scoreless. Jody is grim on the sidelines, but during a time-out, she holds herself in check. She doesn't yell at her players; she speaks calmly, reminding them of the plays they should run, methodically going over strategy. It seems to work.

For the next five minutes, Oregon chips away at a seven-point deficit, with Sally, Red and B all making their shots. Jess is finally playing again after missing seven games and four weeks of practice, but she isn't starting tonight. Jody is giving her plenty of playing time, though, hoping she will find the groove. That's not happening. Although she manages to sink most of her free throws, she can't seem to hit a basket from the field. She finds her spot outside the three-point line and lofts the ball, pushing from her fingertips. It looks lovely right up until it ricochets off the backboard. She tries another from the opposite side. It swipes the underside of the net. A third attempt hits the rim hard.

With each miss, the expression on her face hardens. She knows she has to give herself time, but it's so hard to have patience, so hard to fight back in your senior year when you should be in the flow, in the zone, playing the best you've ever played. The last time Jess played a full game, she led the team with twenty-eight points. It was just last month, but it seems like years ago. She can't remember how it feels to play that way, to play without thinking, to trust your shot, to play like a senior. But the ankle is rehabbed; that's what counts. She is finally part of the team again, and that thought keeps her going as she tries for another basket and misses.

Sandie, on the other hand, is playing better than she's played all season. Instead of committing fouls, she's drawing them. She's pulling down rebounds. She's even attempting shots rather than passing the ball as if she can't wait to get rid of it. She'll never be a high scorer, but tonight she's a presence. What she does out there has meaning. She is contributing, and it feels good.

It's all attitude, she knows. Her fear is momentarily cloaked by her hostility toward Oregon State, the team that so battered the Ducks last year, the team that made her roommate cry. Her vulnerability, her small-town sweetness are in temporary remission. She is actually enjoying being *big*. It matters also that Jess is back on the court. Sandie loves B but she's happier when Jess is playing. It makes her feel more confident. And Jess gets the passes to her just where she likes them.

When Sandie stands behind the sidelines to in-bound a ball, she looks over at the Oregon bench. Jody looks right back. Pointing at her with one long finger, she nods her head and yells "Yes" over the din of the crowd. To Sandie, that's almost as good as it gets. It's almost as good as earning approval from her father.

Sandie wishes she could pull Eddie along with her, but

Eddie is struggling. She takes two shots and misses both of them. She misses one of two free throws. Her OSU counterpart is a tough, wiry, five-foot-nine Croatian named Boky Vidic, who has all the self-confidence Eddie lacks and then some. Boky has the moves, and she loves to show them off. Eddie does her best to stay with her, to pressure her, to break something open. But nothing is happening. Still, she hasn't let Boky trample her underfoot. She's not being knocked silly like last year. She has turned over the ball only twice. But Eddie, being Eddie, takes little solace in this. She is enormously disappointed in herself. At halftime, with Oregon up by a tenuous five points, Eddie walks alone down the stairs to the locker room. She keeps her head down. She pounds the wall with her fist.

The second half, OSU comes out steaming, and within two minutes, the score is tied. But Oregon begins to show that it has learned something since the USC game. The girls don't panic; they settle down and work their way back into the lead, slowly and methodically, beginning with a fifteen-foot jump shot by Eddie. Finally, she makes something. The pressure is off. She makes another basket. Then, right in front of the OSU bench she throws an elbow at the other guard while muscling her way toward the basket. The official doesn't see it.

"That's an offensive foul!" yells one of the OSU coaches from the bench.

Eddie is secretly delighted. She clenches her fist. It's a private victory. Gotcha, she thinks. This year I'm giving 'em rather than getting 'em.

Under the basket, Sandie continues to play tough. Last year she was shoved, kicked and elbowed. This year she plants her feet and stays with it. Grabbing for a rebound, she jostles one of the OSU players.

"Bitch," the player spits at her.

Sandie says nothing. A few minutes later, when the OSU girl commits her third foul and the coach takes her out, Sandie strides by the OSU bench, gives the girl a look and waves, mouthing "Bye-bye." Sandie never knew playing could be this much fun.

Oregon goes on a fourteen-to-nothing run with Red sinking three baskets from inside. The bench is on its feet, waving towels and hooting. The crowd is deafening.

"They have time for one more run," Jody tells the players when time-out is called. She is kneeling down in front of them, one hand on Roy's knee to steady herself. She keeps her voice calm. She wants the players confident, but not too confident. There are seven minutes on the clock, and Oregon is up by twelve. "You fight this off and you're gonna win," she tells them.

OSU makes the run, as predicted, managing to close the gap to eight before Eddie sinks a three throw, then steals the ball and sends it to Sally for a layup. Only then, with ten seconds left, does Eddie smile. It is just a little smile, and it fades fast.

She hasn't had the game she wanted to. It hasn't been "Eddie's revenge" out there, as she had hoped. She scores only six points, missing five of seven from the floor. She manages to steal the ball only once. But she grabs five rebounds and turns over the ball only three times. She is not happy, but she has proven something to herself: There will be no more "baby games" for her.

It's an important win for the team. The victory over Santa Clara cemented the wins of the preseason, a well-played game against a tough opponent. This game against OSU has shown them that they can play with the big guys, the nationally ranked teams in their conference—and win. They may not yet have garnered national respect, but now they respect themselves. Upstairs in the hallway that encircles the arena, Jess's and Karen's pictures are now hanging on the wall, eight-foot-high framed action shots, just like the men's. Two posters of male players had to be removed to make room for the senior women. Jody made sure that happened in time for the OSU game.

"I'm very proud of you ladies," Jody tells them in the locker room.

They are hugging each other, high-fiving, slapping each other's backs. Jody waits for them to sit down. Then she smiles broadly.

"Hey, if there's anything better than beating the Beavers," she says, referring to the OSU team, "it's beating the Huskies." The sweat hasn't dried, and she's already looking to the next big game, the game against the thirteenth-ranked University of Washington Huskies.

Before the Huskies, though, Oregon has to get past Washington State. The Cougars, eighth in the conference last year, have never been a Pac-10 powerhouse. They aren't nationally ranked. They aren't a particular rival of the Ducks. Jody knows you can't go through the whole season with your foot on the accelerator. You've got to ease up sometime, not on the level of play but on the emotional intensity. This is one of those times. Still, every game in the Pac-10 season is important, and after the OSU win, Jody expects that if the Ducks win against both the Washington teams this week, Oregon will, for the first time this season, earn a national ranking.

Jody wishes she didn't have to be nervous about the game. But she is. In the locker room a few minutes before game time, she is her usual, unsmiling self, game face firmly in place.

"I've got a knot right here," she tells the girls, massaging the back of her neck for a moment. "It's because I never know who's gonna show up for any game. I never know who's gonna play like they mean it. We should be beyond this point now." She sighs, for effect. "So you could do me a lot of good and give yourself a shot of confidence if you went out there and beat their tails."

Since the Oregon State game last week, Jody has struggled with the decision of whether to start Jess in this next game. She was hoping Jess would come back with a vengeance, come back all steamed up, heated not just by her own internal fires but by fear that B might take her spot in the lineup. But against Oregon State, Jess missed five of the six baskets she attempted, including all three three-pointers. She turned over the ball four times. Worse yet, from Jody's point of view, Jess didn't pull down a single rebound.

She was supposed to be better—the doctor said so, the trainer said so—but she was playing as if she were still hurt. She was protecting herself, being cautious. Jody sympathized with Jess's fear of reinjury—she knew that's where the caution came from—but she told herself that she wasn't about to convert this sympathy into welfare, into giving Jess her position back if she didn't earn it.

Jess's practices this week have been okay, nothing special. B's practices have been just as good, and B has had some tremendous games since Jess has been sitting on the bench. If she were going to be scrupulously fair, absolutely objective, Jody would probably be starting B tonight. But she decides to start Jess. She tells herself there is something steadying about Jess's presence on the court. She tells herself Jess's maturity matters. She tells herself this because she doesn't want to admit that she is making an emotional decision, that despite herself, she feels for Jess. She wants to give the girl a chance to have a decent senior year.

B, who is unofficial team cheerleader, perhaps the ultimate, all-time, hands-down cheerleader, takes the news in stride. She is a sophomore with time on her hands. She is happy for the playing time she's gotten, and if she feels any resentment toward Jess, she blankets it with graciousness and good sportsmanship.

"It's all for the good," she says to Jess, nodding her head. "It's the team that counts."

From someone else, it would be pap. From B it's genuine.

Oregon plays a decent game. After a cold first half, Jess finds her rhythm, eventually making four baskets and one three-pointer and working hard on defense. Eddie has a hot hand, the hand she wanted to have last week against Oregon State, and turns in a career-high fifteen points. For the first time this season, all five starters score in double digits.

The stats look good, but it's not a high-intensity game and, even with an increasing point spread in the second half, Jody is never quite sure that she's got the game in the bag. It isn't until the Ducks are up by twenty with only one minute left to go that she puts in Cicely and two other second stringers. Even now, more than a dozen games into the season, she cannot trust the subs.

Sports may be about self-improvement, self-esteem, self-discipline, about building one's character, about learning to work with and trust others. But on a given night in a given arena, what sports is really about is competition, clashing with an opponent, conflict, struggle, a self-contained little war with boundaries and rules, strategies and plans, fought for the amusement of others.

Making money from sports, especially collegiate sports, is about fostering and intensifying rivalries between opponents so that a game is not merely an athletic contest but one team's holy war against a visiting infidel, a jihad in jerseys. The so-called civil war rivalry that feeds every contest between the University of Oregon and Oregon State is a war, for the most part, between equals. The neighboring schools, located in slow-moving, tree-lined, bucolic towns, are about the same size, with about the same money to spend on sports. Neither has the reputation of being an athletic powerhouse, although both have occasionally enjoyed noteworthy seasons.

But the University of Washington is another matter. Located in glossy, gridlocked Seattle, the latest urban setting made hip on the big and small screens, the school is the academic and athletic leader of the Northwest, with more students than both Oregon schools combined. Its football team is always a Rose Bowl contender. Its women's basketball team is always nationally ranked. Seven of the past nine seasons, the women's team has won twenty-one or more games.

Nine of the last ten years, the Washington team has made it to the NCAA tournament. This year the team ranks thirteenth in the nation, and the coach, a former USC player now in her tenth year in Seattle, thinks Washington is about to break through, a good program about to be great, a team poised to go all the way, from winning the Pac-10 championship to making it to the Final Four.

The gulf between the Washington and Oregon teams is symbolic as well as real: It is the Washington *Huskies*—the mascot a big, brawny dog known for its rugged nature (the word husky itself connotes burly, virile athleticism) versus the Oregon *Ducks*, a waddling, web-footed, offbeat, self-deprecating symbol that once earned *Esquire* magazine's Dubious Achievement Award for the worst-named college team.

Tonight's game between the Huskies and the Ducks is a huge one for Oregon, the biggest of the season so far. The two teams are tied for second place with 3–1 Pac-10 records. Of course the conference season has just begun; only four games have been played, but if Jody entertains any hopes of a conference championship this year, Oregon has to beat Washington tonight. Besides Stanford, whom the Ducks have yet to play, Washington is the toughest opponent in the conference. But to Washington, the Ducks are of little consequence: a young and shallow team, a nuisance to be dispatched, a pebble to be shaken out of their Reeboks.

Tonight, four hundred miles from home, the Huskies move into Mac Court as if they owned it. Washington has sent three busloads of purple-shirted, placard-waving fans down Interstate 5 along with a sixty-member uniformed band. The band is both wildly energetic and professionally choreographed. As the two teams warm up on separate sides of the court, the University of Washington tuba players dance on the sidelines in bold, synchronized moves. Six rows of horn players and drummers clap, play and sway from side to side in accompaniment.

Twenty feet away, in the bleachers reserved for the University of Oregon's band, twelve kids in T-shirts, the sum of the band that has been assigned to play at the women's game tonight, sit disconsolately, holding their instruments on their laps, listening to the Huskies play and looking like they wish they were up in Seattle with the rest of the band playing for the men's game. Jody is standing on the sidelines watching the visitors go through their drills. She glances over at the two bands and feels the anger rising. What she sees, right there—in front of her, in front of her players, in front of the fans and tonight in front of a local TV audience as well—is proof of the lack of support and respect her team is getting from its own school. How can I get Washington to take us seriously when it looks as if Oregon doesn't even take us seriously? Jody thinks. Here we are, second-class citizens in our own country. The whole thing embarrasses her. It also pisses her off.

She takes the anger down with her to the locker room, but keeps it close. She is strung tight enough without it. As if the big game were not enough, her mother and younger sister are in town. Her family visits often, and it's both a joy and a pain to maintain these close ties. When she's alone, rattling around in her new house, eating take-out enchiladas from a nearby deli, sweating by herself on the StairMaster at the health club, she craves a social life. But when her family comes, bringing with it ready-made conviviality, she balks.

Before she left for Mac Court earlier this evening, Joanna, her mother, gives her the once-over. Jody is, as usual, impeccably dressed and freshly coifed. "You need more blush," Joanna tells her. Joanna wants her naturally pale daughter to look her best on television. Joanna doesn't know it, but Jody already has her game face on.

"Shut up, Mom," Jody tells her. "Like I care about how much blush I'm wearing, like that's what I care about tonight."

Joanna sits on the couch and cries.

On the board in the front of the locker room, Jody has written: FOCUS, PATIENCE, CONFIDENCE, PERSEVER-

ANCE, TOGETHER. She planned a controlled, inspiring pep talk, but the band has got her so mad she launches into something else entirely.

"Did you see that band?" she asks the girls. "Did you see those fans?"

It's clear they did, and that they're not happy about it.

"They can't come in here and act like they're gonna take over," Jody says, her voice rising. "I'm glad to see you're hot pissed about this because so am I." She takes a second to compose herself. Then, talking so softly that the girls have to lean forward to hear, talking as if she were speaking to herself rather than to them, she says: "No one's gonna promote us here but ourselves, ladies. We have to go out there and show them."

She turns from them to put on the matching jacket to her taupe pantsuit. The girls are sprawled in their usual places, waiting now for her last word.

"If I have to walk out of this place with a loss, I'm gonna puke," Jody says. "Let's go out there and beat their butt."

Out on the floor, it is immediately evident what kind of a game this will be. In the first five minutes, Washington players foul Oregon five times. Roy takes one in the chest and goes down. Sally skids across the floor. Red winces from an elbow in the ribs. Washington wants to intimidate the Ducks with such physical play, but the strategy is not working. Oregon is used to this bang-and-batter play from last week's OSU game, and they've figured out that all they have to do is stay cool, do their jobs and take advantage of all the freebies at the free throw line.

It's one of those rare evenings when everyone is playing well, when everyone, as Jody says, "shows up." Jess seems to have gotten her confidence back after her decent showing at the Washington State game, and she is looking more like the veteran starter she is rather than the tentative injured player she is clearly tired of being. In the first half, she sinks four field goals, including a signature three-pointer, and pulls down four rebounds. Red is 100 percent from the field. Eddie is 100 percent from the free throw line. Sally is everywhere, shooting, stealing, firing passes inside, mixing it up, attracting fouls, sinking free throws. She is having the game of her life.

The baskets keep dropping; Washington keeps fouling. Oregon goes on a thirteen-to-zero streak toward the end of the half, and UW coach Chris Gobrecht, with three of her starters in foul trouble and her thirteenth-ranked team being embarrassed by an unranked competitor, is enraged. She explodes on the court and immediately gets a technical foul. Nine seconds later, another one of her starters gets called for a personal foul. The UW band strikes up a tune, loud and spirited. Across the bleachers, the Oregon band puts down its instruments and starts dancing in the aisles.

At halftime, Oregon is up by twelve points, and Jody is trying hard not to let her emotions show. Here's this young team no one thought would do anything this year—her team— and they're beating the mighty Huskies. They are out there showing everyone what a team coached by Jody Runge can do. Somehow this team of sophomores and newcomers, this team with no bench, is winning. Red may annoy the hell out of her sometimes, but Red is producing. Roy has an off night once in a while, but mostly she's there, inside, blocking shots and scoring in the double digits. Jess looks as if she's going to come through the injury and play like she did last year. Eddie is finally shooting. Sal is exceeding all expectations, doing everything that needs to be done including providing leadership on the court. B has shown she can be a major contributor. Even Sandie looks as if she might have turned the corner.

All this races through Jody's mind as she looks at the girls down in the locker room. They are mopping their faces with towels and sucking on sections of orange, so pleased with themselves they can hardly stand it. But Jody knows there is still a half a game to play and that a twelve-point lead can evaporate in a minute or two if the team slacks off.

She gets their attention. She is careful to say good things about their play without actually praising them. She needs them to still feel on the edge.

"Listen, ladies," she tells them, "when you go back out there, the score is zero to zero." She pauses a moment. "Zero to zero, ladies. *No . . . big . . . heads.*" She emphasizes each word. "You have to play like you're scratching and clawing for your lives."

Back on the court, that's what Oregon does. After trading baskets for a while, the Ducks go on a ten-to-nothing run, with Red, Roy, Sally and Jess all shooting. Meanwhile, the Huskies keep fouling. With more than ten minutes left to play, the first of three Washington starters who will eventually foul out of the game is disqualified. The Washington coach goes to her bench, but even several of the backups are playing with three fouls.

So far, Jody is taking no chances. She is playing her five starters almost exclusively, putting in B and Sandie just long enough to give someone a breather. It's not a particularly good strategy, to run the starters into the ground, but she feels she has little choice. With a margin of ten or twelve points, she can't afford to slacken the pace. Besides, the Oregon bench is really only two deep: B and Sandie. The others can't handle this level of play yet.

Tonight, it looks as if B and Sandie can't either. When Jody puts in B in the middle of the first half, she stays in just long enough to commit two fouls and miss a free throw. Now she puts her in again to give Jess a breather. Maybe, if B steps up this time, Jess can stay on the bench and give her ankle a rest. B has her chance, but makes nothing happen. A minute later, Jess is back in.

Then, with Oregon ahead by seventeen, Jody feels safe enough to substitute Sandie for Red, who has played almost without a break. Sandie goes in looking like the old Sandie, the pre–Oregon State Sandie, the I'm-petrified-to-be-out-here-so-don't-pass-me-the-ball Sandie. Five seconds later, she commits a foul. A few seconds afterward, she makes another foul, and Red is back in.

Now with the starters back, the team fires up, sinking five baskets to Washington's one. It doesn't hurt that two more Husky starters are on the bench after committing their fifth fouls. With three minutes left to play, Oregon is up by thirty. This is what's known in the trade as a "drubbing," and the UW coach is beyond angry and well into livid. It's not just all the fouls the officials are calling, which of course she thinks are unwarranted. It's not just losing. It's losing so badly. It's how Jody is pushing her nose in it by leaving the starters in and continuing to rack up the points. It is etiquette, she thinks, for Jody to put in the bench. There's no way Washington can come back. Leaving the starters in can only widen the point spread and add to Washington's embarrassment.

She stalks over to the far end of her turf, the closest she can come to the Oregon bench without getting called for a technical. She leans forward, jutting out her chin, so she can shout across the timekeepers and scorers to where Jody is standing. She is a slender woman with a pixy haircut. She is in a rage, her face white, fists clenched. She screams at Jody to take out the starters.

Jody doesn't hear her over the din of the crowd. Jody doesn't even see her at first. One of the assistant coaches tells her what's going on just as the TV camera across the court zooms in for a better look. Jody turns her back on the scene. Isn't it just too bad if Washington, number thirteen in the nation, doesn't want to get blown out by Oregon, Jody mutters to herself as she walks away. That's tough, real tough. But in the midst of this victory, the Washington coach has managed to pinpoint the Ducks' big weakness and, while embarrassing herself with her tantrum, embarrass Jody as well.

The reason Jody isn't sending subs in at this point is not because she has it in for Washington; it's because she has no one to send in. Washington has been playing nine people. The bench has scored nineteen points. Jody has played the five starters all game with B and Sandie in and out quickly, together scoring just six points. Now, at the end of the game, with such a large lead, it would be smart to take out the starters and smart to give the other girls on the bench some playing time. But Jody is afraid they will blow the big lead, a lead the starters worked hard for.

Finally, with less than two minutes left in the game, she starts subbing. Cicely comes in for Roy. Timmy comes in for Eddie. Shanthi, a junior benchwarmer, comes in for Sally. Sally is tired. She's played thirty-seven out of the game's thirty-eight minutes, but she leaves the court reluctantly. She has twenty-one points and eight assists. She is having too much fun out there to want to sit down. This is how she used to feel about basketball, all fiery and lit up.

These past few seasons back in Australia she has just been going through the motions, playing basketball because that's all she knows how to do, playing until something better comes along. She hadn't realized just how burned out she was, how flat the experience had become for her until tonight. Tonight she remembers why she loves the game.

Maybe I'll stay here in Oregon, she thinks to herself. Maybe I'll play another season here. From the beginning, from that first phone call with Jody, she made it clear that she is here for only this season. But tonight she feels her resolve melting. Maybe she'll look into what course of study she might follow. Maybe her boyfriend can find a job here. Maybe it's the adrenaline talking. Sally sits down and takes a long drink of water from her squeeze bottle.

Jody puts in Neiman, a freshman who hasn't had a good, hard practice since she arrived four months ago. In these last two minutes of play, Washington, also playing its bench, scores ten points. Oregon, scoreless, makes three fouls.

It is still a wonderful win—although by eighteen rather than thirty—and the team is ecstatic. It means Oregon is in sole possession of second place in the Pac-10. It means when the AP sportswriters' poll comes out next week, Oregon should be ranked in the top twenty-five. It means the Ducks are having their best season in fifteen years.

But Jody is not a happy camper.

"That was a great win, ladies," she says in the locker room. The words are right, but her voice is low and flat, sullen even, and her face is a mask. It's not at all what the girls expect. They are hugging and high-fiving. They are not prepared for what comes next.

"You subs are not pulling your weight. You're embarrassing the team." Her voice is harsh and bitter. She is standing at the front of the room glowering down at them.

Red is sitting on the couch in her usual place near the front, and she can't believe what she's hearing. Sure the subs screwed up, Red is thinking. But this is our moment. We won. You're stealing our moment from us. She leans over to untie her ankle supports and to avoid glowering back at the coach. Red is bold, not stupid.

No one says a word. The fans whir in the background, filling the locker room with white noise. Jody hasn't moved. She isn't finished with them yet.

"I can't even put you in in the last minute," she says. Her anger is palpable. "I'm disgusted with you. You're welfare cases, that's what you are." She looks as if she could go on, but there is a knock at the locker-room door. Dave, the sports information assistant, has come to escort Jody down the hall to the media room. The local press wants to hear all about the great victory.

Three days later, the new national rankings are announced. The University of Oregon is twenty-fourth.

NOTHING BUT A
HARD LESSON

AFTER THE BIG WINS AGAINST WASHINGTON AND OREGON
State, the road trip to Arizona is anticlimactic. These are
bottom-of-the-heap Pac-10 teams. Last year, both teams lost
both of their games to Oregon, at home and away. This year
Arizona State is dead last in the conference. The Ducks, with
their twenty-fourth-in-the-nation ranking, their 4–1 record in
league play and their second spot in the Pac-10, are riding
high, and even Jody, who fears overconfidence more than just
about anything, is smiling. She won't say so out loud, but
she's thinking: sweep. She's thinking: Go down there, blast
'em, come home with a 6–1 record and square off against
Stanford, the only team between the Ducks and the Pac-10
title.

Everyone is feeling good. Everyone is feeling that this
is a team on the move. What they don't realize, what Jody
doesn't realize until it's all over, is that the girls know how
to play when they're underdogs, but not when they are the
team to beat, the feather waiting to be placed in someone
else's cap. When your reputation precedes you, like Stanford,

you learn to deal with it. You learn that every team you meet is gunning for you, that you're going to have to fend off everyone's best game. The Ducks have never been in that situation, never had that reputation—not this year, not last year, not ever. Even in a good year, like last year's third-place Pac-10 finish, the Ducks were thought of more as a scrappy, upstart team, a surprise finisher rather than a threat through the season.

Now the Ducks are a threat. They are number two—thus far beaten only by nationally ranked USC, and only by one point at USC's home court—and that means everyone else is going to try harder. But that's not what the girls are thinking as they fly out of Eugene airport on a cold, drizzly Wednesday morning in late January. They're thinking: We're on a roll. We're contenders. We're gonna blow 'em out. And we'll catch some sun while we're at it.

The first road game, the Arizona game, is the more challenging of the two. Although Arizona's stats don't look good, the team has had a grueling schedule, and most of its losses have been to teams ranked higher than Oregon. The first half looks like an even match, despite the fact that Oregon is not playing well. Jess, who is starting again, is one for six from the field; Red is scoreless after five tries. Even Sally, who has been a rock, can't get her shot to fall. The Ducks are being outrebounded two to one. But with Roy and B stepping up, and the Arizona team not getting much production from its starters, the two teams trade one- or two-point leads.

Then, with three minutes left in the half, Arizona catches fire: a three-pointer, a steal for a quick basket, another three-pointer and, with only five seconds on the clock, a basket and a foul. Any streak like this is demoralizing, but coming right at the end of the half—with no time to answer it and lots of time down in the locker room to think about it—makes it even worse. Oregon is twelve points in the hole at halftime.

Of the three games Oregon has lost all season—the early

game against Drake, the blowout against Vanderbilt and the USC loss—the Ducks have gone down to the locker room at halftime losing. The games they won, they were winning at halftime. This team has never won a game coming from behind. Jody doesn't know how many of the girls realize this. She is not about to point it out. It's too scary.

But Jody is so angry that she barely feels the fear. It's not just that the team is losing; it's how the girls are playing. Jess and Red are having terrible shooting nights, and, as far as Jody can determine, they've given up playing altogether. Their defensive game has disappeared. They're not rebounding; they're not boxing out; they're not giving help. They're just standing around like spectators at their own game.

Jody doesn't get it. Aren't we here to play basketball? Aren't we all after the same thing? It doesn't occur to her that, at some level, they aren't after the same thing. Yes, they all want to win. But the girls are college students funding their education by playing basketball, and these games are the work they do to pay for tuition. They may love the game, they may love playing—at least on some nights—but it is just a game. It is not their life, and it is not their future. For Jody, it is both.

Jody knows everyone has bad shooting nights. She understands that. What she doesn't understand is giving up. That is unforgivable. In the locker room, she is torn between anger and disappointment, but it comes out weariness.

"The only time you seem to play hard is when I'm hateful and mean and get on your case," she tells them. "All right, ladies, you called it."

But hateful and mean doesn't work either, although Jody gives it a good try in the second half. The hole they've dug for themselves is just too deep. They are not a comeback team. They lose 78–74.

In the locker room, Jody pounds them with a speech about selfishness, about players who play for their own glory and not the team's, players who give up when their shots won't fall. Red figures Jody is talking about her. Red scored only six points all game—she has been averaging more than seventeen a game since the Pac-10 season began—and she's disappointed in her performance. But to her, it was just a bad night. Jody is always finding fault with how she plays anyway—at least that's how Red sees it. She doesn't exactly know what the coach expects of her, but whatever it is, it's too much.

But Jody isn't talking about stats, about who scored how many points or who didn't; she's talking about being a team player. Jody thinks what Red really cares about, what motivates her, is her own performance—the baskets she sinks, the rebounds she grabs—and not how the team is doing. But the stats the record keepers keep measure only a narrow band, just a few of the many ways a player can contribute on the court. There are no stats for how quickly a player gets back down the court on defense, how aggressively a player keeps the opposition away from the basket, how much help a player gives her teammates. These are the unselfish contributions, the ones that don't show up in media guides, the ones sportswriters never mention. This is what Jody is talking about tonight.

Down the bench from Red, Jess is stone-faced. Last year she would have listened to a talk like this, nodded, and thought, yeah, we should all be less selfish. This year, her on-again, off-again performances, her threatened position as a starter, her insecurities about her own ability to lead the team—all of this has her on the edge. She is vulnerable as she never has been before. She is raw and open to hurt. So tonight, to her, this speech is absolutely personal, absolutely about her, a targeted insult, an attack both on her ability as a player and on her stature as a senior. Jody doesn't look at Jess directly as she speaks, but Jess knows. Okay, she thinks to herself, I had a bad game. I had a terrible game. She admits that. She hit two of fourteen from the floor, an embarrassing,

god-awful percentage. She admits she was a little pouty during one of the time-outs. But she went back in and played
hard, she thought.

Jess sits there, half listening. It has all been so hard:
Karen's injuries, which cost Jess her only friend on the team;
her own injury, which cost her six games, took her out of the
flow and somehow, she doesn't know how, took away her
outside shooting, the strongest part of her game. And now
this, now insults from the coach. Jess is feeling sorry for herself. She figures, after all that's happened, she has a right to.

But she is also deeply angry. To her, this speech ends
the possibility of communicating with Jody. She knows with
certainty that she will never go to her coach to talk about the
problems she's having with her shot. Jess has a hard time
talking to anyone other than Karen anyway, but she is in real
pain over her shooting. She needs advice and encouragement
more than she would ever admit. But now, after this speech,
she figures if she ever went to Jody with her problems, the
coach would think she was just being selfish.

I am not selfish, she tells herself, I'm just in this rut I
don't know my way out of. Sitting there on the bench, she is
very close to losing control. But it is important to Jess that
no one knows how upset she is. She clamps her jaw shut and
stares straight ahead.

Later, in the hotel room, she lets loose in front of one
of her sisters, who has flown down to see the games. For more
than an hour, Jess paces the small room, yelling and crying.
She throws her shoes at the wall. She tells her sister that she's
fed up with the coaches. She tells her sister that she wants to
quit, right now, tonight. She can't stand to play another game.
She cries some more. Her sister waits out the storm, not knowing what to say.

Slowly, Jess takes control of herself. She is an expert at
that. She clamps down tight. It's okay for her sister to see
this, but no one else must know. She goes over to the table
in the corner of the room, tears a loose-leaf page out of one
of her school notebooks and starts writing. From now on, she

will keep a journal of her thoughts. There will be no conversations with the coach.

Losing on the road, especially losing the first game of a two-game trip, is among the least pleasant experiences in intercollegiate athletics. There you are, stuck in a hotel, stranded in an unfamiliar town, surrounded only by those who've shared the loss, with nothing to do but think about how poorly you played. You eat; you sleep; you practice; you try to think ahead and not back.

The problem is, if you're Oregon on the road and the next game is against Arizona State, it's hard to look ahead the way you should. It's hard to take your next opponent seriously, even if you have just been humbled by a surprise defeat. After all, Arizona State won only four games all season last year, with only two wins in conference play. Arizona State is one of those teams you "look past."

Oregon comes out so strong Saturday night in Tempe that, with only five minutes gone in the first half, the game has blowout written all over it. Oregon is up 17–4, with Roy, Jess, Red, Sandie and Eddie all hitting shots. Jody watches from the sidelines and relaxes. This is gonna be okay, she tells herself. We've got this one.

Her decision not to sub in the Washington game still haunts her. She thinks she made the right choice on that one, but that was Washington, a threat to the end. This is Arizona State. She knows the bench is weak in part because she has not given any of the newcomers significant playing time. Now, with such a big lead early on, Jody figures it's safe to start cycling in the players she kept out of the Washington game. They need some Pac-10 minutes or they will never be useful to the team.

In goes Kirsten McKnight, the one they call Timmy, the skinny, white-blond guard. A few minutes later, Jody puts in Neiman, a player she feels has been coasting all season. Then comes Shanthi Barton, the junior with the nice outside shot. She considers putting in Cicely too, but Cicely still gets confused running the plays. Her presence is unsettling on the court.

With the subs in, the game quickly changes. It's not just that the bench can't play as well as the starters, which is certainly true; it's that the starters don't—won't, thinks Jody—play as well with the bench players in. Jody looks over at Jess and Red on the court and she sees it in their faces. Why are you making us play with them? With them in, I'm just gonna have to play harder, and I don't want to take on the extra load. That's the look she sees.

By the time the three subs have cycled in and out of the game, with Sally, Roy, Eddie, Jess and Red resting on the bench in pairs, Oregon has blown a thirteen-point lead and is in the hole by three. A steal and two three-pointers later, the Ducks go to the locker room shaken, embarrassed and eight points down. Jody knows she's made a big mistake, and as angry as she is about the lackluster bench and the lazy starters, she is angrier still with herself. This is the kind of mistake you don't make in the Pac-10. It's the kind of misjudgment that costs you a game.

In the second half, the starters work hard to pull the game even. They do it, but the Arizona State women have tasted the lead. They didn't expect it, but now they want to get there again. There are no more jitters. They know now that they won't be blown out on their home court. They can play with confidence. As the underdog here, they have nothing to lose and everything to gain. With less than a minute left in the game, the score is tied at 77.

With eleven seconds left to play, Arizona State sinks a basket. Jody can't believe this is happening. She calls a timeout to calm down the players, to tell them this game is still winnable. She's not sure she believes it herself, but she says it. The Ducks inbound the ball. Jess goes up for a jump shot from fourteen feet out. She has missed all but two of twelve attempts tonight. She misses this one too. Eddie grabs the rebound and puts it up with no time on the clock. It doesn't fall.

The Ducks arrived in Arizona two days ago with a chance of being this year's Pac-10 champions. That is gone. They arrived with a national ranking and sole possession of the number two slot in the Pac-10. Those are gone. They leave with nothing but a hard lesson.

The team returns to Eugene late Sunday afternoon, tired and despondent. Monday they are on the court again, back to drills, back to basics, back to running sprints and shooting endless free throws. Jody stands on the sidelines, weary and pale. She came home yesterday to a silent, empty house, the perfect setting to sit and stew about the Arizona games, to watch the tapes, relive the embarrassment, feed the anger. There is nothing in her life but basketball now, and when basketball goes bad, there is really nothing. It seems to her that everything she feared about this team months ago—their youth, their lack of grit, the weak bench—was all justified.

This week Oregon faces its toughest opponent, the best team in the league, one of the best teams in the country, the undefeated Stanford Cardinal. Jody never expected to face Stanford as an equal, but she was counting on coming to the game with a 6–1 record, a record that would force Stanford to take the Ducks seriously. Now Oregon approaches its toughest game with a lackluster 4–3 record after being whipped by the worst team in the league.

Jody accepts the blame for that defeat. She knew it down in Tempe, and she saw it again clearly watching the tapes last night. It was her fault. She put in the subs too early; she let them stay in too long. She is responsible for the weakness of the bench in the first place. These are her recruits. She brought them to Oregon. But the other loss, the loss to the University of Arizona—that one the girls managed all by themselves.

She can glare at the players, yell at them, force them to watch themselves on tape, make them practice long and hard, work out her anger against them that way. But she has no way of working through her anger at herself, no partner to talk it over with, no best friend to console her, no outside interests to distract her. There is just Jody, alone, pissed off and, although she would never say the word or even think it, scared. Her future rides on this team.

"Let's go, ladies!" she yells into the court. "I don't see any hustle out there." The girls are tired. She knows it, and she doesn't care.

Stacy, the equipment manager, walks over. "Coach," she says quietly, waiting for Jody to turn around. Stacy is a small, thin, unsmiling freshman. This job of dispensing water bottles and fresh towels during games and doing laundry on the road is what is paying her way through school. She is very serious about it.

"Coach," she says again, "there's a message that the president is trying to get ahold of you."

Jody nods. The players are scrimmaging on the court. She is absorbed in their game, watching them move, checking their positions, taking note of who is playing hard and who isn't. A minute or two go by.

"Jody?" The trainer is trying to get her attention. She also has a message from the president's office. Apparently the president's secretary has been calling all around Mac Court trying to track her down. Unlike her male counterpart, Jody doesn't have an office or a phone in the building.

Jody is now paying attention. So, the president needs to get ahold of her, and in a hurry. She's never received an urgent call from Dave before. She figures it can be only one thing. It must be news about the donor. That's the only business she and Dave have together. And it must be important news, otherwise why would he be tracking her down like this. She knows the president was supposed to have another meeting with the donor last week. Something must have happened. He must have heard from her this afternoon.

Adrenaline washes away the weariness. Jody leaves the court quickly looking for a telephone. The closest one she can find is a pay phone just outside Mac Court. It is raining. The sky is pewter. She huddles by the phone and makes the call.

It turns out to be about the donor, but it's not what she thought.

There is no good news. In fact, there is no news at all. The president has not met with the donor since the Rose Bowl. That's why he's calling. He has a meeting scheduled with her tonight, in a few hours, and he wants to pump Jody for more information about her program. Jody stands there in the rain, telling the president about how she thinks Oregon can be a Pac-10 contender, how she thinks women's basketball is about to break through, how she wants to market and publicize the game, bring fans in, create a winning tradition. She is ad-libbing her philosophy at a pay phone. She can't believe this is how the president is preparing himself for this meeting. She can't believe this is how he takes care of business, her business.

No coach wants to lose a game, or even admit she expects to lose it, but of all the games this season, this next game against Stanford is the one Jody had thought she could afford to lose. There would be no shame in it. Stanford is, and has been for most of the past decade, not just the shining light of the Pac-10 but a national powerhouse. Under coach Tara VanDerveer, who took over the team in the late 1980s, Stanford has posted seven consecutive twenty-five-game or more winning seasons, won the Pac-10 championship five times and captured the NCAA title twice. Tara is one of the finest coaches in the country, and she has just recruited one of her best freshman classes. This season, Stanford is a force no team has yet learned to reckon with: ranked number three in the nation, not only undefeated but beating its opponents by an average of thirty-four points a game, playing four returning starters and boasting one of the strongest and deepest benches in the nation. If Oregon had come to this game after clobbering the Arizona teams, with its national ranking intact, a loss to Stanford probably would not have cost the Ducks their place in the top twenty-five.

But that's not the situation now. Now a loss would mean a dismal 4–4 record, a fourth or fifth place in the conference and perhaps most significantly, a third consecutive defeat. Jody, who hates losing even more than she loves winning, has never lost three in a row. And, if a loss to Stanford seemed likely before, it now seems certain: Sally, Roy and Eddie have all turned their ankles in practice this week. It's nothing that will keep them from playing, but it may keep them from playing as hard as they would have.

The mood in the locker room minutes before game time is grim as the players listen to Jody go through the matchups, pairing the Oregon starters with their Stanford counterparts. Every Stanford player she mentions has something amazing about her: This one is all-Pac 10; that one pulled down thirteen rebounds in the first half of a recent game; that one is deadly from the three-point line. Usually Jody can find something confidence-building to say at this point, like "She's not quick" or "She's gonna foul out." This time, there's nothing. Every Stanford player, deep into the bench, is a winner.

"We're ready to play these people," Jody tells the team. She looks earnest and pale. She doesn't believe her own words.

Sandie, sitting on the couch, looks down at her feet. She's got a big shiner on her right eye where Cicely whopped her during practice. Cicely always seems to be in the wrong place at the wrong time. On another player, the black eye might look tough. Another player might wear it with attitude. But Sandie looks like a poster child for a battered women's hot line. She shakes her head. She's not buying what Jody is selling. Sally and Eddie, who always sit together now, inseparable in practice as well, stare straight ahead. Even Red looks unsure of herself.

Tonight's game is televised, which is good news for Jody. It means TV time-outs every four minutes, a blessing for a team that will need to play its starters for almost the entire game.

"You've got to play as hard as you can in four-minute spurts," Jody tells the starters.

She will try to use B and Sandie when she can, but there won't be any other help from the bench. This is not the time to get angry again about the bench, but Jody can't help it. It's not just that the talent isn't there. It's that the work ethic, the ambition, the commitment are missing. She knows she's going to have to come down hard on them soon, give them another "You're all slouchers on welfare" lecture. But not now. Now is the time for can-do bravado.

"Just think in terms of four minutes," she tells the starters. "Don't let them get away from you. Don't let them get anything going in that four minutes." Jody looks around the room, making eye contact with each player. "This is what you came here to do, ladies," she says, her voice low and steady. "Let's do it."

The game starts slowly. The Ducks are tentative; Stanford is taking it easy. Tara VanDerveer, the deservedly highest paid coach in the Pac-10, is testing the waters. Just how hard will her team have to play to beat Oregon? Stanford didn't get where it is by underestimating opponents. She is taking this game seriously, but she is not worried. She watches as Anita Kaplan, the hulking six-foot-five senior, sinks the first basket for Stanford. One-hundred-eighty-pound Roy, who looks willowy by comparison, answers for Oregon. By the first TV time-out, Oregon is ahead by one. Throughout the first half, the teams trade baskets, with the lead changing ten times. Then, with four minutes left to play, Stanford begins pulling ahead, opening a gap of thirteen before Sally, with back-to-back layups, closes it to nine.

Sally is everywhere: handling the ball, passing, penetrating, shooting from the inside, shooting from the perimeter, denying, stealing. She doesn't move with Eddie's quicksilver grace. Her shot is not particularly pretty. But she is becoming the one player who can be counted on in both offense and defense, the one who makes things happen on the court and now, just a month and a half after joining the team, the leader. It is she who pulls them together in the huddle, she who bucks them up. She is wearing Missy's number—Missy Crowshaw, last year's spark plug—and now she's doing Missy's job.

Under the basket, the big players are banging each other, bodies on bodies, shoulders down, elbows out. These women's games are often more physical than the men's. Sometimes these big women, these six-foot-three, 190-pounders, seem to have less control over their bodies than the even bigger men who play basketball. Maybe it comes from years of being made to feel uncomfortable about their size.

Since their first prepubescent growth spurt, these big women have had to struggle not to be embarrassed. All around them, they see women taking up less and less space, starving themselves, hunching their shoulders, hugging their arms to their bodies, speaking softly, minimizing. The big women are not sure what to do with their bodies. They may never learn to use them with the same grace and style tall men are capable of, men not just comfortable with their size but admired for it, idolized, idealized. But out on the court, the big women find a use for these bodies that challenge what society deems feminine. They can use their brawn rather than hide it.

Women too are more comfortable being physical with one another than men—another legacy of the different ways boys and girls are socialized. Jody often tells a player to "put a butt on her," meaning back up into the opponent, pushing her away with your body. It's not a move you see many men do.

That's what's happening now under the basket as the big post players try to outmaneuver each other in the key. There is a lot of pushing but no whistle. Red emerges from the knot of players, walking quickly across the court to the bench, holding a bloody nose and cursing. At first she suspects it might be broken, but the trainer and team doctor take a quick look and decide to stuff plugs up her nostrils and ice it. She goes downstairs to the training room.

Jody looks at the bench and, as usual, has few options.

Sandie goes in, and in less than a minute, commits back-to-back fouls. Jody curses under her breath and looks over at the bench again.

"Where the hell is Red?" she hisses to Steph. Either she's forgotten about the bloody nose or she thinks Red is goldbricking downstairs. The relationship between Jody and Red is no smoother now than it was when the season began. These two big, hardheaded women, one player, one coach, have not learned to cut each other any slack. They grate on each other constantly—small things no one else notices: a look, a stance, a few seconds too long at the water cooler. For all their hardheadedness, they are both thin-skinned, and easily rub each other raw. When Red comes back up three minutes later, Jody throws her a where-the-hell-have-you-been look, but immediately puts her back in. Red scores from the inside.

Jody has said to play in tough four-minute spurts, and that's what the girls are doing. By halftime, Stanford, the mighty power, is only nine points ahead.

"We stayed with 'em," says Roy, dropping to the couch in the locker room. "We can play 'em." She claps her hands and looks around the room for support. The starters are too exhausted to respond.

Jody too is pleased, or as pleased as she can be when the team is losing. This isn't a blowout. The girls are playing hard, and she's proud of them. In the locker room, she takes off her beige linen jacket and talks strategy. Her voice is calm. The girls can't remember the last time she didn't rip them apart at halftime when they were losing. They don't know it, but Jody is beginning to entertain the slim notion that Oregon might win this game. That idea has not occurred to the starters, who are already so tired that they don't know where they will get the strength to play the second half. Sally, who has had ten points and a steal in the first half, looks dazed, like she just walked out into the bright sunlight after a week underground. Jody doesn't realize how tired they all are.

In the first four minutes of the second half, Stanford effortlessly opens the lead to fifteen.

"You came out like you're on vacation!" Jody screams at her players during the first time-out. "Now get into the game or there won't be any game."

They come out and play hard. Red and Roy whittle the lead back down to nine. All through the second half, it's the same story: the five Oregon starters battle to cut the margin. Then Stanford whips in and opens the gap. Three times during the second half, Stanford opens the lead to fifteen. Three times Oregon fights back to within nine.

The Ducks do this without the help of Jess, who has hit only two of thirteen baskets. One bad shooting game has segued into another until Jess has found herself so deep in this slump that she can't get out. It blinds her. It grabs her by the ankles and keeps her earthbound. She practices. She gives herself pep talks. She vents her frustration in her loose-leaf journal. Nothing seems to help.

B sits on the bench wondering why Jody doesn't sub her for Jess. In the first half, B was hot, hitting three of four from the field. She knows she could be doing something in there. She tries not to question Jody's decision. She knows that's not the job of a player. She knows that line of thinking will just get you in trouble, like Red. But she can't help wondering.

In fact, Jody has forgotten all about B. She would sub her if she would just look back at the bench for a moment. But she's screaming at the officials, who have called Roy for her fourth personal foul. A minute later, Red gets called, then Jess, then Sally. Jody is so wound up in the moment that she doesn't even think of B.

With four minutes left to play, Oregon begins its final collapse. Sally, who has carried this game with nineteen points and four steals, hits a three-pointer, but nothing else seems to go right for the Ducks. Red fouls again; Jess is called for back-to-back fouls. The game ends with Stanford up by thirteen.

"You have nothing to feel bad about," Jody tells them down in the locker room. "We had a bad shooting night, but we played hard."

They are not used to this kinder and gentler Jody. It takes them a minute to realize they are not going to be screamed at. They stop untying their shoes and look up at her.

"Listen, you play this hard every time, and you'll win every game." She leaves them to their showers, their stack of pizzas growing cold in the corner and their exhaustion.

Down the hall in the media room, she faces the local reporters. "We had a good effort tonight," she tells them. "But from here on out we have to start winning basketball games."

Eddie is exhausted. She doesn't talk about it. She doesn't complain. But, two days after the Stanford game, she has not yet recuperated, neither mind nor body. She played the full forty minutes, twice as much time as many of the Stanford starters and even more time than her own overworked team-mates. And when Eddie plays forty minutes, it's not a few seconds of loping down the court punctuated by long stretches of jostling under the basket. It's hard running, constant, quick motion, hyper alertness looking for the steal, anticipating the moves. For the last thirteen minutes of the game, Eddie played grueling full court press against the Stanford guards, pressuring her opposite number from one end of the court to the other.

But it's not just the playing that's wearing Eddie down. It's the rest of her life: the 8 A.M. chemistry class that meets four mornings a week, the homework that keeps her up past midnight almost every night, the boyfriend who requires care and feeding, and above all, her own insecurities about her skills on the court. Last season—the long, painful and public spiral from starter to three-minute-a-game sub—continues to haunt her.

Now, even as she plays well, which she has been doing, she is thinking to herself: How long will this last? She is waiting to screw up just like last year. Each game she questions her ability anew, as if the starting buzzer erased all her past accomplishments. She forgets the steals, the rebounds, the slick ballhandling. She remembers only the turnovers, the missed shots. Her insecurities threaten to sabotage her. She knows this, and it scares her. She wishes she were more like Sally: calm, steady, quietly confident, secure in knowing she can dig deep and find something there. Sometimes she even wishes she were like Red, so self-assured that she seems untouchable. But she can only be herself and hope to outplay her doubts.

Tonight, too soon, there's another game. Eddie is beat, but she must find a way to play hard.

Tonight's game is against the University of California, Berkeley, known in the Pac-10 as "Cal." The Ducks must win this game; otherwise what can still be called a "temporary setback"—the three consecutive losses—becomes a serious losing streak and the end to any hopes of going to the NCAA tournament. In a month and a half, sixty-four teams will be selected to participate in what sportswriters have dubbed "the Big Dance." The criterion is how many games you've won. Oregon has ten wins so far and ten games left to play. At least seven of those ten have to be victories or there will be no hope of a trip to the tournament.

Cal is a team Oregon should beat, but then, so was Arizona State. As the coaches are fond of saying in this tough conference: On a given night, any team can beat any other team in the Pac-10. The Ducks must win tonight not just to shore up their record but also to help repair their flagging self-esteem. Losing makes you think of yourself as a loser.

It's been one of those extraordinary days that take western Oregonians by surprise once or twice every February, a sweet, soft spring day, cloudless and blue, the air light and fresh, the parks suddenly overrun with people wild and joyous at seeing the sun for the first time since October. Jody has spent the day indoors watching game film. When she walks into the locker room in black stirrup pants that make her legs look a mile long, she is pasty faced and haggard. Her voice is hoarse from the Stanford game.

"I'm really nervous, ladies," she says as she stands almost motionless in front of the room. "Time was when whatever we did, people would say, 'Oh wow, look at those women.' We were getting three hundred people to a game. No one knew us. We were staying in bad hotels." She's not talking about ancient history; she's talking about last season.

"But now you've got a new locker room. You've got a chartered bus when you travel. You've got a generous per diem. You've been given a lot, ladies. We've been given a lot. We've got two thousand people coming to our games now, and they expect us to win." She stops and repeats the line for emphasis: "They expect us to win."

Jody is talking about herself as much, maybe more, than she is talking about the team. She has made a lot of noise in the year and a half she's been coach. She knows you can't demand respect and then go out and lose basketball games.

"This is serious business, ladies," she tells them. They think she means this basketball game. She means women's basketball. She means her career.

The Ducks come out flat. They are not just physically exhausted from the Stanford game, they are mentally spent as well. Their heads have to be in this game if their bodies are to follow, and right now their heads are somewhere between the last ten minutes of the Stanford game and the homework they need to finish this weekend. After a quick basket by Sally, there's a long dry spell. Jess's shot is still off. Roy has a cold hand. Cal is everywhere, grabbing rebounds, shooting three-pointers, penetrating inside. They've come to win, and they're acting as if they can do it. They take a seven-point lead before Oregon starts paying attention.

It's Red who catches fire, sinking three baskets in a single frenzied minute, the last a left-handed hook that looks as if Balanchine choreographed it. The bench is up waving towels. With six minutes left to the half, the Ducks start playing, going on a fifteen-to-two run. Even Jess, who's missed all four of her previous attempts, finally sinks a basket. By the end of the half, Oregon has opened a ten-point lead.

The girls go down to the locker room in high spirits, all except Eddie. On the way down the stairs, she mutters to herself and bangs her fist against the wall. She's hit just one of five baskets and grabbed only a single rebound. Worse yet, she's committed three turnovers. She's giving it what she has to give. She just doesn't have a lot. When other players play flat, Jody figures they're being lazy or they've got an attitude problem or they're planning on letting someone else carry the load. With Eddie it's different. Jody thinks Eddie is the hardest-working player on the team. She thinks Eddie has heart.

In the second half, Jody gives Eddie a rest, the first rest of any kind she's had in several games and the first long rest she's had all season. Eddie is struggling out there. She's racked up two more turnovers, missed a basket and a free throw. Jody knows the mistakes come from exhaustion, not lack of effort.

It's hard to rest Eddie because there's no one on the bench ready to step into her position. Taking Eddie out means switching Sally to her spot and rearranging the others. Jody makes the adjustments. Eddie watches morosely from the bench.

When Jody takes out a starter in the middle of a game for more than a minute's rest, everyone knows it's meant as punishment for a job poorly done. She's done it with Red a couple of times, pulled her out after some bonehead move or some real or imagined slacking off on the court, had her sit there on the bench cooling her heels for a while, pondering her transgressions before Jody got good and ready to put her back in again. Eddie figures that's what's happening to her now. She tries to block the other thought she's having as she watches her team play well without her: This is just like last year. I'm playing like shit, and the coach is shifting someone else into my position. I'm one step away from losing my position. She sits there and stews about it. But she's wrong. Although she isn't having a good night, she's on the bench for only one reason: Her coach knows how tired she is.

On the court, Red is pouring it on. All the moves are working: the head fakes, the pivots, the L-cuts. If she has the ball and she's near the basket, she either sinks one or draws a foul. Jess is struggling but hitting more than she has in a while. Sally is a rock.

With four minutes left, the Ducks are up by twenty-two, and Jody is confident enough to start subbing. B comes in, then Timmy, then Sandie, then Shanthi and finally Cicely, the player she had hoped would be a force on the team, now one of her biggest disappointments.

Cicely sprints down the court, knees high. The subs have allowed the twenty-two-point lead to dwindle to sixteen. Cicely has the ball and a clear shot. She puts it up fast. It falls just right. It is the first Pac-10 basket of her career.

When she sinks it, the players on the bench stand in unison and cheer. They may not be her friends, she may not have earned their respect in practice, but they know this is her moment. They understand the importance of that first basket. Cicely looks over at the cheering bench, and for the first time in the five months since she's worn an Oregon Ducks jersey, she feels as if she belongs.

The clock runs out with Oregon up by eighteen. It is the convincing win the Ducks needed, and Jody is more relieved than happy. The losing streak is over. Next week begins the second half of the Pac-10 season. It's time to get back to winning.

IN THE HOLE

ALL WEEK, THE DUCKS HAVE BEEN PRACTICING A NEW scrimmage drill: The starters are down ten points with five minutes left to play. They have to come from behind and beat the subs. In practice, it's working fine, but beating your own subs on your own court with nothing at stake is one thing; coming from behind in a real game, especially a game on the road, is something else. It's something the Ducks have not been able to do.

Oregon has now played every Pac-10 team once, beating five of them and losing to four. It is not a great record. It is not the record Jody thought the team was headed for just two weeks ago before the Arizona losses. But it still leaves open the possibility of an NCAA berth if the Ducks do better in the second half of the season. The problem is, the team now faces its three toughest opponents on the road, and away games are much more difficult to win. First comes the rematch with intrastate rival Oregon State, then regional rival University of Washington, then Stanford. The ability to come from behind will be essential. Without it, the Ducks are likely to lose all three games.

Jody is in perpetual ill humor these days. If it's not Jess's uneven play, it's Sally's ankle, twisted in practice. If it's not Red's attitude, it's the bench's laziness. She misses Kim, her close friend and the team's former trainer, who left for a new job in Boston last month. She is disgusted with the university's lack of progress on corralling the big-money donor. She has come down with another cold. Deer are mauling her garden.

But nothing lowers her spirits more than the news she receives Saturday night from Corvallis: Oregon State has beaten the unbeatable Stanford. She cannot imagine worse news. The Ducks' game against Oregon State this week was already going to be hellish, an away game in front of a big, unfriendly crowd with the opponents, a brash, physical team to begin with, whipped up to avenge their loss to Oregon last month. Now it looks as if Oregon State is playing at the top of its game, and the players will not only be vengeful, they will be suffused with confidence, so buoyed by their win against Stanford that they may be impossible to beat.

Jody wants to think that one of the reasons Oregon State was able to beat Stanford was because of the tough, physical full-court-press game the Ducks gave the California team two days before.

"We tired 'em out," she tells the girls in practice. "We gave them a game they couldn't recover from."

Everyone wants to believe this. It may even be true. But it is also true that while Oregon was busy losing three out of four games the past two weeks, OSU was busy winning. In fact, the Beavers are on a five-game winning streak, having dropped only one game since losing to Oregon back in mid-January.

In the basement locker room of Oregon State's Gill Coliseum minutes before game time, Jody searches for a way to make the game sound winnable. She has already detailed the strategy, including a new offensive pattern OSU has never seen. She has already catalogued the matchups. Now it's time for the inspiration. But Jody doesn't feel inspirational. She would never say it out loud, but she thinks this OSU team is probably too hot to beat tonight.

Practice this week has been okay, but team morale is shaky. Nothing has been the same since the Arizona road trip. Sally has come down considerably from her high after the University of Washington win. She is no longer contemplating staying for another year. She is tired and homesick and ready for the season to end. She has a boyfriend waiting for her in Australia and a mother and sister she's close to. She wants her real life to begin again. The coaches have finally stopped trying to talk her into playing another season. She tries to keep her weariness to herself, but her pale skin is looking even paler, and there are dark circles under her eyes. She knows exactly how many days it is until the end of the season.

Jess is fighting her own demons, suffering silently through the worst shooting slump in her career, watching her senior year slip by without figuring out how to pull herself together. She has neither been the ace shooter she used to be nor the team leader she hoped to be. One failure feeds the other. Her iffy playing makes it hard for her to assume leadership on the court. And without Karen around to perk her up, to form a partnership of seniors, she is more stoic and silent than ever.

She is struggling too with her feelings toward Red. There's probably some jealousy there: Red, a sophomore, has become so much more important to the team than Jess is. Red has had a bad game or two but she's scored in the double digits nine of the last ten games, outrebounding almost everyone almost all the time. Red is an undeniable presence on the court.

There is such a gulf between the two women's personal styles that even under the best of conditions they would not be friends: Jess, serious and fierce; Red, cool and nonchalant.

So Jess is not predisposed to like Red, and Red does not go out of her way to be liked.

Jess tries to separate her personal feelings for Red from her feelings about Red as a player and teammate. But it's hard. Jess is of the opinion that Red cares only about herself and not about the team. It's the same selfishness problem Jody worried about, the one she lectured the team on after the Arizona game. What Jess and some of the other players see is that when Red has a good game, she's happy, regardless of how the team does. When the team loses, Red seems less affected than the others, as if she didn't care as much.

Red too is in turmoil. She and Jody have not worked out a détente. In fact, their battle of wills is escalating. Red thinks she's working hard. Jody thinks she isn't. Red thinks Jody picks on her. Jody sees it differently: She expects more out of Red because Red, alone, has the potential to be an all-American. It's Jody's nature to push and push to make that happen. It's Red's nature to resist, to push back.

Eddie isn't in good shape either. When the Ducks beat OSU at home a few weeks ago, everyone slapped her on the back and told her she was over her "thing" about playing Oregon State. That game was supposed to have exorcised the evil spirits that haunted her since last year's debacle, Eddie's "baby game," the game that ended her run as a starting player. But Eddie doesn't see it that way. Although her team beat OSU this season, she doesn't think her own game was very good. She didn't prove anything to herself with that game, despite what her teammates thought. Last year's humiliation is still with her, a constant drain on her small reserve of self-confidence.

Jody takes a long look at the team sitting on the hard benches in front of her and searches for something the girls can hold on to as they go out on the court.

"What do you think their coach is telling them right now in the locker room?" she asks. "She's telling them: 'Ya gotta win, ya gotta win. Ya gotta win if ya wanna be number two in the conference.' " The girls fiddle with their sneakers, wondering where this is going. "Listen," says Jody, speaking almost confidentially, "the pressure is all on them. We're just where we want to be. We're the underdog, and it'll be a big feather in our cap if we beat them." She is talking herself into something here, gaining confidence as she speaks. "They have an overinflated idea of how good they are. Do you think they gave even one thought to the role we had in them beating Stanford?" She leaves them with that idea.

Upstairs the OSU band is playing to an already overwrought Corvallis crowd, at 5,233 the largest group to date ever assembled at Gill Coliseum for a women's basketball game. In the bleachers behind the Oregon bench sit several hundred stalwart Duck fans, including a busload of Daisy Ducks who trekked forty miles up the freeway to be at the game: two women with faces painted bright green, a group with yellow pom-poms, another group with GO DUCK placards. As always, Jess's parents are in the stands, and tonight Red has an entourage: mother and grandmother, father and stepmother. There is no Oregon band. The band is at home, playing for the men's game.

In the huddle before the tip-off, Sally gets them going. Increasingly it is Sal acting as team captain even though Jess holds that title. Sal reminds the starters what they've been telling each other all week: "Let's not let them get fired up. Let's not let them get started."

It's hard to know exactly what goes wrong. Maybe it's the new, more difficult offense Jody has been teaching them all week. They are still clumsy with it. Maybe it's the cockiness of this Oregon State team, with its Croatian point guard who prances backward up the court, revving up the crowd, playing to the stands. Maybe it's the loud, unfriendly fans and the eardrum-shattering band. Maybe it's just sagging morale. Whatever it is, it's bad for the Ducks.

In the first two minutes, Eddie, Sal and Roy all turn over the ball, and each time Oregon State scores. It's 10–0 before anyone even has time to work up a sweat.

Jody doesn't call a time-out. Let them calm down by playing, she thinks. Let them work it out. They come together on the court for another huddle as OSU lines up at the free throw line. Sally and Jess exchange glances. Jess is scared. She sees something in Red's eyes, in Eddie's eyes, that she doesn't like. She sees defeat. Sal holds herself in check, waiting for Jess to say something. Jess is the senior. She needs to step up.

"We can do this," Jess says to her teammates. This game, whatever happens with her own shot, she is determined to be a leader.

"We can do this," echoes Sally. Slowly, they work themselves into the game. They're still turning the ball over; they're still playing wretched defense, but at least some of the shots are falling. Jess and Sally are cold, but Red sinks five baskets in three minutes, and Roy hits three of her shots. Halfway through the half, the Ducks have scratched their way to a tie.

But they don't hold it for long. OSU is playing with the confidence and vitality that befits the only team in the conference to have beaten Stanford. The Beavers have no intention of letting their intrastate rivals look good, especially on their home court in front of a record crowd. It has taken Oregon eight minutes to fight back from a ten-point deficit. It takes OSU less than two to open it up again, going on an eight-point run. The lead is ten, then thirteen, then sixteen.

Jody watches in silence, her anger growing. She can't understand what's happening out there. Where's the defense? What the hell is Red doing standing around under the basket? What's happening to the guards, Eddie and Sally? They've turned over the ball seven times. She paces back and forth in front of the bench, stiff-legged and white-faced.

"Shit," she says, just loud enough for Steph and Joe, sitting on the bench, to hear. She is careful to turn away from the cameras that are catching the action for the local sports network. She is careful to speak low enough so the fans in the first row can't hear her. A minute later, she turns back to the bench again:

"What the hell are we doing?" Even if Steph or Joe knew, they know this is not the time to answer Jody.

Red takes the ball out of bounds and passes to Eddie. While Eddie is dribbling up the court, Red bends to tie a shoelace. Jody is following the ball, but she catches Red out of the corner of her eye. What she sees isn't an untied shoelace; it's an attitude. It puts her over the top.

"Get in the game, Red!" she screams so loud Red can hear her over the band, over the din of the crowd. Red finishes what she's doing and then looks over at Jody with that what's-your-problem look that even in good times drives Jody nuts. Then Red runs the length of the court, grabs a pass, drives to the basket and sinks one. It doesn't matter. She's still on Jody's shit list.

At halftime, Oregon is fourteen points down.

Jody yells and stamps her way through the locker-room talk. She rips them for not playing defense. She rips them for the twelve turnovers that converted to twenty-four points for OSU. "You're reacting," she tells the girls. "You've got to start dictating." Her sentences begin slowly and work themselves into screams. Her voice echoes off the steel lockers and the painted concrete walls. The girls sit there and take it in silence.

It doesn't seem to make a difference. In the second half, the defense is tighter, but OSU is hitting everything. Effortlessly, it seems, the Beavers' lead grows to twenty. In the huddle, Jess and Sally again try to rally the team. This is what "heart" is all about. When coaches talk about "digging deep" or "sucking it up," this is what they mean.

Jody doesn't give them let's-do-it-for-the-Gipper speeches during the time-outs. Maybe she should, but she's just not that kind of coach. The girls give each other the speech in huddles, on the free throw line, in those seconds when the officials are talking to the timekeepers.

But as the game wears on, Jess is getting increasingly

frustrated. She is trying hard to provide leadership on the court tonight, but every time she says something, Red has a quick answer, an excuse. Jess doesn't want to hear excuses. She wants the team to pull together as a team. It takes the Ducks fifteen minutes, but they whittle the deficit back to nine after Jess hits a three-pointer, only her second in the game. There are two minutes left, just enough time to win.

Red thinks she can help make it happen. She is having a good shooting night, six of eight from the floor, and she knows she could be helping out there. But she is sitting on the bench. Jody took her out with eight minutes left in the half. It's punishment: Jody thinks Red isn't playing defense. Red, of course, doesn't see it that way. "I just don't understand her," Red mutters under her breath as OSU goes on another run.

The Beavers have opened up a fourteen-point lead with a minute left in the game. The Ducks still don't give up, but it's too late. They lose by ten.

Down in the locker room, Sally and Eddie sit next to each other, oblivious that they have struck identical poses: elbows on knees, heads hung low, foreheads cradled in hands. No one speaks. You can hear the whooping of the OSU team through the concrete walls. The only other sound is scissors snipping tape as the girls cut their ankle wrappings. They are all waiting for Jody, not knowing which will be worse, this tension, this waiting, or what will happen when the coach comes in. Jody is pacing the hall outside the locker room trying to collect herself. She is not having any success.

When she finally comes into the locker room, all activity ceases.

"All right, ladies," she says. Already she is yelling. "What did they do that we didn't prepare for?" It is a rhetorical question. "Nothing!" she screams at them. "Nothing. We played like crap. You kids don't work hard until you're down by twenty."

She pauses, but not for long. "You've got to decide what you want out of the rest of the season. What are you willing to sacrifice to win? How hard are you willing to play?" Her voice is under control, but she is almost shaking with anger. "We scout for you. My assistants work off their asses for you. I don't know, ladies. I just don't know. If you're not willing to give what is needed, then I don't know what to do."

She stalks out of the locker room and into a knot of sports reporters. When she returns a few minutes later, the locker room is empty. Most of the players are already on the bus. A few are still in the showers. She sits alone on one of the benches, shoulders slumped, running her finger around and around the top of a can of soda. A minute goes by, then two. She sits there, staring at the floor, motionless except for that one finger inscribing a circle around the can. If Kim, the old trainer, were here she might be able to say something to Jody. But no one else dares approach.

On the bus, Eddie immediately buries herself in her chemistry book. She doesn't want to think about her eight turnovers. She doesn't want to think about the game. She doesn't want to think about basketball at all. The reading light over her seat is dim. She moves her head closer to the page.

Red saunters on the bus, holding a paper plate piled high with cookies and two loaves of zucchini bread wrapped in silver foil.

"Hey, who wants some of my grandma's cookies?" she yells to the back of the bus. "She's all worried we'll be hungry on the way home." No one answers. She passes the plate of cookies back anyway. "Here's some zucchini bread." She cocks her hand back as if getting ready to toss the loaf like a football.

Sandie is sitting in the very back of the bus, sprawled across three seats. She only played two minutes tonight, but she feels as if she's been through the wringer. She doesn't want a cookie. She doesn't want zucchini bread. She can't believe Red is acting like nothing happened. Doesn't she even care? Sandie closes her eyes and blots it out. Red is getting few takers. Finally, she sits down and tears into one of the loaves herself.

Jody steps on the bus a few minutes later. Some of the girls are talking softly in the back.

"I want quiet in this bus!" Jody yells. The anger that seemed spent just minutes ago in the locker room is back again, full force. "I want you to shut up and sit here and think about the flippin' game." Eddie sinks her head deeper into her book. Red sighs. She wishes, not for the first time this season, that this part of her life were over.

The OSU defeat pushes them deeper into a hole, not just statistically—the team now has a 5–5 Pac-10 record—but emotionally. Red tries to remember the last time she thought it was fun to play basketball, and can't. Sally crosses off a few more days on her calendar. Jess stews. Sandie sleeps. Eddie lies in bed, wide-eyed at 2 A.M., replaying each turnover, alternately swearing she'll never have another game like that and fearing she will. They drag themselves to classes. They drag themselves to practice. And they all work on letters to Jody.

She has asked them to write their answers to "What do I want for the rest of the season?" It is the half-punishment, half-therapy technique she has tried before, with this group and with last year's team, and she knows that sometimes the exercise can shake something loose by compelling the girls to stop and think about themselves and their commitment to the team. Jody figures she might glean a few insights from this forced introspection.

But Sally isn't sure anyone will be honest with the coach. She knows that she won't write: "I'm tired. I'm lonely. I'm counting the days until the season is over," even though that is what she is feeling. Red figures the coach doesn't really want the truth. She figures Jody is looking for the pat answers about working harder and going to the NCAA tournament. Although a few players do write the expected rah-rah-let's-all-pull-together letters, many use the assignment to say, at least partially, what's on their minds.

B wants Jody to know that there's a problem with, as she delicately puts it, "coach-player communication." Timmy says much the same thing but with less diplomacy, writing that harsh criticism and negativity are pulling the team apart. Eddie, as expected, beats herself up in print. "I haven't played well," she writes. "The only reason I am in now is because there is no Missy to go to," she tells Jody. She still can't shake last year's experience.

Sally doesn't tell the coach the whole truth, but she does use the letter to vent anger against one teammate who remains unnamed. "I question where everyone's heart is," Sally writes. "Actually, not everyone's. I only have a problem with the efforts of one person. Consistently, it's the same person letting everyone down." Jess also lights into this unnamed teammate who "won't listen" and "makes excuses for every little thing that goes wrong."

Red, the unnamed teammate, is as oblivious of what her teammates think of her as she is to any faults in her own performance. She uses her letter to vent her anger against Jody. "I'm tired and I'm tired of always having to explain myself to people. But what I'm most tired of is fighting," Red scrawls on blue-lined paper pulled from one of her notebooks. "We go to a place like OSU and have to fight off the crowds, the officials and the other team. I don't think we need to fight off our own coaching staff." Remembering how Jody yelled at her from the sidelines, Red writes: "I don't need to be humiliated from the bench."

She also lights into the coach for saying negative things about the team to the press. "You make your players look horrible. We never say anything against the coaches. We're professional." Red really lets Jody have it at the end, calling her way of dealing with the players "the abuse method." Then she writes something no one else on the team would ever dare write, even if they dared think it: "I would like to ask you to look inside yourself and see if you are being the coach you want to be coached by. Are you your own role model or have you turned into something other than what you started out to be?"

Jody has grown accustomed to Red's attitude. She continues to be bothered but is no longer startled by Red's temerity. The kid will say anything to anybody. But the vehemence and anger of this response take her by surprise. It is not that she is overly concerned with how Red perceives her. Jody is who she needs to be to get the job done. If she's tough, if she yells, if she doesn't cut them much slack, that's the kind of coach she is—and wants to be. Red's opinion changes nothing. But this latest essay makes Jody realize that she's got more of a problem on her hands than she thought. She is beginning to fear that the player on whom the long-term future of the team depends is becoming uncoachable.

Down the hall from the suite that houses the women's basketball staff is the small, windowless, but somehow still cheerful office of Karen Nelson, sports psychologist. Karen has made a career out of helping collegiate athletes come to grips with everything from injuries to body image, slumps to homesickness, dating problems to sexual identity. Sometimes athletes seek her out; other times coaches send their troubled players her way. This time, a coach seeks her out.

Jody doesn't know what to do about Red. What works with the others—from screaming to alternately withholding or bestowing approval—doesn't work with her because Red isn't as vulnerable as the others. It comes off as arrogance, but Jody thinks it is really lack of vulnerability. Maybe Red's skin grew a little too thick when her parents divorced; maybe she was just born without a vulnerability gene. Jody has thought a lot about what makes Red tick. She hasn't figured out much, but she has figured out that somewhere along the line, Red learned not to defer to authority, whether it be her mother's, her teachers' or her coaches'.

The two have been waging a mostly silent war all season long. Jody would probably have let it go on this way—both because she didn't know how to stop it and because she had

other worries—but now Red's attitude is affecting more than
Jody's blood pressure. It's affecting the team. So Jody walks
down the hall to Karen Nelson's office. Maybe Karen will
know what to do about Red.

Karen does. It's Karen's commonsense philosophy to approach people from where they are, not where you wish they
would be. Jody wants Red to be more of a team player; Karen
understands that. Jody wants Red to be motivated by the same
techniques that motivate the rest of the players; Karen understands that. But what about Red? she asks Jody. What does
she want?

Jody has never thought of it that way. It takes her a
minute to respond. "Red always knows how many points
she's scored, how many rebounds she has," Jody tells Karen.
"She keeps a mental tally, and if she's doing well in the
stats, she's happy with her game."

"But you're not?" Karen asks.

"Those stats have nothing to do with defense, with how
much help she's giving to the other players, with her position
on the floor. That's where she's letting everyone down," Jody
says. "I just can't get her to see that."

Karen understands immediately. She was once a girls'
high school basketball coach. She smiles. This is an easy one.

"Okay," she tells Jody, "let's not try to change the fact
that she pays attention to her statistics. Let's not try to make
her feel guilty about being selfish. Let's work with how she
views the game." Jody listens carefully. "How about if we
create new statistical categories for Red?" Karen asks. "Like
how many times she gets in front of the post. Like boxing
out even if she doesn't personally get the rebound. Let her
pay attention to stats all she wants—just expand the categories."

That sounds good to Jody. In fact, it sounds brilliant.
She calls Red that afternoon to arrange for a conference the
next day.

Red comes prepared for confrontation. She's proud of
herself for writing that last sentence about Jody not being a

good role model, but she's a little scared too. Red speaks—
or in this case, writes—first, then thinks through the impli-
cations later. Now, a few days after writing the letter, she is
just beginning to realize how brash she has been, even for
her. Another kid might be contrite or repentant or maybe
subdued.

Not Red. She figures she started this, she might as well
finish it. She strides into Jody's office, ready for battle. The
best defense is a good offense. Jody lets her blow off steam
first. Red needs to say again how much she hated it in the
OSU game when she was yelled at from the bench, first by
Jody, then by the assistant coaches who ragged on her for
missing free throws. She needs to tell Jody again that she feels
picked on, singled out, held to a higher standard than the other
sophomores. Jody lets her go on for a while. It's nothing new,
nothing she hasn't heard before a half dozen times, but she
knows Red needs to say it.

Then it's Jody's turn. What she says takes Red by surprise. "You and I are very different, Red," she says; "that's
why we don't get along." Actually it's probably because Red
and Jody are so much alike that they don't get along: two
stubborn, outspoken, self-assured women with something to
prove. But Jody doesn't see it that way. "I realize that what
motivates me doesn't motivate you."

That gets Red's attention. She's told Jody every way
she's known how that yelling and getting tough don't make
her play harder.

"I know you're different, not just from me but from the
other girls, and I'm not gonna try to put a square peg in a
round hole."

Red is sitting there wondering whether she's being insulted. But Jody says quickly, "It's okay to be different, but
we've got to make this work." So Jody tells Red about the
statistics idea, about Red keeping mental count of some new
categories that cannot be found in the box scores.

At first, Red balks. She tries to persuade Jody that she
really isn't motivated by statistics. She thinks this is Jody's

way of saying that she's a selfish player—which, in fact, it is. They go back and forth about this for a while. But when Jody starts saying nice things about Red, how she thinks Red could be an all-American if she learned to round out her game, Red calms down. She agrees to try the statistics thing. She agrees that she has to work hard these last eight games. She leaves the office smiling. It is the first time since she can't remember when that she hasn't been angry with her coach.

To Jody, it feels as if the barrier between her and Red is beginning to crumble a little at the edges. It is a barrier that has short-circuited communication and blocked mutual respect. It's made for two angry women who waste energy blaming one another. Maybe a truce is in the air. Jody feels buoyed at the thought. But maybe it's that she feels buoyed in general. On the long windowsill in her office sits an impressive bouquet of long-stemmed yellow roses.

It's Valentine's Day, and Jody has a boyfriend.

It is all David the hairdresser's doing. David takes it as a personal challenge that Jody says to him one day while he's combing her out: "There just aren't any good men in this town." So David has been on the lookout.

It turns out that one of his clients has just broken up with her boyfriend, a mid-thirties businessman, and, as luck would have it, a women's basketball fan. David knows the ex-boyfriend—there aren't many people in town David doesn't know—and when he sees him a few days later, he casually brings up the subject of Jody Runge. The ex-boyfriend is more than a little interested. Yes, he tells David, he would love to meet Jody. David takes him to one of the home games, then briefs Jody by phone before the guy calls for a date. As it happens, he calls at an opportune moment, a week when the team has only one game, no road trips. Jody says yes. Her policy of not dating frivolously is fine, theoretically, but makes for long, lonely weekends. She has been lonely for a long time. She's delighted that a man has seen her in action, seen her screaming and pacing and cursing, and still wants to take her to lunch.

Lunch is good. Next is a movie. Then a men's basketball game. Then a dinner party. Then watching game films in Jody's living room on a Sunday afternoon. This is all in a week and a half.

He treats Jody like a rare specimen. At the men's basketball game, sitting beside her in the bleachers, he studies the distance between her hip and her knee. "Your legs are so long," he marvels. Another time, looking down at her elegant hands, he says: "Wow, look at those fingers. They're so long."

This man is a mere six feet to Jody's six-three, and he has what she thinks of as "this height thing." She's waiting to see if he'll grow out of it. She's also waiting to see how he will feel about her once the novelty wears off. Right now, he is in the throes of astonishment. He can't believe that this fierce, aggressive, loudmouthed woman he sees on the sidelines going mano a mano with the officials is the same woman he's dating. With him she is charming. She laughs. She cooks dinner. He thinks of this as his little secret.

The girls have more than a week to mentally recover from the OSU defeat, and they need it. They need to put the memory of that game behind them and concentrate on the eight games that remain. There is no talk of winning the Pac-10 anymore, of course. There is not even talk of placing as high in the conference as last year's team did—third. But there is still talk about going to the tournament.

In the world of collegiate basketball, success is measured by whether a team is invited to the NCAA tournament. Then it is measured by how many consecutive years a team is invited to the tournament. Finally, among the privileged programs, success is measured by how far a team goes in the tournament: first round, second round, regionals, Elite Eight, Final Four, the championship.

Going to the tournament is more than a goal for a particular team during a particular season, more than the rallying cry for a group of twenty-year-olds in sweaty jerseys. It is how a team is identified and identifies itself. It is how programs are built and sustained, one success mortared on another, a good recruiting year following a good showing at the tournament. It is how coaches are measured—and recompensed. It is how programs are viewed by their own athletic departments and the university administrations that fund them. Jody's future at Oregon—the kind of future she wants: a high-profile, well-paid future—depends on her success in winning enough games to get an invitation to the tournament this year.

Going to the tournament . . . going to the tournament. It is a litany; it is a mantra; it is a prayer. At this point, with a 12–7 overall record and five wins and five losses in conference play, tournament hopes are just that. Each defeat dims the hope. But there are many games left to play, and if the Ducks can recapture some of that confidence, some of the ebullience that marked their play back in December and early January, the season might end well. Ending well means winning enough games to be invited to the tournament. For Oregon, eighteen wins would secure a berth. Anything less would be iffy. That means winning six of the final eight games.

Jody has the team practice hard most of the week. It begins as a punishment for losing to Oregon State, but as she slowly works herself out of that state of mind, the practices become more productive and less punitive. She has private talks with Red and Eddie, wishing she could perform a confidence-transplant operation on Eddie with Red as the donor. She brings in Jess to try to talk about her shooting slump. She works on Cicely, trying to make her feel part of the team. Cicely is lonely and unhappy and is not doing herself or the team much good. Her brief moment of feeling accepted when she sank her first Pac-10 basket has only served to bring into sharper focus her usual state of isolation.

By the time Thursday rolls around again, a week past the OSU game, Jody is feeling pretty good. She sits behind her big desk checking the itinerary for the team's Washington road trip. Everything seems squared away, she thinks. We're back on track.

A few miles away, in the small house that Sally, Roy and Cicely share, Sally is not so sure. From where she sits, morale looks to be at an all-time low. The team has lost four of the last five games. The grueling OSU game followed by a grueling week of practice has done nothing to ease her bone weariness or dull her homesickness. But she is willing to push past this. For the sake of the team, she is willing to be the spark plug.

But she feels caught between assuming a bigger leadership role and stepping on Jess's toes. More than ever, she feels the precariousness of her position: a foreign player, a student-athlete who really isn't a student, a late arrival who will soon depart and never return. She knows, and she knows the rest of the girls know, that her investment in the team can never match theirs. But still, she wonders if she should take the initiative and suggest a player meeting on the road, a time for the girls to fire each other up without the coach. She likes the idea, but she's worried that she's not the right person to do it.

The road trip begins auspiciously when, on Friday night, Oregon beats Washington State by six points. It's not a great win. Washington State is several notches below Oregon in the Pac-10 standings, so it's no great proof of an Oregon comeback. And it's a narrow win, a sloppy win with too many turnovers and too few free throws going in. With a good share of the turnovers being Eddie's, the game is hardly a confidence builder for her. But a win is a win, and it's certainly better to be heading to Seattle with a victory.

The University of Washington Huskies, second in the Pac-10 and tenth in the nation, are ready for the Ducks. This is what's known as payback time. Less than a month ago, in

Mac Court, the Huskies were embarrassed by a big loss to the Ducks. Now, on their home court with the support of more than six thousand fans who slosh through a deluge that, even by the Northwest's soggy standards, is impressive, the UW team looks tough.

"I'm watching them warm up, and they look nervous," Jody tells the team in the locker room before game time. This is a lie. The UW team looks confident. The players all have their game faces on. Their warm-up has gone smoothly. But Jody knows she has to build confidence here, and one of the best ways to do that is to pick at the other team.

"They have to win this one here at home. The pressure is all on them, and they're scared." It sounds good. It's plausible. But it's just not true. The Ducks know it too. They sit quietly on the locker-room benches, their faces solemn, their eyes averted. Jody sees this is getting her nowhere. She tries a new tack.

"I don't know about you, but I think this would be the sweetest win of the season." She lets them think about that for a second. "You know, they've been popping off for a month now." Her voice changes to a mocking singsong: " 'Just wait until they come back up here, just wait, we're gonna blast 'em.' " Her voice returns to its strident, before-game tone. "Well, ladies, we're here. Now let's go out and do something about it."

They are subdued as they walk down the passageway from the visitors' locker room to the court. Jess walks alone, looking fierce, looking like someone you wouldn't want to run into a dark alley. Red looks all business. Sally is whispering to Eddie, talking strategy, pumping her up, helping her focus on the game rather than her insecurities. The players' meeting that Sal had envisioned hasn't happened, partly because of the numbing eat-sleep-practice routine of a road trip, partly because she just didn't know how to take the initiative.

But she can at least talk with Eddie. Eddie needs it. On top of her usual lack of self-confidence, Eddie feels more than usual pressure to perform well during this game. In the stands

of Hec Edmundson Pavilion sit twenty-five family members
and friends who have driven almost four hundred miles from
Kamloops, British Columbia, to see her play.

The girls are immediately heartened when they come out
on the court. Although Seattle is a solid five-and-a-half-hour
freeway drive from Eugene, hundreds of Duck fans have made
the trip. The stands closest to the Ducks' bench are filled with
people in bright green sweatshirts waving yellow pom-poms.
As the players are introduced, one by one, fans hold up huge
homemade signs: RUNGE'S ROWDIES says one. RED'S HOT 'N
ROLLIN' says another. Sally's sign reads OREGON HAS SOME-
THING TO CROWE ABOUT. Jess's says SHOOT JESSICA SCHUTT.

On the court, the Ducks slowly play their way into the
game. It's like this on the road all the time. Jody wants them
to come out with both barrels blasting, but they are just not
that kind of team. They play cautious and tight for the first
five minutes, getting used to the court, getting used to the
Washington lineup, seeing what works. In the far court, in the
midst of some defensive move, Sally rolls her ankle, the same
one that gave her trouble a few weeks back, and limps upcourt, wincing. Jody doesn't see it. But the new trainer, Kim's
replacement, does.

"Sal's hurt," Moira says, rushing up to Jody, catching
her in midstride as she paces the sidelines. "We've got to get
her out of there."

"Shit," Jody says under her breath. Sal comes out. She
too is cursing. The ankle hurts, but she wants to be playing.
The last time she played Washington was the last time she
felt completely happy. She wants to feel that way again. On
the bench, she takes off her shoe, unlaces her ankle support
and strips off her sock. The trainer retapes the ankle, giving
it more side support. Sal is impatient with all the fussing.

"I'm ready. I wanna go back in," she tells Jody.

Out on the court, the Ducks are down by three. Eddie
has scored her first basket, an icebreaker that helps her self-
confidence. But then, under the Duck basket, she makes a bad
pass.

"Jeezus, Eddie, look . . . will ya!" Joe, the assistant coach, yells from the bench. Eddie doesn't hear him. She is sprinting down the court ahead of everyone, including the Husky player who stole the ball. The player comes loping down and Eddie, composed and in position, bats the ball away from her. It's another steal. Eddie races back to the Duck basket and puts it in. Oregon is one point down.

Jess scores, then Eddie penetrates for another layup, putting the Ducks ahead by three. It is Oregon's largest lead of the half, but the Ducks can't maintain it. By the buzzer, they are down by four. Eddie, with eight points, is the team's high scorer, a position she has never been in before. But she also has four turnovers already and, of course, it's the turnovers, not the points she thinks about as the team heads to the locker room.

Jody is as calm as anyone has ever seen her at halftime. They haven't yet figured out that she is calm when she thinks they are playing hard, regardless of whether they are winning. She praises the players for a great effort.

"We're ready to go. We just have to go out there and battle them," she says. There is very little emotion in her voice. She holds herself very still. It's as if she doesn't want to do anything that will change the players' state of mind. They have played a good half. Washington, with its national ranking and its home-court advantage, expected to blow out the downwardly mobile Ducks, the team that lost four of its last six games.

But Oregon hasn't let that happen. Jody is allowing herself to think that the Ducks can win this one, that finally this will be the game the team comes from behind to win. It looks more possible now than she could have imagined twenty minutes ago.

Joe, who never predicts anything, says softly to Steph, "We got 'em. It'll be a fight, but we got 'em."

The Ducks come out and immediately go on a six-point run, recapturing the lead. Jess goes on a shooting spree, hitting a layup, a three-pointer and four free throws in the first three and a half minutes of play. She is somehow managing to get herself fouled by just about everyone on the Washington team. Each time she goes to the line, cool and expressionless, like she hasn't been in the worst shooting slump of her career, she makes it. But the Ducks can't seem to keep the lead. Roy is not having a great shooting night and neither is Red. They aren't blowing it; they just haven't caught fire. The Huskies have adjusted their defense so that Eddie can no longer penetrate the way she did in the first half. She is scoreless. The subs off the Washington bench contribute thirty-three points while giving the starters a rest. Once again, there is no bench for Jody to go to. Her starters are beginning to tire. Nothing big is going wrong for the Ducks; they are just being outplayed.

Still, with three minutes left to play, the Ducks are down by only six points. Steph and Joe are perched on their seats, leaning forward, alternately yelling plays and screaming at the officials. Joe especially is going nuts tonight. He leaps from his seat after what looks to him like a terrible call. His hands are so sweaty that his clipboard slips through them and clatters to the floor. The top pages where he keeps track of fouls and shots for Jody are soaked through. The ink is smeared. The crack of the clipboard hitting the floor startles a young campus cop sitting by the timekeepers' desk to the right of the Oregon bench. Each time Joe explodes, the cop looks over at him uneasily. The cop's left hand seeks out his baton and grabs hold of it. He almost gets up, but thinks better of it. He reminds himself that he's there to control the crowd, not the coaches. Still, all through the rest of the game, he keeps one eye on Joe.

On the sidelines, Jody is concentrating her efforts on the officials. There has yet to be a game—whether Oregon has won or lost—that she has thought the officials did their job. The way she sees it tonight, these three officials are costing her the game. When it's this close, every call, missed or made, counts. A questionable foul on Roy, her fourth, means she takes fewer risks, and the Oregon defense suffers inside. A change of possession that leaves everyone on the floor, both teams, mystified, translates into a four-point advantage for Washington.

Maybe it's the officiating. Maybe it's the home-court advantage. Maybe it's just that nine points up with only two minutes to go, the Huskies smell blood. Oregon keeps fighting, whittling the difference to five with a basket by Sally and two more free throws by Jess—she's 100 percent tonight, fourteen of fourteen—but time runs out. Washington wins 85–78.

"You have nothing to be ashamed of," Jody tells them in the locker room. "You played tough." But tough or not, the Ducks go back to Eugene with another loss. Their record in the Pac-10 is 6–6. Only six games remain. If they don't win five of them, they will not go to the tournament.

SOMETHING TO FIGHT FOR

TWO DAYS AFTER THE TEAM RETURNS FROM SEATTLE, JODY is sitting in a quiet little restaurant near campus lunching with the president, the athletic director and the wealthy woman they are trying to court. The potential donor is a sixtyish businesswoman whose husband's family made its fortune in logging back when it was possible for families to do that. A stout, square-shouldered, plainly dressed woman, she looks to Jody less like a benefactress and more like one of her Iowa aunts. There is nothing about the woman that says money except what's parked curbside: a sleek new Mercedes.

Jody has been waiting a long time for this meeting. The endowment idea has been the only solution proposed to her salary concerns and the other equity problems in the program. This woman is the sole prospect. Jody isn't nervous—she is too much of a public creature for that, long accustomed to making a good impression in front of strangers, from Rotarians to sportswriters to the parents of high school recruits— but this afternoon she is particularly careful when she chooses her words. She knows how important it is for this woman to like her.

Jody talks about the program, about the future of women's basketball, about what she wants to do at Oregon. She's said it all before, to Dave, to Dan Williams, to anyone who will listen, but because she believes in it so fervently, it comes out fresh, spirited, energetic. She is a good saleswoman. The older woman listens. She is silent but Jody thinks she looks interested. The talk turns to promotion of the program. You should advertise in the men's basketball media guide, the older woman suggests. You should coattail on the men's success in attracting fans, get after their fan base.

Jody hides a wince. Women's basketball has its own strengths, its own fans, its own future. It is not a future Jody sees tied to the success, or failure, of the men's program. She understands immediately that the older woman doesn't see women's basketball in this new light, that in all these months no one has presented that vision, no one has planted an agenda in her mind. The conversation continues, low-key, in no particular direction. Jody leaves satisfied that she has made her case but sorely disappointed that it wasn't made months ago, that the seeds were not sown much earlier.

She is glad the meeting finally took place, but it is hard for her to imagine that anything will come of it, that a million-dollar check is in the mail, that a single act of generosity will solve her problems. It is hard for her to imagine that anything short of her own success leavened with her lawyer's threats will get her what she wants. She drives back to the Cas Center thinking not of the endowment but of winning basketball games, of Thursday night's game against Arizona State and Saturday's game against Arizona.

Oregon finds itself in the unenviable position of having to win both Arizona games but, assuming this is accomplished, not being able to take pride in the wins. In fact, the bigger the wins, the harsher the criticism is likely to be. Jody can imagine the sportswriters making hay of this in their col-

umns, taking Oregon to task yet again for the embarrassing
losses in the desert last month, losses made to seem even more
egregious should Oregon win these home games decisively.
These are games Jody is not looking forward to.

The players see it more myopically. Weaned on the rhetoric of competitive athletics, they are looking for "revenge."
They are in high spirits this Thursday evening in late February. It has been a soft, breezy surprise spring day. Midterms
are over. They can see the end of the season. They are ready
to play.

Jody, in her three-inch black pumps—the ones that leave
her feet throbbing at the end of a game, the ones she chooses
when being six-foot-three is just not enough—is ready to
coach. She is dressed impeccably, as usual, hair coifed, as
usual, by David. Standing in front of the locker room, chin
high, one hand on a slim hip, she looks momentarily like a
model poised for a photo shoot. Then she drops her chin and
surveys the troops with a cold eye.

"Don't be out there dicking around," she tells the girls
sternly.

From the tip-off, which Roy gets, batting it to Sally, who
puts in an easy layup, the game is never in doubt. Roy steals
the ball four times in the first half; Red and B each score
twelve points. The Ducks open up a twenty-point lead with
two minutes left in the half. They do it without Eddie and
Jess, neither of whom is playing well tonight.

Eddie rips down the court and passes to no one, an un-
forced turnover that makes her blush. Later, she has a clear
shot but passes instead. It costs the Ducks the possession. Jody
pulls her out. It kills Eddie to see that everything is working
fine without her. In fact, everything is working better. She sits
on the bench berating herself until Jody sends her in again.
She needs to do something to get in the game: a steal, a fast
break, anything. Finally, she makes a shot. But it is the only
shot she makes all night.

Jess is also struggling. She turns over the ball on a bad
pass and gets a foul early on. Jody pulls her out immediately,

substituting B. There will be no mistakes tonight. When she goes back in, she can't seem to connect. She's zero for four from the field, including two three-point misses. She's had a week of good, tough practices. She's stayed late working on her shot. She doesn't know what else to do. She tries to buoy herself with the memory of her perfect fourteen for fourteen from the free throw line against Washington last week. She tries to put energy into her defensive game. But mostly, she sits on the bench and watches B take command of her position as she plays her way into the "B-zone" again, the place where every shot falls. B racks up twenty-four points in less than thirty minutes of play.

Despite Eddie and Jess, Oregon effortlessly increases its lead to thirty points and holds it there. Jody starts subbing deep from the bench. There are more than fifteen minutes left to the second half. Her chest tightens when she does it, putting in first Timmy, then Cicely, then the others. She doesn't trust them; she doesn't know what will happen out there. But she figures with a thirty-point lead, she's got enough of a buffer. She knows it won't be a repeat of the last time she did this down at Arizona State, when the bench blew a thirteen-point lead and cost the team the game. Still, she's nervous when she pulls out Red and Sal, then Eddie and Roy, careful to leave at least one starter on the court until the game is almost over.

The bench holds on. Cicely makes six points, grabs four rebounds and finally seems to know what plays are being run. Tonight she is playing basketball the way Jody envisioned her playing back when she was recruited. Cicely looks focused and in control, using her speed rather than letting it over-whelm her or bowl over her own teammates. Jody thinks Cicely may have turned a corner.

It's not that Cicely has all of a sudden metamorphosed into a gregarious, high-spirited young woman who mixes it up and makes friends easily. But she has gone outside the team to find friends, hooking up with a group of Christian athletes who share some of her values. Cicely has made some friends among this group and that's bolstered her self-confidence. She seems more relaxed, more able to handle the stress of coming off the bench, more able to tolerate the loneliness of still not having made a friend on the team. Jody isn't sure if it's the new group she's in or just the passage of time. But whatever accounts for the change in Cicely, Jody is happy to see it. She watches her lead the second-string players as they widen the margin of victory to thirty-nine points.

In the locker room, Jody lets them have a moment of revelry.

"Great bench," she says, smiling.

Then she sits on the couch, slips off her black pumps and rubs her stocking feet together. She watches the girls congratulate each other. She sinks back into the couch for a moment and shakes her head.

"Okay, so now everyone in the free world is wondering how we ever lost to those guys," she says. Her voice is purposefully low. Only Steph, standing next to her, hears.

Sure enough, in the newspaper the next morning, the story about Oregon's victory begins: "Even the neighborhood rocket scientist was hard-pressed to understand how Oregon could have lost to the Sun Devils a month ago." Jody reads the story standing at the counter at Starbucks, sipping a latte and suppressing a groan.

Later that day, after practice, Jody walks up behind Jess, who is standing on the sidelines drinking water from a paper cup. Jess's hair is matted to her scalp, as wet as if she had just washed it. There are twin rivulets of sweat running from her temples to her jawline. It has been a tough practice. Jody taps Jess on the shoulder. "I'm starting B tomorrow night, so don't get in a tink about it," she says. Then she walks away.

Jess is so angry she is almost breathless. She has just finished a good practice. She is working hard. She has been telling herself that she'd only played thirteen minutes against Arizona State last night because Oregon was winning so decisively that Jody wanted the bench to get some minutes. After all, most of the other starters played less than twenty minutes. But really she'd played the thirteen minutes because Jody wanted her out of there, because Jody thought she was playing so poorly she was bringing down the team. Jess hasn't figured this out. Her pride would never allow her to see it this way. She knows B had a good game. All right, B had a great game. But as the senior, as the veteran, Jess expects to be in the starting lineup. That's the way the game is played.

Jess doesn't know which makes her angrier, what the coach just told her or how she said it. Ever since the road trip to the desert last month and that speech about being selfish, there's been a wall between Jess and Jody. Jody is out of patience waiting for Jess's shooting problems to end. What started as "everyone has a bad game" and deepened into a slump has now become a permanent nosedive. Most times she thinks Jess just isn't trying hard enough. Sometimes, because Jess is so silent, so stone-faced, Jody thinks Jess doesn't care. The coach knows that starting B tomorrow night is a slap in Jess's face. But maybe, thinks Jody, the slap will wake her up. Jody doesn't know that this isn't how Jess operates because she doesn't know Jess. Jess doesn't know Jody is just trying to motivate her because she doesn't know how Jody operates.

Jess steadies herself and approaches Jody, who is walking off the court. "Why is B starting?" she asks, keeping her voice level.

"I'm rewarding her for having such a good game," says Jody, starting to walk away.

"You mean this is about *one* game?" Jess asks. She struggles to keep her voice down. She stands there looking up at Jody and feeling herself get emotional. That's how she thinks of it: I'm getting emotional. "Getting emotional" is the woman athlete code phrase for crying. Jess makes her face expressionless and carefully clears her throat. "Okay," she says. "I just wanted to know." She walks away dry-eyed and as angry as she's ever been in her life.

Jess'll just have to suck it up, Jody thinks to herself.

The next night, the night of the University of Arizona game, Jess's anger is a banked fire. She sits on the couch in the locker room staring straight ahead as the others trade jokes. None of the other starters know yet that Jess won't be in the opening lineup. They learn it for the first time when they look up at the board where Jody has written the match-ups. There's B's name, sandwiched between Sally's and Red's, where Jess's name usually is. The players stare at the board for a long moment. No one looks over at Jess.

Jess is glad to be ignored. The worst thing right now would be if she thought anyone felt sorry for her. She couldn't handle that. Her face is a mask. Better that they think I've got a heart of stone, Jess says to herself. She looks down at the carpet and half listens to Jody's pep talk, which concentrates on how much the University of Arizona wants to win this game.

"This is their last chance to go to the NCAA," Jody says, trying to fire up the players. "If they can win this game, they've got a chance. If they lose, that's it for them. So they're gonna be pumped."

The girls are getting restless. Eddie is shifting a basketball back and forth in her lap; Red is playing with her mouth guard, propelling it out of her mouth with her tongue, then whipping it back in by grabbing on with her teeth. B is standing in the back stretching; Sal and Roy are lacing their sneakers. Only Jess is motionless.

"Okay, ladies," Jody says, "let's go out and take care of it like we did the night before last."

Of course, it isn't that easy: Arizona is a much stronger team than Arizona State and has something important at stake tonight. The Ducks will have to play better than they did Thursday night.

Red comes out tough, grabbing rebounds, planting her

feet, swiveling her torso with elbows out until she's cleared a space around herself. It's the most aggressive, most territorial move she has, and it works: She not only gets the ball, she also intimidates. In that split second when the Arizona defenders back off a half step, maybe daunted by Red's power, maybe grazed by an elbow, she muscles in for the basket. No other player on this team moves with such force.

B gets inside for two baskets, then hits a three-pointer, then an outside jumper; Roy shoots four for five from the floor. Oregon pulls ahead by fifteen. This is just what Jody likes, aggressive first-half play, a big early lead. But before she has time to feel confident, Arizona comes back with an eight-point run to bring the halftime score to 39–32.

Seven points, thinks Jody, as she stalks down to the locker room, disgusted. Seven points. That's very much a ball game. Arizona is still in it. That's not what Jody wants. She wants a nice, fat thirty-point lead at halftime. It's the same old story, she thinks. They get ahead by a few points, then relax, get lazy. The defense falls apart. She spends all of half-time walking them through the defense, anger in check. But just barely. She doesn't tell them what's uppermost on her mind: A loss tonight will mean the only way Oregon can get to the NCAA tournament is by beating Stanford in Palo Alto next week. In other words, a loss tonight means no invitation to the Big Dance.

In the second half, Eddie catches fire. It's odd how this happens, how a player can be flat for half a game and then suddenly turn it on, interesting how physical skill is sometimes so much less important than mental attitude. When Eddie digs deep and finds that place in herself that knows and trusts her abilities, she plays like a winner. Every basket she makes gives her permission to go for another. Every steal makes her more aggressive. There are long moments when she is perfectly attuned to the game, when her pace and the game's pace are indistinguishable. She senses rather than sees a pass, plucking it from the air even as she looks the other way. She is in control without making a big show of it the way some other point guards do. She is quick and graceful and unrelenting. Jody watches her for a long moment. This is how Eddie can play, she thinks. If only she could get the girl to see how good she is when she plays like this, to believe wholeheartedly in her own talent. Jody figures it's going to take more time. She wishes she could have Eddie full power every game right now, but she knows that's not yet possible. Maybe next year, when she's a junior. Maybe the year after. It will happen. Jody knows it.

Jess, though, is out of time. She desperately needs a good game but isn't having one. For a while after she came back from her injury, she expected her shot would return, and she put the ball up each time with optimism. Now, as the ball leaves her hand, she expects a miss. She sees a miss before it happens, like how sometimes a bowler can see clearly just how the pins will fall while the ball is still gliding down the alley.

"Off," Jess says aloud as the ball leaves her hand. Most times she's right. The shot is off. Tonight she's right six out of eight times. But tonight the team doesn't need Jess. B, Red, Roy, Eddie and Sal all score in the double digits, Red leading with fifteen points and ten rebounds. Playing better defense, the Ducks pull away and win decisively, 73–55.

Jody walks off the court, relieved. Another one down, another step closer to the tournament. She doesn't take a moment to enjoy the win. She can't help herself: Before she is out of the arena, before the band stops playing the Oregon fight song, she is already thinking of next week's road trip— Cal and Stanford. Gotta beat Cal.

There is waking at 6 A.M. on dark, rainy Saturday mornings to sweat while the world sleeps. There is sitting on hard benches in drafty basement locker rooms listening to the coach scream at you. And then there is hopping a flight to San Francisco, where you are met by a chartered bus and whisked to the Berkeley Marina Marriott, a sprawling complex that hugs the shores of the bay, where the air smells of eucalyptus and escallonia, where out your window across the piers and the yachts and the houseboats, across the choppy, iron gray water, you can see the Golden Gate and the city skyline, the distant buildings soft and silvery, almost luminescent. This is as close as it gets to payoff time for women who play basketball.

It is the final road trip. The team will play the University of California, Berkeley, tonight and Stanford Saturday. A few hours before game time Thursday afternoon, Jody is out jogging around the marina. She is in decent spirits, but she's nervous. There are just four more games to the season, and the Ducks must win three of them to earn an NCAA tournament berth. She is prepared to lose to the virtually unstoppable Stanford, but losing to anyone else will cost the team, not just in win-loss statistics but in the "power rankings" that determine which teams make the tournament.

These rankings factor in the strength of the opponent (more points are awarded for beating a nationally ranked team or a team higher than yours in the conference than for winning against a less worthy opponent), the size of the win (the bigger the point spread the better) and the location (winning on the road is more impressive than winning at home). When the Ducks beat Oregon State and the University of Washington, those wins boosted the power rankings, although wins on the road would have been better. But when the Ducks beat Arizona State, the worst team in the Pac-10, in a home game, the win didn't do anything for Oregon's stature. If the team loses to Berkeley tonight, a team below the Ducks in the Pac-10, the damage will be irreparable.

Jody tries to jog away the jitters. She goes out with Moira, the new trainer, but soon leaves her a quarter of a mile behind. Jody's stride is too long to run with a partner. It's best for her to run by herself anyway. She doesn't want to talk; she wants to think. She goes through the roster in her mind.

She figures she's pretty squared away with Red. Their relationship is not free and easy but at least Red is no longer looking daggers at her. Red is playing well, and Jody is trying to stay off her back. The combination seems to be working. Jody isn't worried about Eddie, who is playing with increasing confidence and even when she doesn't play well, still works harder than anyone else on the team. Sal and Roy—thank God for them—are rocks. It is once more Jess who concerns her this afternoon. Jody has decided not to start Jess again tonight. She thinks it's the right decision for the team—Jess is not shooting well, B is—but she feels guilty about it anyway. This is Jess's last road trip, her final four Pac-10 games. Jody knows that. But she also knows that it is her job to win.

Jess, meanwhile, is up in the hotel room stewing, still angry, not just about losing her starting position but about how she lost it and what she sees as Jody's coldheartedness. She still doesn't understand why she was yanked from the spot. Why not just give B more playing time to reward her for doing well? She's got two more years to play. It's not that Jess is angry at B, or even jealous. She's glad the girl is playing well. It's the coach she'd like to throttle. Up in her room, stuffing her gear in her game bag, Jess feels as vulnerable as a freshman coming off the bench.

In the locker room at Berkeley, Jody launches into her pregame talk, the object of which is to make sure the girls take this game seriously, even though they beat Cal by eighteen points the last time the two teams met.

"Look," she says finally, searching for what will ignite the team tonight, "we cannot lose this game and go to the tournament." She sighs audibly. "Does everyone want to go to the tournament?" The room is silent. Maybe they've heard this too many times. Maybe they don't understand this isn't a rhetorical question. She asks it again, louder.

"Yeah." Sally breaks the silence. The others chime in until there is a chorus of yeses.

"All right, then," says Jody, sternly. "Go out there and take care of business."

Oregon plays a fits-and-starts game at first, surging ahead

by four, six, even as many as twelve points, before relaxing on defense and letting Cal get back in the game. Twice in the first five minutes, Cal comes back to tie the score. But the Ducks wake up, start to play again and pull away. Eight minutes into the game, Jody signals Jess to sub for B, who is not having a particularly good night. Jess stands up, takes a deep breath, pulls her ponytail tighter and checks in at the timekeeper's desk. Here she is, a senior starter coming off the bench having to prove herself like some new recruit. She has felt so much pressure this year that she's almost numb to it. Her face shows nothing. She stares that wide-eyed stare of hers, an almost blind stare, and jogs onto the court.

A minute later, on an inside pass from Sandie, Jess sinks one. It's not her usual shot, just some little lob she popped in, so she doesn't give herself much credit for it. Next time down the court, Jess puts another one in, an off-kilter shot from inside the key, something she just pushed up on a prayer when a Cal player banged her arm. She doesn't take credit for that one either. That one was luck. But the next one is a good one, a drive past a defender that ends in a sweet little jumper from the right side. When her feet touch down after the jump, she pushes off again. It is, literally, a jump for joy. She hits four of five and suddenly the world is a friendly place again.

At halftime, the Ducks are up by twelve, but Jody doesn't like how Cal has managed to come back two or three times to tighten the margin.

"We need to put them away, ladies," she tells them in the locker room. "Let's not make this into any more of a game than it has to be."

Despite the warning, the Ducks let Cal come back early in the second half, whittling the lead to five before Jess sinks her first three-pointer. She goes on to make two great passes, two assists, and then sink another three-point basket. She is remembering how it used to feel—it seems like so long ago— when playing was a pleasure. When she gets the ball again in three-point position and first looks to pass, Sal yells, "Shoot, Jess, shoot!" That makes Jess feel the best she's felt in a long time. To be trusted, to be counted on, that's what she's missed. She's grateful to Sally for that. Jess takes the shot. She buries it.

With Jess, Red and Roy all having great nights, the Ducks are solidly ahead now, and it's clear to everyone on both teams, as time passes and the lead stabilizes at sixteen to eighteen, that Oregon will win. But that doesn't stop Jody from calling an angry time-out when the Ducks' defense gets sloppy. She squats on her haunches in front of the bench where the starters sit mopping their faces and squirting water into their mouths.

"They're goddamn midgets out there!" she screams, neck veins popping. The crowd is small and quiet, only seven hundred people in the stands. Women's basketball is not big in Berkeley. Jody's voice carries far. Two rows behind the bench sits a sweet-faced junior college girl who just announced her intention to play for Oregon next year. She stares at Jody, transfixed. She has never seen anything like this before. She gulps.

Out on the floor, with five minutes left and Oregon ahead by fifteen, Jody starts putting in the subs. With one minute left, she takes out Jess, who has scored seventeen points, including three three-pointers and has played all but the first eight minutes of the game. As Jess passes by Jody, the coach extends her hand to be slapped. Other coaches do this routinely. Jody rarely does. For a second, Jess is so surprised that she doesn't respond. Then she slaps the coach's hand and walks on by to find a seat on the bench. Jody pivots and follows her down the line, placing a hand on her shoulder.

"Way to fight back for your position, Jess," she says.

Jess knows this is supposed to make her feel good, but it doesn't. It isn't like she needed the coach to threaten her like this for her to play well. Or is it? She doesn't know. She just knows she's back in the lineup and will start against Stanford Saturday night. She sits down and blots her sweaty face with a clean towel. The subs are doing fine. Oregon wins it by sixteen.

The Stanford game two days later is a nightmare that begins badly and ends worse. In the middle it feels like being caught in a tornado, a force of nature that jerks you from your moorings, bats you around, bloodies and bruises you and then swoops on back for another go at it. When sportscasters talk about a team getting pasted, throttled, shellacked, hammered or bludgeoned, they are talking about a game such as the Ducks have against Stanford on a warm, rainy night in early March.

It is not that Jody ever expected to win. In fact, she has been discounting this game for weeks, assuming a loss. Stanford is just too big, too talented, too deep, too well coached. For Oregon to win, the Ducks will have to play better than the best game they've had all season, and Stanford will have to play poorly, shoot cold, get in foul trouble early. Neither scenario is likely. No one actually remembers the last time Oregon beat Stanford, at home or away. It hasn't happened in Jess's four years.

A win tonight will clinch the Pac-10 championship for Stanford, now ranked number five in the nation. It would be the team's thirty-eighth straight conference win at home. As if that were not incentive enough to play hard, this is also Stanford's final home game of the season, the last time the seniors can show off in front of the home crowd, the last chance the fans have to show just how much they love this team.

Despite all this, the Oregon players are telling themselves they can win this game. It is ninety-nine parts bravado, one part confidence. In the Stanford locker room, Eddie and Sal are writing "#30 JS" in black pen on the backs of their Nikes. "JS" is Jessica Schutt; 30 is the number on her jersey. Sal hands the pen to Roy, who writes on her sneakers.

"We're gonna win this one for Jess," Roy tells Sandie, handing her the pen. "Jess has never beat Stanford."

Jess doesn't hear them. She sits by herself in the corner, missing Karen, as usual, and tense about being back in the starting lineup. If she could only count on her shot tonight. But she can't. The confidence she felt during the Cal game has evaporated.

In front of the room, chalk in hand, Jody is in a foul mood. The bus driver was late picking up the team from the hotel. Jody hates it when the team isn't treated well, whether it's a surly waiter at the Olive Garden complaining about setting up another table or a fractious clerk at the hotel arguing about room assignments. She has a short fuse anyway; road trips make it shorter. And right now, she has the unpleasant job of describing Stanford's lineup to the Oregon team: There's six-five senior Anita Kaplan, not just tall, but big, broad-shouldered, tough, a terrific shooter who is averaging seventeen points a game. There's six-three senior Rachel Hemmer, her frontcourt partner, averaging fourteen points and eight rebounds. Along with Kate Paye, another returning senior, they have led Stanford to two Pac-10 championships and, in 1992, won the NCAA tournament. What can Jody say about them? They're shooters; they're penetrators; they're passers; they're rebounders; they're defenders. There's nothing they can't do.

"Everybody's got to show up tonight," Jody says. "It has got to be a great effort."

If ever there was a time for a spirited pep talk, this is it. But Jody has no energy for it or maybe no heart. Maybe she just can't think of anything convincing to say. She hesitates for a moment at the chalkboard. The girls sit quietly, waiting for her to say something else. But that's it. If they want inspiration, it will have to come from within tonight.

The girls file out of the locker room, down a long hall and into an arena packed with more than seven thousand fans. Before the game begins, the Ducks must sit quietly on the bench and listen to a twenty-minute salute to the Stanford seniors with congratulatory speeches, beaming parents, tearful players and big bouquets of long-stemmed blood red roses. The fans go nuts, stomping so loudly that they drown out the announcer. The Ducks sit on the sidelines looking uncomfortable, like children at a grown-up party, wondering when they can go home.

The stomping continues, unabated, as the game finally begins. From the opening whistle, it's all bad news for the Ducks. In the first seven minutes of the half, Oregon commits seven fouls, turns over the ball five times and sinks just two baskets to Stanford's eleven. Sal takes a shot and misses. Stanford gets the rebound. Stanford runs the fast break. Stanford gets the layup. The Ducks miss again, and again are muscled out of the way for the rebound. Again Stanford scores. It goes on like this, exactly like this, with Oregon taking and missing one shot, Stanford grabbing the rebound and scoring, so that the game takes on a surreal quality, as if both teams were stuck in a endless loop of instant replays. It's not just Stanford's size that makes the team so dominant, not just talent or even maturity. It's that their coach, Tara VanDerveer, has given them a sense of themselves as winners without somehow also giving them big heads. They move with confidence, but they don't take anything for granted. They are a great team because they play each game as if it matters.

Twelve minutes into the half, Oregon is down by twenty-eight, and Jody is speechless with anger, with embarrassment, maybe even with fear. She doesn't know what to do to turn this around. She's not even thinking in those terms, of "turning it around"; she just wants to leave this place with a little dignity. But it doesn't look as if it's going to happen that way.

She calls a time-out. The starters come off the court panting and wide-eyed, frightened, unsettled, like they've just had a close encounter of the third kind. They make their way to the bench in a trance. They sit heavily, staring at their feet. Jody gets down on her haunches in front of them.

"I suggest you snap out of this stupor you're in or you're gonna get beat by fifty points."

They look as if this thought has already occurred to them.

Back on the court, Heather Owen, a Stanford freshman who is built like a tank, crashes into Red and sends her flying into the Stanford bench. The officials don't make the call. Sal is right there. She stalks over to the nearest ref.

"How the hell did she land out of bounds?" Sal yells at the guy. The ref turns his back and calls Sal for a technical. Stanford sinks both free throws. At the half, Oregon is down by thirty-three.

"We're in a horrible place—but this is where we are," Jody tells the girls in the locker room. "We're just gonna have to suck it up and do better." Sal stares at the floor. Jess has her eyes closed. "I don't know what to tell you," Jody says. "They're beating the living hell out of us." Outside in the arena, the crowd is stomping in time to the Stanford fight song. "Listen, ladies," she says quietly, "we've got to go out there and play another twenty minutes. We've just got to do it."

The next twenty minutes are even uglier than the first. Roy tries an overhead pass, but the long arm of a Stanford player plucks it out of the air. Sal tries a bounce pass. Stanford intercepts. Eddie misses everything. Red can't get a shot off. Every call goes against the Ducks, or so it seems when a team is losing this badly. Jody is stalking the sidelines, muttering and shaking her head at the calls. She turns her head toward the bench and curses.

"Getting too tough for you, Coach?" someone in the stands yells in. It is all Jody can do to keep from jumping into the bleachers and strangling the woman.

Now it's Stanford's second string that's pasting the Ducks, effortlessly upping the margin to more than forty points. With four and a half minutes left to the game, Jody calls a time-out. She has no strategy to share, no new plays to run. She hunches down facing the bench and steadies herself with a hand on Roy's knee. "Let's not go out like this," she says just loud enough to be heard over the din of the crowd. "Let's chip away. Let's go out fighting."

But it doesn't work that way. The shots are starting to fall a little better, mostly because Stanford's defense is easing up, but Oregon can't seem to keep Stanford from scoring. So, for the final four minutes of the game, the teams trade baskets. Roy fouls out with only eight points in the game. Red fouls out next, with ten points. Eddie, who has made only one basket all game, turns the ball over, her fourth and the team's seventeenth. Never have the Ducks been ahead in this game. Only once, at 2–2, were they tied. They end the game down by forty-two, the biggest loss of the year, the biggest loss in Jody's tenure at Oregon.

The Stanford crowd surges onto the floor, waving banners, dancing to the band, inching forward to high-five the players. The Pac-10 championship is theirs, no matter what happens in the conference for the final two games. The Oregon players, led by Jody, make their way through the crowd, heads down, moving as quickly as they can. The locker room is their safe haven.

Jody stands at the head of the small room, her eyes bloodshot, her face pale and blotchy under the makeup. She waits for all the players to come in, then clears her throat.

"We need to take a minute here," she says, and then pauses, not knowing what else to say. She shakes her head. "We didn't have to lose like that." No one is making eye contact. Outside, the band is blaring, and a parade is getting under way.

"Let's take a minute," Jody says again. "We've worked too hard and gone through too much to not go to the tournament." The girls are not listening. The NCAA tournament is far from their thoughts. They are numb, like a roomful of disaster survivors who need time to understand that what they've experienced is actually over, that they can begin slowly to become themselves again.

Jess is in the corner, covering her eyes with a towel,

fighting to keep from crying. Sal goes over and hugs her. She's the only one who would dare interrupt Jess's grieving.

"I'm sorry," Sal tells her. "We tried." Jess keeps her head buried in the towel.

Red is sitting motionless on a small stool in the middle of the room. Usually she's one of the first ones out of the locker room. Usually she has something to say. Tonight, even though her father and stepmother are out there, she can't get herself to move. Finally, when the locker room is all but empty, Red heaves herself up and walks slowly out the door and down the corridor. At the end of the passageway, her father is waiting. They look at each other for a moment. Mr. Boyer puts his arms around his six-foot daughter and cradles her head against his shoulder.

Jody sends word for the bus to take the girls back to the Hyatt hotel. She is staying on campus for a while longer. She's been asked to appear before the Stanford women's basketball booster club. Oregon has an organization like this too, called the Fast Break Club, with fifty loyal supporters. At Stanford, the booster club is four hundred strong. Tonight the members are celebrating Stanford's victory by raffling off prizes, cheering the seniors and listening to speeches by a California state senator who used to play six-on-six basketball in high school, by Stanford's associate athletic director, by winning coach Tara VanDerveer and, as a surprise, by coach Jody Runge.

Tara, who was a guard for Indiana in the mid-seventies and still looks as lean and fast today, is gracious in her introduction of Jody. Jody has been sitting off to the side of the crowded room, almost hidden behind a table that holds four huge trophies. She has sat through the raffle. She has sat through the senator's speech. She is about to have to sit through the athletic director's speech when Tara intervenes and changes the order of events. This is the second time tonight she has gone out of her way to be sensitive to Oregon. Earlier, at the beginning of the introductions of Stanford's

seniors, Tara handed Jess a single long-stemmed rose to recognize her senior standing. Now she introduces Jody, noting
that she was last year's Pac-10 Coach of the Year.

Tara is a compact woman with dark, close-cropped hair.
Next to Jody, most women look diminished. Tara doesn't. In
fact, her very compactness makes Jody look attenuated, frag-
ile. Her darkness makes Jody look too pale.

Jody's talk is mostly question and answer, and she handles it well. It is hard to realize that this composed woman
making small jokes about Oregon's underdog status is the
same person who stood speechless and near tears in the locker
room a half an hour ago. She feels humbled in Tara's com-
pany and humbled by the size and enthusiasm of this booster
crowd. They love her humility.

"I am so encouraged to see this kind of support for a
team," Jody says. They cheer themselves. "This gives me
hope. It gives me something to work for." They cheer again.
"Tonight you've given me a vision of how our program can
grow so that we can have a team that can come down here
and"—she pauses for effect—"not get whomped by forty."
The crowd eats it up. They love to hear just how good they
are. They applaud Jody long and loud. She stands at the po-
dium, long arms relaxed at her sides, a small smile on her
face.

DOWN TO THE WIRE

FIVE DAYS LATER, OREGON BEGINS ITS FINAL HOME STAND.
Karen is suited up tonight, and she has a big smile on her
face. The fans think it's her triumphant return after a full
season of injuries. In the press box, the sports reporters are
already writing her into their leads. But it isn't what it looks
like. Karen is back for this game and the next, the last games
of the season, not because she has triumphed over her injuries
but because she has finally faced the fact that her injuries are
ending her basketball career.

These past four months, as she struggled back from hip
problems only to break her hand, she fooled herself into thinking that what she was doing on the bench in street clothes
every game was "redshirting."

Redshirting meant she was sitting out this year, saving a
year of eligibility so she could play next year when she went
to graduate school. The idea of redshirting has sustained her
emotionally. Whenever the frustration, the anger and the sad-
ness of this awful senior year have threatened to do her in,
Karen has taken solace from this idea of redshirting. She'll

be back next year. Next year she'll be part of the team again, packing for the road trips, signing autographs after home games, bitching about tough practices at training table. It won't be as good as it would have been this year, with Jess by her side, the two seniors playing their last season together. But it'll be something.

This is what Karen has been telling herself, and while it has made life bearable for her this winter, it has also allowed her to delude herself, to avoid coming to terms with the seriousness of her physical problems.

But five days ago, that all changed. Five days ago, walking home from class to the apartment she and Jess share, Karen felt that deep, dull ache in her left hip, and it scared her. It felt just like last summer, just like the pain that sent her to the doctor in the first place, then to specialists, trainers and physical therapists. She had just started practicing with the team a few days before. Finally, the doctors told her that her hand was sufficiently rehabilitated. The practices were going well, she thought. Her shot was looking good. But all it took was a few days of light practice, and her hip was bad again.

Karen tried to ignore it. She went back to practice a second day, and running up and down the court with the pain firmly settled in her hip, she knew she was doing herself harm. That night in bed, her hip throbbed. She couldn't sleep. On Tuesday, two days before the Ducks' second to last game of the season, Karen called her specialist in Utah, the one who had been giving her the "let's wait and see" lecture for four months. Now, hearing about the return of the pain, he told Karen what she most feared and least wanted to hear. If you're feeling pain, you shouldn't be playing, he said. Do you want to be in a wheelchair at thirty-five? Do you want a life punctuated every five years by hip-replacement surgeries? He told Karen that he really didn't know—no one knew—the consequences of her playing in her condition. But why take the risk? For what?

None of the other doctors had ever talked to her that

plainly, but she knew the truth when she heard it. That night, she called home and told her mother that she wouldn't be redshirting this season. She wouldn't sit out the final two games. There was no sense to keeping her eligibility for another year because she wouldn't be playing again. This summer she'd go in for surgery, followed by a four- to five-month rehab regimen, and that would be the end of basketball.

Her mother cried, and then she agreed. Karen was relieved that her father wasn't home, and not surprised at all when he didn't call her the next day. He's probably taking it harder than I am, she thought.

The next day she told Jody, who was both sympathetic and relieved. The sympathy she showed Karen; the relief she kept to herself. Jody understood that Karen had come to a painful, life-altering decision, and that Karen would remember this day for a long time. Jody understood the devastation of serious injury. Her sister had been permanently sidelined by an injury early in a promising college career.

She felt for Karen, but she had no idea what she would have done with her on the roster next year. Karen would never have been able to play as a starter. She couldn't last that long on the court. Yet she would have been there, a veteran, a player she would have to use as a sub, perhaps to the detriment of the team. Karen's hand injury had cleared the way for Sally. Now her congenital hip problem left the number two guard spot wide open for next year. And that's how Jody wanted it.

So tonight, Thursday night, Karen is suited up and sitting on the bench next to Jess. She won't actually be on the court tonight. If she plays now, she might be in too much pain to play Saturday afternoon in the Ducks' final game, the game that will honor the seniors. That's the game she wants to be part of.

It's just as well Karen can't play tonight, because the Ducks need Sally full time. The game is against the twenty-third-ranked University of Southern California, who beat the Ducks earlier in the season. In fact, the Ducks haven't beaten

USC in five years. But this game and the Saturday game against UCLA are must wins. The USC game in particular, against a ranked team, is Oregon's last chance to boost its power ranking high enough to secure a spot among the sixty-four teams to be chosen for the tournament. A loss, on the other hand, would almost certainly keep Oregon out of the tournament.

Jody is solemn in the locker room. Here it is the next to last game, and she still doesn't know what to expect from the team. Will Jess shoot well? Will Eddie be a threat? Will Red be tough on defense? There shouldn't be so many unknowns so late in the season.

"We need to come out and make it go our way," Jody says quietly, after she maps out strategy. The girls are sitting in their usual places: forwards at the front end of the long couch; Sal and Eddie together on folding chairs. It's the seventeenth time this season that they've sat in the home locker room listening to the coach tell them how to win a game. They listen carefully to the strategy, sitting forward in their seats, asking questions, nodding, but they zone out on the pep talk. Jody realizes she hasn't got their attention. She stops talking and sends them out the door. She's got to trust that they want to win this game as much as she does.

Out on the court, Oregon plays with the kind of confidence the team hasn't shown since the early-season wins against Oregon State and the University of Washington. Maybe it has taken the girls this long to fully recover from the demoralizing Arizona road trip. Maybe the Stanford game has shown them how basketball should be played. Maybe they are just glad to be home in front of a friendly crowd at the end of a tough season.

In the first half, everyone plays well. Jess connects on one of two three-point attempts and grabs two steals; Red pulls down five rebounds. Eddie shoots the ball and sinks two. Sandie surprises Jody, and herself, by coming off the bench, attracting two fouls and sinking all four shots. Sal is everywhere, shooting layups, jumpers, three-pointers. Ten minutes into the first half, the Ducks are up by ten and quite pleased with themselves.

"If we can get them down another ten," Jody tells the starters during a time-out, "they're not gonna be able to come back from it. Here's where we wanna push."

Red has a bad cold, and she's in the middle of studying for five finals, but she is playing tougher than she's played in a while. When she gets the ball anywhere near the basket, she goes for it, regardless of how many players surround her. She grabs a pass from Sally, throws her signature head fake to see if her defender will fall for it. The USC player doesn't and stays with her. Red bends her knees and pushes off, pretending to take a shot. The idea is to make the defender go up, then wait a split second and, while the defender is on the way down, get off a shot over the player's head. This fake doesn't work either but Red keeps at it. She doesn't pass the ball out to the wings. Instead, she pivots, dribbles and lunges toward the basket again. But now she has two USC players on her. One goes for the fake but the other stays with Red. Now there's a third USC player under the basket. Red goes up for one more fake, comes down fast and, triple-teamed, sinks the basket. The whole sequence has taken three seconds.

B, sitting on the bench, is mightily impressed. She jumps up and waves her towel. "All right, Red Dog!" she yells.

Oregon pulls away: twelve, fifteen, eighteen points. USC's big player, all-American candidate Tina Thompson, has been averaging twenty points a game, but tonight she is, as one of the local sportswriters later puts it, "a surprising nonfactor."

Still, Jody is taking nothing for granted. She paces the sidelines; her gaze never leaves the court. With two minutes left in the half, Jody feels confident enough to start seriously subbing, meaning she will go deeper than B and Sandie. She puts Cicely in with a minute remaining. Cicely's mother, up from Los Angeles for these final games, is sitting in the row behind the bench. She puts down her tub of popcorn and sits forward. Cicely bolts from one end of the court to the other, lifting her knees like a drum majorette, almost leaping as she runs. With one second left to go in the half, she sinks one. Cicely's mother breaks into a big smile. That second was worth the plane trip.

"We can't let them get back into the game," Jody tells the girls at halftime. Oregon is ahead by seventeen points. "They are very capable of doing so, believe me. You need to put them down by thirty." She looks out over the locker room, steely-eyed. "You need to squash every hope they've got of getting into this game."

Her speech notwithstanding, in the second half, the Ducks come out with less intensity. For the first six minutes, they do nothing more than trade shots with USC. Although that means Oregon is still ahead by the same margin, Jody is not happy. She pulls Roy and Jess from the lineup, subbing in Sandie and B. She watches the two subs take their places on the court, then pivots sharply and marches back along the bench until she comes to where Roy is sitting.

Roy is the Ducks' high scorer this season and probably the most consistent player on the team. She also understands the game of basketball better than any of the others. Jody respects her.

"You're not playing hard out there!" Jody yells at Roy. "You're just out there cruising." Roy stops mopping her face with a towel and looks up at Jody. It's true. During the entire first half, Roy took only three shots and pulled down only two rebounds. "You sit there and think about that," Jody says. Her tone is icy. She pivots again, and in two long strides she is down at the far end of the bench watching the play.

She couldn't have spoken to Red this way. It would be like slapping the girl in the face with a glove and challenging her to a duel. She couldn't have spoken to Jess this way. She has done too much to Jess already this season. And she would never have spoken to Eddie this way. Eddie is too vulnerable. But Jody knows how tough Roy is, and she knows that what might anger or intimidate the others will get Roy moving. She's right.

Roy goes in and works hard under the basket, attracting four fouls and sinking six of the seven shots. Sally catches fire. Jess finds her range and sinks two three-pointers. The Ducks score fifteen straight points, widening the margin for a twenty-six-point win. If they had played like this all season, they would be right behind Stanford now, number two in the conference, instead of tied for fourth. That's what Jody is thinking as she walks down to the locker room. Still, it is a very big victory. It probably means an invitation to the tournament. Jody forces herself to take a minute to enjoy it.

Two days later, the Ducks face their final opponent of the season, UCLA. This is the team the Ducks beat in their very first conference game, the heady, on-the-road victory that got everyone talking about winning this year's Pac-10 championship and celebrating with strategically placed tattoos. It seems so long ago that Jody can hardly remember the game, but barely two months have passed.

That first game down in Los Angeles was vital to win, an opening volley, an announcement, a proclamation of Oregon's intention to be a contender. This last game is even more important. A victory this afternoon will mean an uncontested fourth place in the conference behind Stanford, Washington and Oregon State, a far cry from the championship the girls dreamed of but still respectable enough to earn that berth in the tournament. A defeat means fifth place and a vulnerable position. A defeat means that for Oregon to get to the tournament, NCAA officials will have to offer bids to five Pac-10 schools, half the conference. Jody knows that it is rare to go that deep in one conference. If the fifth school is USC, last year's conference champs, Jody thinks five teams will make it. But if Oregon is fifth, she doesn't think the Ducks command the requisite national respect to make the cut. It is down to the wire. This is yet another must-win game.

It is also senior night, the time when the veteran players are recognized and honored, their statistics touted, their athletic careers summarized by deep-voiced announcers as the crowd cheers and their parents accompany them center court to receive corsages and kudos. In the stands, fifty of Jess's friends and family have come to watch her last game. Her parents have not missed a game in four years. With Jess, their youngest, finishing her career tonight, they will be at loose ends until their first grandchild starts to play.

Karen's parents are in the stands tonight too. It hasn't quite sunk in with Karen's father that his daughter will be playing her final game tonight. He was counting on her red-shirting even more than Karen was herself. Karen has adjusted to the idea much better than her father. They've decided to not talk about it. It's better for their relationship.

The announcer calls Sally's name. She is not a senior, but because she won't be back next season, she is being honored tonight along with Jess and Karen. Sally has been worried about this for weeks. She doesn't want to step on any toes. She's not falsely humble—she knows how important she has been to the team—but she is also sensitive to the fact that she hasn't earned a senior's right to be honored. She hopes Jess and Karen won't be offended.

As her younger sister, who has flown in from Australia to be with her, looks on, the announcer extols Sal's virtues. The crowd of almost 2,700 cheers loudly. Sal is a favorite: fun to watch on the court, unpretentious off. Her teammates stand and clap. Sal walks down the line, hugging every one of them, eyes bloodshot. These are some of my best friends, she thinks. After just three months, these are some of my best friends. She has never played as well as she has this season on the Oregon team, and never loved—or hated—the game as much. She hugs Sandie, one of her favorites, and the tears start. When she gets to Eddie, she gives her a bear hug, and the two stay locked in each other's arms for a long time, neither willing to let go.

Karen's moment in the spotlight is less dramatic. She hasn't played with the team for months. She hasn't gone on road trips. Her injuries have put her so much on the outside that she barely feels like this is her team. Her expectations for this game are limited. She isn't starting, and she knows she won't be playing a lot of minutes. She has no idea what will happen for her on the court tonight. It's just going to be a relief to be out there, a relief that the season is finally over, that there can be no more disappointments. Karen has a steady boyfriend. She has plans for graduate school. She is more than ready to let basketball go and start the next phase of her life. She walks down the line, awkwardly hugging each player with her long, bony arms. Her eyes are dry. She has done her crying already.

Jess, though, is openly bawling even before the announcer calls her name. This is one of those rare times that it is acceptable to cry in public. In fact, the ceremony is designed to wring emotion from the players. Jess cries all the way through the introduction, all the way through the somewhat perfunctory hugs she gives her teammates, and then stands crying in the middle of the court as she hands her mother a yellow rose corsage tied with bright green ribbon.

Jess can't stop the tears. She is not even trying. She is crying for all those missed shots, for those six games she didn't play after she injured her ankle, for the senior year that didn't happen the way she dreamed it would. More than Karen, who has had time to distance herself emotionally from the season, more than Sal, who came here on a flier and can return to as many seasons of play in Australia as she wants, Jess is conscious of this as an end, as the end.

The announcer introduces the team for the final time. The starters sit by themselves on the bench. The coaches and bench players stand on the court forming a double line in front of them. As each player is announced, she gets up, slaps the hands of the starters still on the bench, then runs through the double line, high-fiving everyone. When the announcer says: "Five-nine senior from Sunnyside, Washington . . . Jessica Schutt," drawing out the "Schutt" until he's almost out of breath, Jess is still crying. She lopes between the lines of her teammates, slapping their outstretched hands. What she wants to do more than anything is go out strong. She knows there's more to the game than shooting, but what Jess prays for as she takes her place on the court for the last time is a good shooting night.

The game begins slowly. Jody watches the sluggish play, pacing, nervous, increasingly exasperated. How many times does she have to tell them to come out strong, to come out threatening, to dictate from the beginning? This tentative play only serves to give the opponent time to acclimate to the court, to check out the Oregon players, to study their moves. After twenty-seven games and eighteen victories, these girls still don't come out playing as if they believe they can win. Jody stifles the urge to call a time-out and berate them. It is too late for that now. She waits, stalking the sidelines.

She is not just waiting for the pace to pick up on general principles. She is very specifically waiting for Oregon to pull ahead so that she can put in Karen. She has to wait almost eight minutes. That's how long it takes the Ducks to sink three baskets and pull ahead 6–5.

Jody turns to the bench and casually, as if it's something she's said all season, she says: "Karen, get Sal."

Karen sprints to the timekeepers' table to wait for the ref's signal, and the entire bench stands and claps. Karen looks back and flashes a big grin. But her elation is short-lived. Once in, she misses a shot, commits a foul and, a scant minute later, she's back on the bench.

Jody gives her another chance three minutes later, and Karen tries for a jump shot. As the ball heads toward the basket, the girls on the bench stand and raise their arms above their heads. They want Karen to sink one. The ball rattles around the rim and pops out. When Oregon next gets the ball, Karen tries again from the other side. It seems to take forever for the ball to travel from her fingertips to the basket. Her teammates are up again, arms raised. The crowd is silent. The ball ricochets off the rim.

Then, with three minutes in the half, Sandie fires a great pass to Karen, who is standing fifteen feet from the basket with no defenders around. Karen takes her time. She lets the ball go in a long arc, pushing from the wrist. She knows it's good before it gets there, and so do her teammates. They are waving towels in the air. The fans are yelling. Karen has broken through.

But Jess is struggling. She is one for eight and has missed all four of her three-point attempts. At halftime, Oregon up by six, Jess stands alone in the back of the locker room staring her wide-eyed stare. She is always silent during halftime, even when the Ducks have a big lead and the others are loose and joking. But tonight, she is not just silent, she is lifeless, inert, hollowed out. She has had bad nights before, many bad nights, but has never stood alone like this in the back of the room. She has always assumed her regular place on the couch, the special place where the starters sit. This afternoon she is purposefully, literally, distancing herself from the team, easing herself out, first to the back of the room, then away from basketball, forever.

But before that happens, she desperately wants a decent game. Okay, she tells herself, my shot is just not going to fall. That's tough, but that's how it is. I've got to suck it up and start playing. I can still have one hell of a defensive game. I can still go out strong.

Out on the court in the second half, Jess plays with a growling intensity that is scary. She is throwing elbows, pressing hard, riveting her opponents with that fierce stare, almost snarling in their faces. Not surprisingly, she finds herself with four personal fouls with more than ten minutes left in the game. Jody takes her out and puts in B, who has been having a decent shooting night.

Jody is not thinking about Jess's problems right now. She is busy watching the team pull ahead decisively. She is busy watching Sally, marveling at her tenacity, her focus, her ability not just to do everything on the court but to know from second to second what most needs to be done. Sally makes a steal. Sally sinks a twelve-footer. Sally sinks a layup, grabs two rebounds, makes another layup. She doesn't have Eddie's speed or grace. She doesn't have Red's power. But she has those attributes Jody most admires. She has guts. She has heart. Jody cannot imagine the team without her and is already mourning her loss even as she plays.

Yesterday, to no one's surprise, Sal and Roy were named to the all–Pac-10 team, an honorary list of the ten best players in the league as voted by the coaches. Jody wishes there were something more she could say to Sal to make her stay another season. But everything that can be said has already been said many times over by Jody and her assistants, by the players, even by a group of fans who have attached themselves to Sally, and still she is determined to go home next month.

The Ducks are up now, for good, with a solid sixteen- or seventeen-point margin. Jody's expression doesn't change— the game face is a fierce mask—but inside she's singing. Inside, she's celebrating. The Ducks will go to the tournament. Jody will be the first woman's basketball coach in Oregon's history to take a team to back-to-back NCAA appearances. She savors the thought for a moment, then forces her attention back to the game.

Out on the court, the girls are ferocious. Jody is always on them for slacking off once they get ahead, but right now they are giving her nothing to complain about. It's not just that they want badly to win this game—in fact, they know they have already won it—it's that this is the last time this team will play together in Mac Court, and they are making the most of it. They are playing some of the best basketball of the season.

Red, who was an honorable mention on the Pac-10 team, is having a huge defensive night with fourteen rebounds. Eddie is all over the court, dogging her opposite number, pressing, challenging, controlling the ball with ease, playing with the confidence of a Pac-10 starter. She loves having Sally in the two spot next to her. Sally is unflappable. If Eddie starts getting jittery, she looks at Sal playing hard, coming up the court by her side, and that settles her down.

Jess has been sitting on the bench with four fouls for a minute and a half, and she wants back in. Jody feels compelled to do it, more to honor Jess's senior status than to help the team. In her place, B has scored fourteen points. Jess, on the other hand, is one for ten, including six three-point misses. With nine minutes left, and Oregon up by eighteen, Jody calls for the substitution, and Jess is in. On the very next play, standing two feet from a UCLA shooter, Jess, playing tough defense, tips the ball from her hand. She thinks it's a good, aggressive move. The referee thinks it's a foul. Jess can't believe it: her fifth foul. She is disqualified. She has fouled out of the last game of her career after scoring only two points.

She stands under the UCLA basket for a moment, stunned, motionless, her head down to hide the tears from the crowd. Everything freezes on the court, like someone has hit the pause button and suspended the characters in a movie. Then, one by one, Roy, Eddie, Sal and Red walk over to Jess under the basket. They surround her, grab her arm, pat her on the back, say a few words to help her through the moment. Jess walks slowly back to the Oregon bench, her head low. The fans understand what's happening. They clap; they yell; they give her a standing ovation. She isn't listening.

As Jess approaches the Oregon bench, Jody walks toward her.

"Keep your head up, Jess," she says, bending close to talk to her over the din of the crowd. "That's a good job."

Jess doesn't look up. She walks past the assistant coaches, past the regular subs, past the freshmen, past all the players on the bench, and takes the very last seat, way down where Stacy, the equipment manager, sits next to the water cooler. Stacy hands her a towel, and Jess covers her head with it. She sits like that, slumped, head covered, in the last seat, for a long time.

When she composes herself enough to remove the towel, she looks up to see that the Ducks are winning by more than twenty, and Karen is letting loose a three-point shot from the top of the key. She has missed all five previous attempts, although she's managed to sink three regular baskets. Sal, who gave her the pass, watches the ball as it arcs. The bench is up, arms raised, waiting for the shot to fall. It falls just right, a soft swish of the net, that perfect basket that doesn't need the backboard and doesn't touch the rim. Forty seconds later, B finds Karen in the same place. Karen arcs in another, and gets it. Her father is going wild in the stands. She comes out of the game with ten points after having played only fourteen minutes. Flushed, grinning, caught in that moment when everything works just right and it seems the gods are smiling, she walks the length of the bench and finds the empty seat next to Jess.

"Nice job," Jess says, unsmiling, staring straight forward. She doesn't begrudge her roommate and best friend this terrific ending. But that doesn't mean it is any easier to take. That's how I wanted to go out, Jess is thinking. Why couldn't I go out that way?

Jody puts in the subs for one last time. Timmy, the skinny white-blond guard, goes in. Cicely goes in. Shanthi, the junior with the three-point shot, goes in. Sandie and B provide the stability. The subs don't do much. They don't have to. It has been Oregon's game for most of the second half. At the buzzer, the score is 83–65, and the place erupts. The noise generated by these 2,700 fans in this cozy old arena is only a few decibels off the din made by the much larger Stanford crowd down in Palo Alto exactly a week ago.

Jody listens to it for a second, smiling, before she strides out of the arena, across the hallway and down the steps to the locker room. The girls follow behind like ducklings. The crowd is still screaming.

The season is over. Oregon has finished number four in the Pac-10, one game behind third-place Oregon State and two games behind second-place University of Washington. Jody doesn't have to wait for the box scores in tomorrow's newspaper. She knows the standings. Two games out of second place, she thinks to herself walking down the steps. Those are the two games we lost down in Arizona. She shakes her head. She has not yet forgiven herself or the players for those losses, and she is not likely to.

But by the time she opens the door to the locker room, she is smiling again.

"We made it, ladies," she says over the noise of their cheers. "There were times when it looked like we might not. . . ." She pauses, waiting for a laugh like a stand-up comedienne. The girls laugh obligingly. "But we did. We made it." They cheer themselves again.

"That was a great effort tonight," she tells them. "Now get back up there and say hello to your fans."

The players throw their warm-up shirts over their sweaty jerseys, grab pieces of lukewarm pizza and rush back upstairs. Immediately, they are surrounded by gangs of little girls, the eight-, nine- and ten-year-olds who come to all the games, watching the players with big eyes, memorizing the moves, imagining themselves in Mac Court some day. Sandie is surrounded, Gulliver in the land of Lilliput. She has to be careful not to trip over these little kids who press forward at her knees, begging for autographs. Roy and Sal, Karen and Eddie, Red and B all float in a sea of little girls. Some have scraps of paper in their hands. Others have brought basketballs to be signed. Some extend their billed baseball caps or hunch over and have the players sign their names on the back of their T-shirts. A few hold up their arms, collecting autographs from wrist to elbow, shouting back and forth at each other.

"Kimmy, I got one! I got Sally!"

"I got Red! I got Red."

The little girls are tireless. The players are still smiling, still signing, but they would like to move on, talk to their friends, take a shower, go celebrate. The little girls won't let them go. After twenty minutes, the mothers and fathers, who have stood in an outer circle, smiling and watching, move in to grab their daughters by the arms and haul them away.

Jess has not yet come upstairs. She sits alone in the locker room for a long time, dry-eyed, numb, unthinking.

With great effort, she gets up and takes a shower. Then she wanders the deserted basement halls. After the crowd has thinned, after the little girls have been dragged off by their parents, Jess walks upstairs. There are only a few people left in the hallway outside the empty arena. They are Jess's family, waiting for her: her mother and father, her sisters and brothers, her uncle, her cousins. They surround her, a human cocoon.

PART THREE

GET
EVEN

TIME TO WIN

THE MORNING AFTER THE FINAL GAME OF THE SEASON, SUN-day morning, three hundred of the faithful find their way to Mac Court. They are here to watch the televised announcement of the teams selected to play in the NCAA tournament. They sit, dressed in combinations of green and yellow, in the bleachers behind the Oregon bench. On the court, under the near basket, a TV projection system converts the small screen to a garish, grainy movie theater–sized image. Everyone is sure Oregon will be chosen this morning. But there is still a drama to be played out: How will the Ducks be seeded? Whom will they play against in the first round? Where will they play? That is what the faithful are here to find out.

Of course, they could have stayed home on this chill, overcast morning. Right now they could be sipping cups of hot coffee, lounging on living-room couches and tuning in to CBS on their own TV sets. But it is not just the news they want; it is the experience. Being a fan is a public, communal activity. They need each other this morning as much as they need the team.

The girls sit in their usual places on the bench, dressed in street clothes that don't quite manage to mask their identity as athletes—Red's shoulders are just too impressive, Sandie and Roy are too tall. Jody stands to the side, smiling, shaking hands, drinking in the praise, half relaxed, half very consciously working the crowd. The university band is here. The mascot, a fat white duck, is waddling up and down the sidelines. The local sportswriters are here with their narrow spiral notebooks and their serious expressions. They hang close to Jody as the announcements begin on-screen.

The NCAA chooses sixty-four teams to compete and divides them into four regions, West, East, Mideast and Midwest. The top sixteen teams in the nation are seeded first and spread across the four regions regardless of actual geography; then the remaining forty-eight teams fill in the blanks, also regardless of geography. The idea is to prevent teams from the same conference facing each other early in the tournament.

First to be announced is the West region. Vanderbilt, a Southern school, is seeded number one, says the sportscaster. Stanford has the number two spot. The announcer's voice is uncomfortably loud. The volume is jacked up, and the sound is ricocheting off the empty wooden seats in the arena. Still, the fans in the bleachers lean forward, as if straining to hear. There is a chance that Oregon will be placed in this region, even though that could mean facing Stanford, a conference opponent, early on. That's because five Pac-10 schools are expected to make it to the tournament this year—Stanford, the University of Washington, Oregon State, the University of Oregon and USC—and there are only four regions. The announcer reads the names slowly, but Oregon is not on the list. USC, ranked fifth in the Pac-10, has been placed in the West.

Next comes the East region, where the University of Connecticut is seeded number one. Jody clenches and unclenches her fists as she listens. The players stare at the big screen unblinkingly. Oregon isn't on this list either.

The show breaks for a commercial. The band strikes up,

and all of a sudden, as if on command, everyone sitting quietly in the bleachers comes to life. They stand, shake out their legs as if they've been sitting for hours, clear their throats, talk, laugh and reassure each other that Oregon will be announced in the very next segment. When the announcements begin again, they freeze midsentence, mouths caught open, muscles locking. They don't sit down for fear that the old bleachers will creak at just the wrong moment.

Now it's the Mideast region being announced, with Tennessee the top seed. One by one, the sixteen schools are listed. When Oregon doesn't make this list, Jody's hands go damp. Could it be that Oregon hasn't made the cut? It is not a possibility she has seriously entertained since the Ducks won their final two games. She doesn't want to entertain it now, but it comes unbidden. All the other Pac-10 teams that were supposed to get bids to the tournament have already been announced. Maybe Oregon, even though the team ended the season one game ahead of USC, is not going to make it. Maybe the power rankings worked against the Ducks. Maybe the Ducks just didn't have the requisite national reputation to make the cut. Jody ponders this all through what seems like an endless commercial break.

The last region is the Midwest. Jody restrains the impulse to start pacing in front of the players' bench. The announcer starts the roll call. Colorado is seeded first. Jody only half listens to the first four teams. She knows Oregon is not among the top sixteen in the nation. At number five, though, she comes to attention. Five is . . . Drake, the first team that beat Oregon back in November. Mac Court is as silent as deep space. Six is . . . the sportscaster stares at the TelePrompTer . . . the University of Oregon. The Ducks will be playing the Louisville Cardinals, seeded eleventh in the region.

The players on the bench are up hugging each other. The crowd, not knowing whether to sigh or cheer, issues an odd collective whoop, like a windstorm howling at the door. Jody's fists are unclenched. She's surrounded by well-wishers, back-patters and handshakers, towering over them, bending her long neck to listen to their congratulations. She is smiling, working the crowd again. But Jody is also thinking fast: Louisville is a beatable team; that's the good news. The bad news is that Oregon will have to travel farther than any other team in the tournament, all the way to Athens, Georgia, to play its first two games.

In the stands, Barb Walker, the associate athletic director, is also thinking about travel. It is her job to work with the official NCAA-appointed travel agency to get the team, its small entourage and the band to Georgia in the next few days. It will not be easy to arrange flights on short notice between two small cities at diagonal ends of the country, especially during spring break. She rushes out of Mac Court as the band begins playing the sixth encore of the Oregon fight song. The faster she gets to her office in the Cas Center, the faster she gets on the phone to the travel agency, the better chance the team has of getting where it needs to go.

Jody lingers in the arena. The fans won't let her go. After everyone who could possibly congratulate her congratulates her, she walks to center court to field questions. They all want to hear that Oregon is ready to beat Louisville, and Jody has no problem telling them what they want to hear. After she's finished, the crowd calls for the players.

Jess walks onto the court, quietly acknowledges her parents and family for support and walks back to the bench. Sal tells the fans she will be sad to leave. Eddie aw-shucks her way through a few thank-yous. Dave, from the sports information office, asks if any other players would like to say a few words. He is orchestrating this event. For a long moment, no one on the bench moves. Then Red gets up, saunters to midcourt and holds the mike in her hand as if she's been doing stand-up gigs for years.

"Hey," she tells the faithful, "everyone talked about this being a rebuilding year. Well, we didn't rebuild." She pauses for effect. "We reloaded."

It's a cliché, but it doesn't matter. The crowd eats it up. When Jody gets home in the early afternoon, there's a message on her machine from her lawyer, Alan, in Atlanta. He congratulates her on Oregon's bid to the tournament and proposes a meeting. Let's talk in Athens after your game to figure out our next step, he tells her.

The travel agency comes through with a grueling itinerary, but it is the best that can be arranged to connect these distant towns. The team flies out two mornings later, first from Eugene to Salt Lake City, then from Salt Lake City to Atlanta. In Atlanta, past midnight, there is a bus waiting to take them an hour east to Athens. It is 2:30 in the morning before they check into their hotel. The air is thick and warm, like pudding on the stove. The girls fall into bed and sleep well into the next day, rousing themselves just in time for a late-afternoon practice session at a local high school gym.

Jody is tired too, but optimistic. Just being back at the tournament for the second consecutive year is a big boost to the Oregon program—and to Jody's career. But of course, that's not enough. Now that the team is here, Jody wants to win a few games. She feels reasonably confident that the Ducks can beat Louisville in the first round. Louisville plays in a much weaker league than the Pac-10 and is seeded eleventh to Oregon's sixth, a good indication of the two teams' relative strengths. Jody is not saying this out loud, but she's already looking past Louisville, looking to the second round in the tournament. She figures Oregon will be playing the University of Georgia in that round on Georgia's home court. This, not the Louisville match, will be the tough one. It is a game that will pit her against Georgia coach Andy Landers, her old friend, the coach whose salary Alan Manheim managed to almost double by threatening a suit.

On the University of Georgia campus, the pear trees are in bloom, and magnolias line the campus streets. At game time, 6 P.M., the billboard on the university track flashes the temperature: seventy-eight degrees. It is a muggy, breezeless Southern evening. The girls are sweating as they bend to lace up their Nikes in the Georgia Coliseum locker room. They haven't yet warmed up, but their jerseys are damp and clinging to their backs. The heat has made them cranky. They've been talking about the weather since they arrived two days earlier, and Jody is sick of it.

"Shit, how hot can it be?" she says under her breath, watching them ready themselves. "We're here, we're in the tournament. Who cares what the thermometer says."

Inside the seventeen-thousand-person arena, there are perhaps a hundred people. Empty gray and red seats stretch up to the ceiling. The Ducks have never played in such a vast and vacant space before. About thirty fans sit behind the Oregon bench: Karen's, Jess's and B's parents, Sally's sister, Jody's father, Barb Walker and a few other university people.

The game begins well for Oregon, with Red and Roy making fast baskets. A few seconds later, Eddie, quick and sure, steals the ball and sinks a layup. Then Jess nails her first shot. Then Sal makes a three-pointer. The Ducks build a nine-point lead. Jody, adrenaline surging, yells encouragement from the sidelines. If this keeps up, Oregon will have a twenty-point lead by halftime, and that's just where she wants to be.

But the rhythm of games can change quickly. The Ducks relax on defense. They suffer a bit of a shooting slump. In the final four minutes of the half, Louisville starts hitting from the outside, four three-pointers in rapid succession, and Oregon's solid ten-point lead is whittled to three. The heat and the anger redden Jody's face as she stalks off the court and down to the locker room. She doesn't wait for them to find seats on the long wooden bench before she starts in on them.

"You are making them look like goddamn all-Americans out there!" she screams. "You're dragging up and down the court with your tongues hanging out." She makes her voice whiny without lowering the decibel level. "*It's too hot and you're too tired.* I am just not interested in hearing that, ladies. You should never have let them back into the game. Never. Now go back out there and *play.*"

Despite the locker-room drubbing, the Ducks come back

with little intensity. The passing is sloppy. The shots are not falling. Three and a half minutes into the second half, Louisville ties the score for the first time, and Jody, barely keeping herself under control, calls a time-out. The veins along her neck are thick and ropy. She hunches down in front of the bench, facing the players.

"What is your problem?" she screams at them. "They want it more than you. Don't you see that?" She stares at them hard and pounds her fist on her thigh. Then she says, slowly, accenting each word, as if she is talking to errant preschoolers: *"If you don't play hard now we will not win this basketball game."*

Eddie gives it everything. She is scoring. She is stealing. She is running the full court press every time Louisville has the ball, dogging the other team's point guard, hounding her, pressuring her, combining speed and confidence to play her finest game of the season. But it isn't enough. Louisville is hitting everything, pulling away by two, five, eight, then ten points.

Jody signals Eddie to come out for a breather. Eddie walks slowly to the sidelines, her face expressionless. She doesn't make her way to the Oregon bench but just stands near the scorers' table, arms hanging at her sides, looking lost. Jody walks over to her.

"What can I do?" Eddie says to her coach. "Tell me what I can do so we can win this game."

Jody wishes she had an answer. But Eddie is already doing everything she can. Eddie is not the problem. Sally is not having a big scoring night and neither is Roy. Jess, after a promising start, is shooting cold. But it's not so much that Oregon is playing poorly. It's that Louisville is playing far better than anyone expected. The three-pointers are killing Oregon.

Jody puts her long arm around Eddie's shoulder. The two of them stand this way for several seconds as the game goes on in front of them. At this moment, Jody respects Eddie more than she ever has. Eddie is a fighter. Eddie cares. This means more to Jody than just about anything. She leans down to reassure her, to tell her to keep on doing what she's been doing. Then she sends her back in, hoping her energy will spark something on the court.

Something does happen, very slowly: The defense tightens. Louisville commits a few too many fouls. Eddie, who is not an outside shooter, hits a three-pointer. B, who has been in and out of the game not doing much, sinks a jumper. Red performs one of her classic moves under the basket, the graceful fake-spin-layup dance. Oregon works itself back into the game, tying the score with six minutes left to play. The bench players are on their feet yelling and waving towels. The band fills the empty arena with the Oregon fight song. On the sidelines, pacing, Jody hears nothing but the bounce of the ball and the squeak of sneakers, sees nothing but her five players, thinks nothing but the game. Time slows.

For endless minutes, the two teams trade the lead. Now Oregon is up by two, now down by one, then up again. With thirty seconds left on the clock, the Ducks are down by one. Red, who has had a wonderful game, muscles in to the basket and, along the way, manages to attract a foul. When it's called, she looks over at Jody and flashes a grin. The two chances she'll get from the line will probably be the two most important shots in the game, and the girl is grinning. Red never ceases to amaze Jody. If Red makes both shots, Oregon will take the lead.

Red goes to the line. She stands at an angle to the basket, loose limbed, bouncing the ball, as relaxed as if this were some ratball game back in Mac Court. The first shot is up—and no good. Jody looks down at the floor and curses. Red takes a good look at the basket. She bounces the ball, exhales and releases the second shot. It's good. That means the score is tied again. Oregon must keep Louisville from making a basket now.

The defense steps up. Everyone is playing hard. The clock is running out, and Louisville can't find a shot. With three seconds left, Leatrice Scott, Louisville's top scorer, finds a hole and charges in to the basket. Red, who is right there with her, has no choice but to foul her. Otherwise, Louisville will score and win.

Scott, who is a fine shooter but poor from the line, has missed two of three free throws this game. The players line up, waiting for her to shoot. She holds the ball for a second, then steps back from the line and laughs. It's pure nerves. When she laughs, it means she's tight. It means she usually misses. But not this time. Both shots go in. Louisville is up by two, and Oregon, with only three seconds, can't score. The Ducks lose the first-round game of the 1995 NCAA tournament.

Down in the locker room, no one is talking. Through the walls, the girls can hear the University of Georgia players firing up for their game. Their enthusiasm is almost too much to bear. Jody walks in, sets her jacket down on the table and begins to speak so softly that the players in the back of the room can't hear her.

"You should have put them away in the first half," Jody says, almost wistfully. She shakes her head. "You are a much better team than what you showed tonight."

The girls have elected to take the bus back to the hotel right away. Jody goes up to the arena to watch the next game, Indiana against Georgia. She finds her father sitting in the section under the Indiana basket. She sits down next to him, her jaw clenched, her lips a thin, tight line. He puts his arm around her. They don't look at each other—both are staring at the game on the court—but they talk. Dennis tells his daughter not to take the defeat so hard. You had a young team, he tells her. She stares at the game and nods, unsmiling. You never thought they'd get this far, he tells her. She nods again. He pats her arm. She is not listening to his words, only to the consoling tone of his voice punctuated by the bounce of the basketball. She stares straight ahead, not seeing the game, thinking: We came all the way across the country to get beat

in the first round. The buildup to this night has been so long.
Now suddenly it's over. Jody feels like a diver who has come
to the surface too quickly.

She has only a few minutes to get her bearings before
she sees Alan Manheim sitting in the bleachers above the
Georgia bench. One of her battles this season may have ended
with the Louisville game, but another one is yet to be decided.
She rouses herself and joins Alan. They watch the game and
talk in spurts in between the action.

Alan tells her that this trip to the tournament has strength-
ened her position. They talk about how her team and the men's
team have identical records. Alan likes the symmetry of it, the
neatness. He thinks it enhances the parity argument he has been
trying to make. Alan tells her that their next move is to set up a
conference call and see what the university is going to offer
now that Jody has completed a second successful season. Jody
doesn't feel successful right now, but she knows that what
Alan is saying is right: Just getting to the tournament has
increased her stock back in Eugene.

Another conference call. Jody sighs and shakes her head,
but remains silent. After all these months, after all the faxes
and phone calls, after talking and waiting, playing cat and
mouse with the local media, listening to Alan's threats of legal
action, listening to Dave's promises of a big-money donor,
she is in mid-March no closer to the contract she wants than
she was nine months ago.

Back in the fall, when Alan first started making serious
noises about a lawsuit, Dan Williams, the acting AD, told the
press that he saw no reason to negotiate with Jody. She had
just recently signed a contract and was bound by it. The time
to negotiate would be when that contract expired, after the
season was over, he said. Jody had been fighting that position
for months, and she had lost. Well, now the season was over,
and it was time to win.

Getting back home to Eugene the next day was a grind:
a bus to Atlanta, a flight to St. Louis, a layover, a flight to

Salt Lake City, a layover, a flight to Eugene, a bus back to the Cas Center parking lot. Flying economy class is not particularly comfortable for anyone, but it is even less so for a six-foot-three traveler with long legs and a short temper. Jody does a considerable amount of traveling but never enjoys these cross-country treks, folding herself into and out of airplane seats, sitting with her knees hard against the back of the next seat, breathing recycled air until her throat goes dry.

Today it is even worse because Jody is bone tired and still nursing her anger over the loss to Louisville. When she isn't stewing about the game the Ducks should have won, she is worrying about her contract, about her future and wondering how—or even if—this whole thing is going to be resolved. She is silent most of the way home, wearing her game face. The girls sleep.

It is after 11 P.M. when the bus pulls up in front of the Cas Center. Jody is sitting in the front as she always does. When the bus stops, she stands up and turns to face the girls. The driver flips on the overhead lights. They cast a greenish glow that makes everyone look a little sick. The girls stay in their seats, waiting for the coach to speak.

Jody has given so many locker-room orations, so many halftime speeches, threatening, scolding, cajoling, prodding, admonishing, analyzing, strategizing. This will be her last speech to this group of women.

"I don't think anyone wants to be driving all the way home tonight," she says tersely. By "home," she means home to their parents. The university is still on spring break. The girls have two days before the next term's classes begin. "It's too late to be driving far," she says. "Get some sleep. Go home tomorrow if you want." Her voice is a monotone. "Just get your butts back here Monday."

They wait for the rest, for the part about what kind of a season it has been and what they've accomplished and how far they've come. But Jody is too tired, too distracted and too angry. She does an about-face and walks down the steps of the bus.

EVERYONE PLAYS NICE

JODY IS BACK AT WORK MONDAY MORNING, STILL WEARY, still disappointed about the first-round loss, but now eager to set up a meeting with Dan Williams. She figures they will talk about what coaches and athletic directors always talk about at the end of a season—how the team fared and why, what to expect next year—but they will also talk about much bigger concerns: the equity issues Jody began raising almost a year ago, the status of women's basketball at the university, Jody's future. But it turns out that Dan Williams doesn't want to talk, not yet anyway. Go to the Final Four, he tells Jody. We'll talk when you get back.

The NCAA women's Final Four is almost two weeks away in Minneapolis. Jody has had her ticket for a while. Women's basketball coaches from around the country will be there, checking out the competition, picking up tips, watching the game at the top of its form and, not incidentally, investigating—or being investigated for—new coaching positions. Like national conventions in many fields, the Final Four competition doubles as a job fair. That's why Jody is so surprised that Dan doesn't want to at least begin serious contract negotiations before Minneapolis. Without a new contract, Jody will essentially be a "free agent," a young coach with a winning record from a top conference, an attractive and—given her modest salary—easy catch for another university.

Does Dan want me to go looking for another job in Minneapolis? Jody wonders. Is that what this new delay is about? It may be, but there is at least one other explanation, one that gives Jody an equally clear message about her standing in the athletic department and the respect accorded women's basketball: It turns out that the men's basketball coach, Jerry Green, whose team also lost in the first round of the NCAA tournament, has just flown to Las Vegas to interview for the head coaching job there. Jerry is a popular coach who has posted a winning season. Dan wants to counter whatever UNLV offers. He wants to negotiate with Jerry as soon as he returns. Jody will have to wait in line.

Jerry Green is already making $200,000 a year in salary and other compensation from the University of Oregon. He comes back from Las Vegas with a $300,000 offer. But Las Vegas is offering only a three-year contract, and it is common knowledge that the job has already been turned down by a UCLA assistant coach and by the coach at Utah State. And the UNLV program has an iffy reputation in the world of intercollegiate athletics, having been routinely slapped with sanctions for serious violations of NCAA rules during the past few years. So the job is no plum, regardless of salary. There is some conjecture about whether Jerry is even serious about the position or whether he went on the interview merely to gain a bargaining chip with the university.

Whatever the case, Dan Williams takes the threat of losing Jerry seriously, and the university instantly mobilizes to counter the offer. Twenty-four hours after returning from his Las Vegas trip, Jerry is presented with a new, perpetually renewing four-year $249,000 contract with an athletic booster–funded annuity to guarantee long-term financial security. He signs immediately.

"I am delighted Jerry made this choice," Dan Williams
tells the local media. The generosity of the new contract, he
explains, is "in recognition of the extremely fine performance
of Jerry and his staff in turning around our men's basketball
program."

When Jody hears this, she doesn't know whether to
laugh—ruefully—or cry. Instead, she reaches for the phone
and unloads on her lawyer. She tells him that Jerry is being
swiftly and richly rewarded for posting a season identical to
the one her team just completed. They've gone over this before, but Jody has to recite the litany again: Both the men's
and women's teams won eleven of eighteen conference
games, both were nationally ranked during the season, both
finished fourth in the Pac-10, both won a berth at the NCAA
tournament and both finished the season with a first-round
loss. Jody is seething. Alan assures her he'll be on the phone
to university counsel Pete Swan immediately.

Even the local media, which jump on the keep-Jerry-at-
all-costs bandwagon, see the problem. A celebratory editorial
that happily recounts the signing of the new contract and calls
Jerry Green "popular, personable and productive" ends with
this admonition: "Now that it's kept Green, the UO must now
exhibit a similar commitment to retain women's coach Jody
Runge."

With Jerry's negotiations over so quickly, with the
Register-Guard calling for action and with Alan presumably
dogging Pete Swan, Jody figures something will happen now,
during the week and a half until she leaves for Minneapolis.
But the days go by with no word from either her lawyer or
the university administration. She spends her time in individual meetings with all her players, debriefing, troubleshooting,
talking about attitude and commitment, extracting promises of
hard work and perseverance. Then, a few days before she is
set to leave for the Midwest, she gets an interesting phone
call from a stranger, a man named Martin Fisher.

Fisher is a second-year law student at the university who
has been following the Jerry Green story in the local press.

Earlier in the season, he followed, with the interest of a would-be attorney, the media coverage of Jody's contract dispute. He likes basketball, although classes, evening meetings and studying have kept him from attending most games. Still, through the season, he's kept tabs on both the men's and women's teams by reading the sports pages. This past week, reading about Jerry Green's new contract, he asks himself the same question Jody is asking herself: Why is everyone falling all over themselves for Jerry Green and no one is doing anything for Jody Runge?

Martin starts talking to some of his friends about this. Martin's friends happen to be student senators. Martin happens to be president of the University of Oregon Student Senate, a governing body that controls millions of dollars of student fees, including more than $1 million given annually to the athletic department. Some of that money goes to providing free tickets to sports events for students. Some goes to supporting nonrevenue sports, like women's basketball.

Martin doesn't think it makes much sense for the student senate to give the athletic department $1 million if the department is not spending its money equitably. As a law student, he questions the legality of students supporting an athletic program that may be in violation of Title IX. He wonders what the student senate can do about it. He talks to his fellow senators. He talks with the president of the student body.

In the midst of these conversations, he calls Jody to introduce himself and outline his concerns. Jody thinks the kid sounds earnest enough on the phone. She's impressed, but she has no idea whether anything he could say or do would be meaningful to her negotiations. At any rate, she has little time to consider the matter. She leaves for Minneapolis, disgruntled and anxious about her future.

She spends some time in Iowa with her family. She spends long hours watching world-class women's basketball in a packed arena with network television cameras trained on the action. This is the kind of basketball she wants her team to be playing. This exciting, fast-paced game, attended by thousands, watched by millions, is the future of women's basketball. March *Maid*ness, they are calling it.

She watches the invincible Stanford crumble before the University of Connecticut. Then she watches UConn outplay Tennessee with a potent combination of skill, swagger and heart. When UConn wins the championship, the *New York Times* plays the story big. *Time* magazine features a page-high photograph of six-foot-four Rebecca Lobo, heroine of the UConn team, next to a breathless story about the glories of women's basketball. A Sunday supplement that reaches 38 million newspaper readers puts women's basketball on the front cover. Jody is buoyed by the sudden national enthusiasm almost as much as she is embittered by her own situation, not just her contract but the general lack of support—and she thinks respect—for women's basketball at her university. But in Minneapolis she does not look for other coaching positions. She has started a fight she intends to see through. She renews her resolve to bring Oregon women's basketball into the 1990s.

Martin Fisher calls her as soon as she returns. He has been busy reading bylaws, checking documents and conferring with his fellow student senators. He has learned that while the senate does not have the power to tell the athletic department how to spend the $1 million in student fees, the senate does have the power to veto the entire allocation. He likes that idea, vetoing the entire million, and so do his fellow senators. It would be a dramatic act, a bold statement that he thinks could materially strengthen Jody's position. Martin figures on calling a big press conference to announce the veto.

When he phones Jody to tell her of his plans, she is caught off guard. She is, as always, delighted by spontaneous expressions of support, but she tells him to hold on. She is sure she will be talking to the university any day now. It is not just that Dan Williams told her weeks ago that they would talk when she got back from Minneapolis, and not just that her lawyer is presumably busy pressing the point. It is also the Jerry Green situation. The university *must* deal with her now. On top of that, there is the just-announced legal decision in a case against Brown University that is giving jitters to athletic directors nationwide. In a sixty-nine-page ruling, a U.S. district judge has just said that Brown, which has one of the largest women's athletic programs in the country, is in violation of Title IX. Although there are just as many women's sports at Brown as there are men's, the percentage of female athletes is lower than the percentage of women at the university. All of a sudden, Title IX is back in the news and back on the national agenda. "If they think *we* have a problem," the Brown attorney tells the press after the decision is announced, "other schools are in big trouble."

Alan calls her later that day. She expects to hear that he's been talking to Pete Swan while she's been away. She expects to hear that at least he has set up a conference call. Instead he tells Jody that nothing has happened. He has been playing phone tag with Pete for a week and has not made contact. Jody is not sure just how diligent her lawyer may have been returning phone calls. She knows from personal experience that this is not his strong suit.

But whatever has happened, whoever is at fault, Jody wants the situation remedied immediately. She presses Alan to action. He says he will send a fax to Pete threatening to file the lawsuit if there is not a quick response to Jody's concerns. He tells Jody he will be on a plane out to Eugene on Sunday, six days from now, lawsuit in hand, if the university has not offered her a contract to her liking. Jody has heard this all before, several times in fact. But this time, she hears new conviction in Alan's voice.

Two days later, Pete receives the fax. In it, Alan accuses Pete, Dan and university president Dave Frohnmayer of responding neither "appropriately nor diligently" to what Alan calls "the serious problems" regarding Jody's salary and the women's basketball program. He and Jody have patiently waited since last winter, he writes, but nothing has happened.

"The University of Oregon acted swiftly and with great

caring for the men's head basketball coach," writes Alan, immediately playing his trump card. "The callous indifference to Jody's situation cannot and will not be endured. I do indeed intend to file a complaint against the University of Oregon and/or others regarding the treatment of Jody Runge, the women's basketball program in general, women's sports and/or other facets of the University of Oregon's blatant violations of Title IX and the Equal Pay Act," Alan writes. "I am very sorry that you have chosen to ignore these serious matters."

At the end of the fax, Alan tells Pete that he will be available in his office that afternoon to discuss the case. He makes it clear he means business: "A mere recitation of previous requests for indulgences by you and the administration will not be worthy of such a phone call," he writes.

Two days later, Jody walks down the hall to Dan Williams's office to sit in on a conference call between Pete and Dan on one end and Alan on the other. She is glad it is finally happening, now more than three weeks since she and the team returned from Georgia, but she is also very uneasy. She doesn't know what to expect. Earlier that day, when Dan stuck his head in her office to set up a time for the meeting, he told her he was going to make a fair offer, that he didn't want to dicker with Alan. But Jody doesn't know what "fair" means anymore. Will the offer be another $4,000 raise and a one-year contract? She is bracing herself for disappointment. In Dan's spacious Cas Center office, Jody sits quietly and listens as Pete lays out the offer to Alan.

It is a four-year $70,000 contract—a $22,000 raise over her current salary—with $5,000 raises for the assistant coaches.

Jody is staring at Pete as he talks to Alan over the speakerphone. Dan is staring at Jody. To Dan, it is a positive sign that the three of them are in an office together, that the mood is quiet and measured, not adversarial. He has a good feeling about this. He looks over to judge Jody's reaction to the offer, but Jody has her game face on, and Dan can't read it.

She may not be showing it, but Jody is very pleased. This offer is quite a bit more generous than the one she would have happily settled for last spring. A year ago, even six months ago, Jody would have jumped at this offer, and that would have been that.

But times have changed. The team no one thought would do well did well. Her male counterpart, coaching his team to an identical season, just signed a fat contract. Title IX compliance is a hot item. And Jody has a lawyer who smells blood.

Alan asks Dan and Pete if he and Jody can talk privately for a few minutes. They leave Jody alone in the office.

"If they offered this much right off, they're willing to do more," Alan tells her.

They quickly discuss a counteroffer, which ups the ante to an $80,000 base salary for Jody and includes a supplement of $10,000 a year in Nike money as well as bonuses for Jody should the team return to the NCAA tournament (with additional bonuses if the team goes on to win successive rounds), a retirement annuity similar to Jerry Green's, bigger raises for her assistant coaches and the promise to mount an aggressive marketing campaign for promotion of women's basketball, including direct-mail advertising, radio broadcasts of games and a radio show for Jody.

All this is making Jody's head spin. She walked into Dan's office fifteen minutes ago, a second-year coach with a $48,000 salary, the lowest paid women's basketball coach in the Pac-10, not sure if she'd be in a courtroom testifying against her employer or out looking for a new job in a few months. Now Alan is telling her that they should negotiate for a $90,000 salary package that, with NCAA bonuses, will easily exceed $100,000. Not only that, he's telling her that everything she dreamed about that would help create a strong future for women's basketball at Oregon, her whole wish list, can and should be part of her new contract.

She sits quietly, taking it all in, relieved that Alan will be doing the talking. When Pete and Dan come back in, Jody has her game face back on. She is giving away nothing. Alan tells them what he wants for Jody. They are surprised—after all, their $70,000 offer was just what Alan said he wanted a few months ago—but they are not stunned. It's Alan's job to get as much as he can. Everyone in the room knows that. Pete and Dan listen carefully. They tell Alan they need time to discuss this. They'll get back to him.

"Gentlemen," says Alan, "this is either going to be an active case on the court docket at five p.m. Monday afternoon or we will have these contract talks resolved. The choice is yours."

Before they hang up, Alan pulls back from that position slightly, giving Pete until 9 A.M. Tuesday morning to get back to him. It is now Friday afternoon.

Later that day, Pete is on the phone to Alan. Pete has spent the last few hours checking on what it might be possible for the university to do. He doesn't say what is or is not acceptable with the counteroffer, but he does say that he thinks there will be a problem with broadcasting the women's basketball games on radio, as the men's are. The university's long-standing contract is for the men's games, and the men and women usually play on the same night at the same time, one a home game, the other on the road. He also tells Alan that the NCAA incentive package, which rewards Jody with a percentage of her salary as the team advances in the tournament, is not what the university has traditionally done. Alan calls Jody with the latest report. She has the weekend to stew about it.

Monday is wild and windy, half rain, half sun, with a little hail thrown in, a typical April day in western Oregon. Jody watches the show from the big picture window in her office. She sticks close to the phone all morning, meeting with a few players, conferring with her assistants, reviewing travel and recruiting plans. Every time the phone rings, she is sure it's Alan. But it never is. At 2 P.M., she breaks down and calls him. He tells her that he has not heard anything from the university. He will call her when he does. She leaves at five without hearing from him.

At nine the next morning, Jody calls her lawyer again. She has been awake for hours waiting to hear from him. Nine is the deadline Alan gave Pete at the end of the Friday afternoon conference call. Either the university responds to the counteroffer by nine or Alan books a flight to Eugene. That's what he said. Alan tells Jody that he hasn't heard from Pete yet this morning, but he was just about to call him.

Pete seems taken aback by Alan's morning call. He is under the impression that the deadline is five this afternoon. The two lawyers debate that for a while with no resolution. Then Pete says that he was working until eleven the night before writing up Jody's contract.

"So that means we've come to an understanding on the issues?" Alan asks.

Not all of them, Pete tells him. Dan Williams has "philosophical reservations" about the NCAA tournament bonus structure Alan proposed. The objection may be philosophical—that is, no other coach benefits from such a plan—but it is also monetary. Under Alan's plan, Jody would receive a bonus equal to 25 percent of her base salary if the team got a bid to the tournament, another 25 percent if the team made the Final Four and a third 25 percent for winning. That translates into three $20,000 rewards. Her current bonus is two weeks' salary if the team goes to the tournament, which would be about $3,300 under her new contract.

"So if you're not going to go for the bonus structure, does that mean you are ready to compensate Jody in salary to make up the difference?" Alan asks.

Pete says no.

Alan snorts. Since Jody's winning season, but especially since Jerry Green's new contract, Alan is infused with confidence. He has never felt more sure about winning a lawsuit than he does at this moment, and never more serious about doing it.

"So why are you staying up late at night to write a contract if we have no agreement on the terms? You're just wast-
ing our time." He pauses just long enough to get Pete's
attention. Then he goes on the offensive. "Listen," he says,
"when I file this lawsuit, don't come to me with a settlement.
There will be no settlement."

The conversation ends abruptly on this less than amicable note. But Alan doesn't put in a call to his travel agent to
book a flight to Eugene. He doesn't think that's going to be
necessary, regardless of the unsatisfactory discussion he has
just had with Pete. No, he's got this contract sewn up. He can
feel it. The university has little room to maneuver after what
it did for the men's basketball coach. The Brown University
decision doesn't hurt either. He feels sure that Pete and Dan
understand the vulnerability of their position. He'll let them
work on this today and see what happens. Sit tight, he tells
Jody.

She feels as if she's been sitting tight forever. *When is
something going to happen?* When is she going to regain control over this part of her life? Despite Alan's new confidence,
Jody still believes, as she has believed for many months, that
the university will do nothing for her unless forced. She still
sees a lawsuit in her future, and the future is now. She goes
to sleep that night, anxious, keyed up, fully ready to hear from
Alan the next morning that they are going to court.

Instead, she hears that the university has accepted the
counteroffer—not all provisions of it, not every clause, but
enough to move forward, enough to announce to the media
that she and the university have come to terms. Alan and Pete
work it out over the phone that morning: the $80,000 base,
the $10,000 Nike money, the raises for the assistants, the new
level of visibility for the program. Jody is stunned, numb, like
someone who has just survived a week in the wilderness and
doesn't yet realize that the ordeal is over. She has felt embattled for so many months that anxiety and bitterness have
become her normal state. She tries to cast them off immediately, to feel free of them, to celebrate, if only in her own

head, her victory. But she can't. It will take a while to uncoil.
It will take a while to remember who she was before all this
started.

She has only minutes to collect herself before Bob Rodman, the sports reporter for the *Register-Guard*, is on the
phone asking questions. Alan has called him with the news,
and he wants Jody to comment. For all of Jody's surprise and
confusion, she knows how to flip the switch and become the
public persona she needs to be, the quotable coach, the mag-
nanimous winner, the consummate university employee. She
knows what public relations is all about. She knows that bad-
mouthing the university as this point would be in no one's
best interest. She tells Rodman that the university has always
dealt with her "from a place of integrity." Dan Williams also
knows what to say: "This is the time to step up, to give her
a proper reward and to give the proper support to the women's
basketball program." Everyone is playing nice. The next day,
the *Portland Oregonian*, the state's largest newspaper, runs
the story under the headline OREGON REWARDS RUNGE'S SUC-
CESS, AND AVOIDS SUIT. Jody figures they've got the order
switched around on that, but what the hell.

It is now mid-April. Pete has to send the contract to
Alan; Alan has to read it, okay it and send it back to Jody for
her signature. Jody figures that will take a week, tops. But
Alan disappears on her. He is suddenly unavailable again and
not returning phone calls. His secretary says he is now in the
midst of a rape trial. Jody waits a week, two weeks, three
weeks. She leaves angry messages on his answering machine.
She curses at the secretary. Her impatience is many layered.
It is not just that after more than a year, she wants to get this
thing settled and behind her. It is also that every week that
passes, she is losing considerable money—the difference between her old $48,000 base salary and her new $80,000 deal.
If Alan delays a month, that costs Jody almost $3,000.

She is also impatient because she needs to hire a new
assistant coach, and Dan has told her that she can't do that
until the contract is signed. Jody is not adding a staff member.

She is replacing the voluble Joe Jackson, the coach who rants and raves from the bench. She hired him when she arrived last season. Now she is firing him. After two years, Joe failed to complete the few credits he needed to earn his bachelor's degree, a stated requirement of his job. If Joe were a superior coach, a real asset, Jody might sit down with him for a heart-to-heart, try to straighten this thing out. But Jody has not been all that impressed with Joe. Now that she has the money to hire a more experienced assistant, she lets him go.

Scouting for a new assistant keeps her busy for most of the rest of April. Then there's a top recruit who comes for a campus visit and must be courted. There are inquiries to make in Australia. Jody hopes to find another Sally Crowe there, another seasoned player for the shooting-guard position. Spring arrives. Jody weeds her yard. She plants flowers in her window boxes. She curses Alan daily.

Finally, on May 18, after she's hounded him for more than a month, Alan faxes Pete a few relatively minor changes to the contract. It's another three weeks before this is straightened out. When Jody finally gets ahold of Alan, he tries to blame the university for the delays, but she knows by now who is at fault. She grits her teeth, tells herself she couldn't have done this without Alan and goes back to waiting.

One morning in mid-June, with the sun warming the open field under her office window and the alders out by the river bright green with new leaves, the phone rings on Jody's big, orderly desk. It is Alan calling to tell her that he's about to fax the final contract. Jody gets to the machine just as the pages start to come through. She stands there for a while. The contract is twenty-seven pages long.

Back in her office, door shut behind her, she sits at her desk and reads every word. Then she calls Alan, and they have a long discussion. Jody is happy to see much of what she wants reflected in the contract, but she is concerned with language that says the university will make its "best faith effort" to get radio and TV coverage for the women's games.

She wants a clear commitment, not vague promises. If she doesn't get it now, she's afraid she will never get it.

She also doesn't like that the contract says she is to report to the athletic director *or whomever the director deems appropriate.* She doesn't want to find herself reporting to Barb Walker again. It's nothing personal. In fact, it is entirely political. The football and men's basketball coaches report directly to the AD; all the other coaches report first to Barb, the associate AD. This whole battle has been about forcing the university to look at women's basketball in a different way, as equal or soon-to-be equal to the traditional male revenue sports. Jody wants the institutional hierarchy to reflect the university's new thinking.

She was concerned about these same two issues weeks ago and thought that Alan was working on them for her. He did try—his May 18 fax specifically addressed the chain-of-command question—but the university stood firm.

Alan tells her it's okay. She's gotten just about everything she wanted, and she's not getting anything else. At least not this time. Sign it, he tells her. Celebrate. You've got a great contract.

Jody knows she should be feeling good right now. But even with the contract in front of her, which almost doubles her salary and commits the university to a new way of thinking about women's basketball, even with this clear victory in black and white, she does not feel victorious. Even as she picks up a pen to sign, she is angry with Alan for the delays and angry with the university for giving her reasons to hire Alan in the first place. Anger has been a constant companion this past year. It is as if she is a little reluctant to let it go. Or perhaps she doesn't know how.

She takes a deep breath and scrawls her name on the bottom of the last page. Then she takes the contract and walks it down the hall to Dan Williams's office. But Dan isn't in. Jody hands the contract to his secretary, suddenly aware, as if she were in a movie, of the anticlimax of this scene.

She calls her parents to tell them the news, and they are more delighted than she is. Dennis, who is fond of proclaiming that his daughter comes from a long line of take-no-prisoners women, is not surprised that Jody has pulled this off. Joanna marvels at her daughter's strength and inner reserves. That evening, Jody and the man she's been seeing on and off all spring, the guy who sent her flowers on Valentine's Day and has been pursuing her ever since, go out for a nice dinner. That's the extent of the celebration.

The next week, Jody treats herself by buying a few things for her house. Then she writes a check to Alan for $6,500. The size of his bill comes as an unpleasant surprise. From the beginning, they had talked little about money. Alan had said only that his payment would come out of the settlement of the lawsuit. Jody had no inkling of what he was going to charge once it became clear that there would be no suit. She supposes now that she should have asked, but there were so many other pressing matters, and Alan was always so difficult to reach. She writes the check in anger. It will eat up more than two months of her salary increase.

She is still finding reasons to be upset. It takes her weeks to come to terms with her own victory. She works it through the way she works everything through: alone, by immersing herself in work. A week after she signs the contract, she conducts the first of several summer basketball camps she will offer for young girls. Two weeks later she is on the road—Dallas, Lubbock, Indianapolis, Los Angeles—living out of a suitcase while she scouts camps and tournaments for players.

By the time she comes home to Eugene in midsummer, she is thinking not of the season past but of the season to come. She has a line on this terrific Oregon high school player, a big girl, six-foot-five, strong and smart. With a girl like that, she could win the Pac-10 championship. With a girl like that, she might go to the Final Four.

She picks up the phone.

EPILOGUE

THE INHERENT DRAMA OF ATHLETIC COMPETITION IS THAT somebody always wins, and somebody always loses. But that season at the University of Oregon, Jody Runge's second year as head coach, it seemed that everybody won: The fans got a winning team, with back-to-back NCAA appearances for the first time in history. The girls got a bit of glory. The program got an infusion of money. University officials came out of it looking like forward-thinking fellows who understood that women's basketball was going places. They avoided a nasty lawsuit while making it appear that rewarding Jody and her program was what they had planned all along. The coach, the heroine who delivered the goods in a tough year, got a whopping salary increase.

It was a public relations dream. From Johnson Hall, the imposing campus home of the president and all his men, and across the river from the Cas Center, the upscale digs of the athletic department, there came a collective sigh as the insiders, who knew just how bad it could have gotten, exhaled.

The crisis was over, and in its wake, women's basketball

had come of age at the University of Oregon, just as it was coming of age at schools all across the country.

By the time the new season began the following fall, Duck women's basketball had a different face. The team's locker-room facilities in the basement of Mac Court were expanded. Like the men's basketball coaches, Jody and her assistants now had an office, a space adjoining the existing locker room that doubled as a "team room" where the players could watch game films. Jody was able to equip it with a ten-thousand-dollar state-of-the-art video editing system that made it possible for the coaches to put together special practice and instruction tapes.

As part of the promised boost in marketing, full-color brochures touting the women's basketball program and soliciting season-ticket sales were sent to thousands of fans and would-be fans. A series of radio ads on the most popular area stations reinforced the message. Billboards popped up on the outskirts of town featuring a photograph of Jody alongside the men's basketball coach. Staff at the athletic department worked on special promotions for the women's games, offering two-for-one tickets and other incentives to boost attendance at games and introduce new fans to the sport.

The university negotiated with the local transit system to provide a bus to pick up fans off campus and deliver them to Mac Court on game nights—a service that had been routinely provided for men's games. Making good on its promise to Jody, the university contracted with two local radio stations to carry live broadcasts of all but one of the women's games. Ten of the games were televised as well. In another move that showed increasing attention to Jody's program, the athletic department hired a new sports information assistant, the first and only woman in that office, to handle, among other responsibilities, women's basketball.

It worked. The next season, a combination of advertising, special promotions and fierce intrastate rivalry translated into more than 9,700 fans packing Mac Court to see the Ducks beat the Oregon State Beavers. It was the largest crowd ever assembled to see a Pac-10 women's basketball game and the fourteenth largest in the history of the sport nationwide.

Jody emerged from her year of conflict with both public and private victories. Publicly, she had made big strides toward accomplishing what she pledged to do when she first arrived in Oregon—to create a winning tradition. Back at that first press conference in the spring of 1993 when she made the promise and her bosses smiled and nodded, they thought she meant only to forge a team with a winning record. But she had a bigger vision, a vision of women's collegiate basketball as an equal of men's, as a national contender for the attention and affection of sports fans. Although parity between the men's and women's programs at Oregon—and elsewhere—has yet to be reached, Jody and coaches like her across the country are pushing the envelope, moving their programs in that direction as they simultaneously challenge stereotypes of femininity and athleticism. At Oregon and elsewhere, women's basketball is now poised to break out of "nonrevenue row" and become the first women's sport to challenge the twin economic towers of football and men's basketball. It might take years, but it is clear now that it can happen.

Privately, within the confines of the team, Jody felt she had been the role model she wanted to be. Throughout the months of anger and tension and frustration and, underneath it all, loneliness, Jody had persevered. She had continued to believe in herself. She had not cracked. She had sucked it up. She had, she thought, shown the young women in her care how strong a woman could and needed to be to accomplish big things, to fight for what she believed in. Maybe it was a lesson they didn't yet know they had learned, but she had taught it.

Amid the turmoil of that year, Jody's personal life was also in flux. She and the man she began dating midseason broke off their relationship late that spring. He was good-looking, smart, attentive and obviously smitten. But she was still secretly pining for Rich, the man she had left behind in the Midwest when she took the Oregon job. Theirs had not been an easy relationship from the beginning, and that was one of the things that appealed to Jody about it. She liked to work against odds, to set herself a difficult task, to persevere, to win. She and Rich started talking again, tentative phone conversations, fits and starts, sometimes casual and chatty, other times painful and probing. The flame was still burning. She flew back to visit him; he flew out to visit her. That summer he piled some of his belongings in the backseat of his car, drove across the country and settled in Eugene. He and Jody are learning how to be a couple. There is talk of marriage.

As for the team:

Jessica Schutt graduated with a major in psychology and took a job as an assistant women's basketball coach at a small college in Washington State.

Karen Healea got accepted into graduate school and earned a master's degree in special education. She never had the hip surgery.

A month and a half after flying home to Australia, Sally Crowe, practicing with her old teammates, tore the ligaments surrounding her knee. It was the worst kind of knee injury a player could sustain. She had surgery, struggled through rehabilitation and did not play that season.

During the summer, Cicely Brewster made the mistake of accepting money for participating in a local hoops contest. Following NCAA rules, she was penalized and redshirted part of the next season. When she came back, she mostly warmed a place on the bench.

Sandie Edwards suffered a serious ankle injury three games into the next season. She redshirted the rest of the year.

Renae Fegent (Roy), Arianne Boyer (Red), Betty Ann Boeving (B) and Cindie Edamura (Eddie) were all starters the next season. After an unexpected loss to Washington State early on, Jody sent the girls to their hotel rooms to write the obligatory essays. She told them she wanted honesty. She needn't have said that to Red, of course, who never held back anyway. When Jody read Red's essay, she went ballistic. It seemed to Jody that the girl took no responsibility for the loss, that she saw herself outside the team. It was the same old issue—Jody saw Red as a selfish player; Red saw Jody as an unsympathetic coach—and Jody was tired of dealing with it. She suspended Red from the team and sent her home on a plane that night.

Red and Jody stewed separately. Red gave serious thought to quitting the team. Jody gave serious thought to letting her. At Jody's request, Red's father drove down for two days of meetings, after which an uneasy détente was again reached. Jody needed Red to win basketball games. Red needed basketball in her life. She ended the season as the Ducks' high scorer and top rebounder and was honored, along with Roy, by selection to the all–Pac-10 team.

The team ended that next season by going to the NCAA tournament for an unprecedented third time in a row.

Armed with her new contract, the back-to-back NCAA tournament visits and a deeper commitment to women's basketball from the university, Jody Runge began the recruiting season with her biggest victory: She snagged one of the top high school players in the nation, a broad-shouldered, six-foot-five powerhouse from a small town in Oregon, a girl who was being actively recruited by UConn, Stanford and other top-ranked programs. Jenny Mowe became the cornerstone of the new Oregon team.

Jody set her sights on something more than another invitation to the Big Dance. Now she was in it to win it.